BESTSELLING
BOOK SERIES

Active Directory For Dummies®

W9-CGL-221

Not All Active Directory Domain Controllers Are Created Equal

Active Directory uses a multiple-master model, and, supposedly, no domain controller has a special role over any of the other domain controllers. This statement, however, isn't strictly true. Some services can't function in a multimaster environment, meaning that changes can't take place on more than one domain controller at a time. Some domain controllers, therefore, do assume a single-master operations role and are known as *operations masters*.

Here are the five categories of operations masters:

- **Schema master (one per forest):** Maintains the master copy of the schema.
- **PDC emulator (one per domain):** Emulates a primary domain controller for backward compatibility with Windows NT.
- **Domain naming master (one per forest):** Tracks object names throughout a forest to ensure that they're unique. Also tracks cross-references to objects in other directories.
- **Infrastructure master (one per domain):** Tracks object references among domains and maintains a list of deleted child objects.
- **Relative identifier (RID) master (one per domain):** Tracks the assignment of SIDs (security identifiers) throughout the domain.

Usually, the first domain controller that you create in the first domain assumes the operations master roles. You can assign these roles to other domain controllers in the domain or forest, but only one domain controller at a time can hold each operations master role.

Logical Design Checklist

Planning comes before implementing! Make sure that you complete the following steps before creating domains and organizational units (OUs):

1. Using the DNS namespace, identify and name the root domain.

2. Determine whether a tree or a forest is appropriate for your organization.

3. Determine whether you need additional domains.

4. Consult your company's organization chart to decide which domain model is best for your needs and whether you need additional child domains.

5. Analyze business models and processes to determine which OU model is best for your needs.

6. Determine who's to administer each OU.

7. Decide what administrative privileges the OU administrators need.

8. Diagram the logical Active Directory structure.

For Dummies®: Bestselling Book Series for Beginners

Active Directory For Dummies®

Common Types of DNS Resource Records

Type	Purpose
A	*Address* resource records match an IP address to a host name.
CNAME	*Canonical name* resource records associate a nickname to a host name.
MX	*Mail exchange* resource records identify mail servers for the specified domain.
NS	*Name server* resource records identify servers (other than the SOA server) that contain zone information files.
PTR	*Pointer* resource records match a host name to a given IP address. Notice that this type is the opposite of an A record, which matches an IP address to the supplied host name.
SOA	*Start of authority* resource records specify which server contains the zone file for a domain.
SRV	*Service* resource records identify servers that provide special services to the domain.

Delegating Administrative Control

Answer the following series of questions as you create each new OU to help you plan how to delegate the appropriate level of authority:

- ✔ How are people going to use the OU?
- ✔ Who's going to administer the OU?
- ✔ What level of rights does the OU administrator require?

Mixed Mode versus Native Mode

Mixed mode and native mode pertain only to the domain controllers in your domains. A domain can run in native mode and still accommodate Windows 95/98 or Windows NT 3.51 and 4.0 clients.

Designing an Efficient Tree

Keep the following guiding principles in mind as you design your Active Directory tree:

- ✔ Keep the domain structure shallow for efficient navigation.
- ✔ Follow the standard DNS naming conventions.
- ✔ Choose short domain names wherever possible; long names are tedious.
- ✔ Make sure that the root domain name is stable — you can't change it easily.

Hardware Requirements for Windows 2000 Server

Component	Requirement
Processor	Pentium 166 MHz or higher.
Memory	64MB required; 128MB recommended.
Hard Disk	1.2GB required on the boot partition; 2GB or more recommended.
Video	VGA or higher video card and monitor.
Hardware	Must be on the Windows 2000 Hardware Compatibility List.

For Dummies®: Bestselling Book Series for Beginners

 ™

References for the Rest of Us! ®

BESTSELLING BOOK SERIES

Are you intimidated and confused by computers? Do you find that traditional manuals are overloaded with technical details you'll never use? Do your friends and family always call you to fix simple problems on their PCs? Then the *...For Dummies*® computer book series from IDG Books Worldwide is for you.

...For Dummies books are written for those frustrated computer users who know they aren't really dumb but find that PC hardware, software, and indeed the unique vocabulary of computing make them feel helpless. *...For Dummies* books use a lighthearted approach, a down-to-earth style, and even cartoons and humorous icons to dispel computer novices' fears and build their confidence. Lighthearted but not lightweight, these books are a perfect survival guide for anyone forced to use a computer.

> *"I like my copy so much I told friends; now they bought copies."*
>
> — Irene C., Orwell, Ohio

> *"Quick, concise, nontechnical, and humorous."*
>
> — Jay A., Elburn, Illinois

> *"Thanks, I needed this book. Now I can sleep at night."*
>
> — Robin F., British Columbia, Canada

Already, millions of satisfied readers agree. They have made *...For Dummies* books the #1 introductory level computer book series and have written asking for more. So, if you're looking for the most fun and easy way to learn about computers, look to *...For Dummies* books to give you a helping hand.

IDG BOOKS WORLDWIDE ®

1/99

Active Directory™

FOR

DUMMIES®

Active Directory™ FOR DUMMIES®

by Marcia Loughry

IDG BOOKS WORLDWIDE

IDG Books Worldwide, Inc.
An International Data Group Company

Foster City, CA ◆ Chicago, IL ◆ Indianapolis, IN ◆ New York, NY

Active Directory™ For Dummies®

Published by
IDG Books Worldwide, Inc.
An International Data Group Company
919 E. Hillsdale Blvd.
Suite 400
Foster City, CA 94404
www.idgbooks.com (IDG Books Worldwide Web site)
www.dummies.com (Dummies Press Web site)

Library of Congress Catalog Card No.: 99-66509

ISBN: 0-7645-0659-5

Printed in the United States of America

10 9 8 7 6 5 4 3 2

1B/QZ/RS/ZZ/IN

Distributed in the United States by IDG Books Worldwide, Inc.

Distributed by CDG Books Canada Inc. for Canada; by Transworld Publishers Limited in the United Kingdom; by IDG Norge Books for Norway; by IDG Sweden Books for Sweden; by IDG Books Australia Publishing Corporation Pty. Ltd. for Australia and New Zealand; by TransQuest Publishers Pte Ltd. for Singapore, Malaysia, Thailand, Indonesia, and Hong Kong; by Gotop Information Inc. for Taiwan; by ICG Muse, Inc. for Japan; by Intersoft for South Africa; by Eyrolles for France; by International Thomson Publishing for Germany, Austria and Switzerland; by Distribuidora Cuspide for Argentina; by LR International for Brazil; by Galileo Libros for Chile; by Ediciones ZETA S.C.R. Ltda. for Peru; by WS Computer Publishing Corporation, Inc., for the Philippines; by Contemporanea de Ediciones for Venezuela; by Express Computer Distributors for the Caribbean and West Indies; by Micronesia Media Distributor, Inc. for Micronesia; by Chips Computadoras S.A. de C.V. for Mexico; by Editorial Norma de Panama S.A. for Panama; by American Bookshops for Finland.

For general information on IDG Books Worldwide's books in the U.S., please call our Consumer Customer Service department at 800-762-2974. For reseller information, including discounts and premium sales, please call our Reseller Customer Service department at 800-434-3422.

For information on where to purchase IDG Books Worldwide's books outside the U.S., please contact our International Sales department at 317-596-5530 or fax 317-596-5692.

For consumer information on foreign language translations, please contact our Customer Service department at 1-800-434-3422, fax 317-596-5692, or e-mail rights@idgbooks.com.

For information on licensing foreign or domestic rights, please phone +1-650-655-3109.

For sales inquiries and special prices for bulk quantities, please contact our Sales department at 650-655-3200 or write to the address above.

For information on using IDG Books Worldwide's books in the classroom or for ordering examination copies, please contact our Educational Sales department at 800-434-2086 or fax 317-596-5499.

For press review copies, author interviews, or other publicity information, please contact our Public Relations department at 650-655-3000 or fax 650-655-3299.

For authorization to photocopy items for corporate, personal, or educational use, please contact Copyright Clearance Center, 222 Rosewood Drive, Danvers, MA 01923, or fax 978-750-4470.

is a registered trademark under exclusive license to IDG Books Worldwide, Inc. from International Data Group, Inc.

About the Author

Marcia Loughry, MCSE and MCP+I, is a Senior Infrastructure Specialist with a large IT firm in Dallas, Texas. She is president of the Plano, Texas BackOffice User Group (PBUG) and a member of Women in Technology International. Marcia received her MCSE in NT 3.51 in 1997 and completed requirements for the NT 4.0 track in 1998.

Marcia has extensive experience working with Windows NT 3.51 and 4.0 in enterprises of all sizes. She currently is assigned to some of her firm's largest customers in designing NT solutions and integrating UNIX and NetWare environments with NT.

ABOUT IDG BOOKS WORLDWIDE

Dedication

This book is dedicated to my family — my son Chris, my parents, my sister Karen — just because I love 'em all! Thanks for the love, laughter, and support.

Author's Acknowledgments

Special thanks to literary agent Lisa Swayne, of the Swayne Agency, for finding me, taking me on, and introducing me to the fun people at IDG Books.

Many, many thanks to the fine folks at IDG Books: Joyce Pepple, who got me excited about this project; Jodi Jensen, who suffered and planned with me and generally kept me in line; Bill Barton, who didn't strangle me over my consistent use of passive voice; and the rest of the IDG team who made the book and CD possible.

And finally, heartfelt thanks to Jackie, Mary, Sherri, Michelle, Anne, Clifton, Sam, Steve, Kent, Sylvana, Nate, Clay, and all the other friends who make every day so much fun.

Publisher's Acknowledgments

We're proud of this book; please register your comments through our IDG Books Worldwide Online Registration Form located at http://my2cents.dummies.com.

Some of the people who helped bring this book to market include the following:

Acquisitions, Editorial, and Media Development

Senior Project Editor: Jodi Jensen

Acquisitions Editor: Joyce Peppler

Senior Copy Editor: William A. Barton

Technical Editor: John Savill

Associate Media Development Editor: Megan Decraene

Associate Permissions Editor: Carmen Krikorian

Editorial Manager: Leah P. Cameron

Editorial Assistant: Beth Parlon

Production

Project Coordinator: Maridee V. Ennis

Layout and Graphics: Shelley Norris, Jill Piscitélli, Doug Rollison, Dan Whetstine, Erin Zeltner

Proofreaders: Laura Albert, John Greenough, Joel Showalter

Indexer: Ty Koontz

General and Administrative

IDG Books Worldwide, Inc.: John Kilcullen, CEO; Steven Berkowitz, President and Publisher

IDG Books Technology Publishing Group: Richard Swadley, Senior Vice President and Publisher; Walter Bruce III, Vice President and Associate Publisher; Joseph Wikert, Associate Publisher; Mary Bednarek, Branded Product Development Director; Mary Corder, Editorial Director; Barry Pruett, Publishing Manager; Michelle Baxter, Publishing Manager

IDG Books Consumer Publishing Group: Roland Elgey, Senior Vice President and Publisher; Kathleen A. Welton, Vice President and Publisher; Kevin Thornton, Acquisitions Manager; Kristin A. Cocks, Editorial Director

IDG Books Internet Publishing Group: Brenda McLaughlin, Senior Vice President and Publisher; Diane Graves Steele, Vice President and Associate Publisher; Sofia Marchant, Online Marketing Manager

IDG Books Production for Dummies Press: Debbie Stailey, Associate Director of Production; Cindy L. Phipps, Manager of Project Coordination, Production Proofreading, and Indexing; Tony Augsburger, Manager of Prepress, Reprints, and Systems; Laura Carpenter, Production Control Manager; Shelley Lea, Supervisor of Graphics and Design; Debbie J. Gates, Production Systems Specialist; Robert Springer, Supervisor of Proofreading; Kathie Schutte, Production Supervisor

Dummies Packaging and Book Design: Patty Page, Manager, Promotions Marketing

◆

The publisher would like to give special thanks to Patrick J. McGovern, without whom this book would not have been possible.

◆

Contents at a Glance

Cartoons at a Glance

By Rich Tennant

page 37

page 233

page 143

page 5

page 263

page 247

page 97

Fax: 978-546-7747
E-mail: richtennant@the5thwave.com
World Wide Web: www.the5thwave.com

Table of Contents

Introduction

*W*ith Windows 2000, Microsoft delivers the next generation of operating-system technology. Knowledge of Active Directory — a fundamental component of Windows 2000 — is crucial. Yet many administrators dread the transition to Active Directory because of its complexity and learning curve.

My goal with this book is to take the anxiety and stress out of mastering this complex technology. I hope that you find the book a clear, straightforward resource for exploring Active Directory.

This Book Is for You

Whether you've already purchased this book or are browsing through it in the bookstore, know that you've come to the right place. Windows 2000 is poised to be the hottest product of the decade, and administrators are lining up to get more information about it. Windows 2000 also ushers in Active Directory, which promises to change the way that people design and manage networks. This book is for you if you're any of the following:

- A savvy system administrator with previous NT experience

- A newbie (to networking or to information technology) who wants to pick up information on the latest Microsoft technology

- A student preparing for certification exams

- An IT manager investigating new technology

- Someone who's merely interested in intelligently discussing Active Directory

For the experienced NT administrator or other IT professional, *Active Directory For Dummies* provides you with an unpretentious resource containing exactly what you need to know. It presents the fundamentals of the program and then moves right into planning, implementing, and managing Active Directory — what you're most interested in knowing right now!

If you're new to Microsoft technologies, the book takes you one step at a time from the basics to the more advanced Active Directory topics. (And — hey! — Active Directory is new to everyone!)

Welcome! And thanks for making *Active Directory For Dummies* your first resource for figuring out Microsoft's hottest new technology!

How This Book Is Organized

I've divided this book into seven parts, organized by topic. The parts take you sequentially from Active Directory fundamentals through planning, deploying, and managing Active Directory. If you're looking for information on a specific Active Directory topic, check the headings in the table of contents. By design, you'll find that you can use *Active Directory For Dummies* as a reference that you reach for again and again.

Part I: Getting Started

Part I contains the "getting to know you" chapters. These chapters contain the answers to your most fundamental questions:

- What is Active Directory?
- What are its benefits?
- What are the buzzwords?

The information you find here also helps you determine what you must do to prepare for Active Directory in your environment.

Part II: Planning and Building Your First Model

Active Directory contains both a logical and a physical structure that you must carefully design before deployment. The logical structure comes first and includes the following steps:

- Planning the DNS namespace (Chapter 3)
- Designing the tree (Chapter 4)
- Defining an organizational unit (OU) model (Chapter 4)

After you plan your logical structure, you move on to developing a plan for your physical structure, which is discussed in Chapter 5. Then finally, in Chapter 6, you put all this planning into action as you build a test model of an Active Directory domain and create your first objects.

Part III: Migrating to Active Directory

Many roads lead to Windows 2000 and Active Directory. Part III considers the various methods of migrating from an existing environment to an Active Directory environment. Whether you're migrating from a Windows multiple-master domain or from NetWare Directory Services (NDS), you can find a migration strategy here.

Part IV: Managing Active Directory

Part IV covers the daily work of managing an Active Directory environment. Active Directory introduces the capability of delegating administrative authority and also introduces new security concepts. The chapters in this part prepare you for managing security, users, and resources within the Active Directory tree.

Part IV also covers managing replication traffic. Optimized replication traffic is vitally important to the Windows 2000 environment. In these chapters, you discover how to propagate updates, schedule replication traffic, work with the Active Directory schema, and maintain the Active Directory database.

Part V: Active Directory and Changing Technology

Part V describes the *Active Directory Services Interface* and how it works with other Microsoft technology. The ADSI is the access point to the directory database, and new products require an interface to the database. In the past, several Microsoft products (Exchange, for example) required a user database apart from the NT user's database. In the future, Microsoft plans for the Active Directory database to serve as the single directory database for all products.

Active Directory also introduces the possibility of managing network devices through the centralized database. Hardware vendors plan to introduce directory-enabled network (DEN) devices that integrate with Windows 2000 and Active Directory. Chapter 16 discusses directory-enabled devices and networks.

Part VI: The Part of Tens

In true *For Dummies* style, this book includes a Part of Tens. These chapters introduce lists of ten items about a variety of informative topics. Here you find additional resources, hints, and tips, plus other nuggets of knowledge. The Part of Tens is a resource you can turn to again and again.

Part VII: Appendixes

I save some of the more detailed information for last. In the appendixes, you find information that will add depth to your understanding and use of Active Directory. I provide detailed schema information, a listing of tools and utilities from the Windows 2000 Resource Kit, tables of country and state codes, a glossary to help you with Active Directory terminology, and, finally, details about how to use the cool stuff on the CD that comes with this book.

Icons Used in This Book

To make using this book easier, I use various icons in the margins to indicate particular points of interest.

Sometimes I feel obligated to give you some technical information, although it doesn't really affect how you use Active Directory. I mark that stuff with this geeky fellow so that you know it's just background information.

Ouch! I mark important directions to keep you out of trouble with this icon. These paragraphs contain facts that can keep you from having nightmares.

Any time that I can give you a hint or a tip that makes a subject or task easier, I mark it with this little thingie for additional emphasis — just my way of showing you that I'm on your side.

This icon is a friendly reminder for something that you want to make sure that you cache in your memory for later use.

Well, some things out there are strange, but true. What else can I say?

This icon directs you to another source for additional information. Sometimes I talk about technologies that you may want to learn more about, so I tell you where to find information about these topics.

This icon points you to goodies included on the companion CD-ROM found at the back of the book.

Part I
Getting Started

In this part . . .

I've been a system administrator, too, so I understand your overwhelming compulsion to skip right to Parts III and IV. Hands on is just more fun! But beginning at the . . . well, *beginning* is always important. These first two chapters prepare you for a new way of designing, implementing, and managing your network. They help you to figure out the lingo and prepare for the work ahead. Welcome to Active Directory!

Chapter 1

Understanding Active Directory

*W*ith all the media hype surrounding the release of Windows 2000 Server, you may already be a bit intimidated by the prospect of working with Active Directory. You've seen the presentations and articles discussing trees, forests, sites, and namespaces. Not only must you assimilate a new technology, but you must also pick up an entire new language just to understand what everyone's talking about.

But Active Directory doesn't need to be difficult! In this chapter, you find out in clear and simple language what Active Directory is, what it does, and what benefits it brings to your organization — and to your job.

What Is Active Directory?

If you visit the Microsoft Web site seeking a definition of Active Directory, you find words such as *hierarchical*, *distributed*, *extensible*, and *integrated*. Then you stumble across terms such as *trees*, *forests*, and *leaf objects* in combination with the usual abbreviations and standards: TCP/IP, DNS, X.500, LDAP. The whole thing quickly becomes pretty overwhelming. (Appendix D has a glossary that defines these abbreviations for you!)

I prefer to define things in simpler terms, as the following sections demonstrate — drum roll, please. . . .

Active Directory is a database

First and foremost, Active Directory is a database. As is true of all databases, Active Directory contains *fields* of information. A telephone directory, for example, is a database of fields containing such information as names, addresses, and telephone numbers (see Figure 1-1).

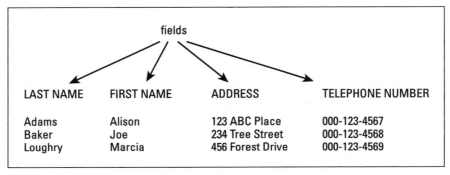

Figure 1-1: A telephone directory is a database containing fields of information.

fields

LAST NAME	FIRST NAME	ADDRESS	TELEPHONE NUMBER
Adams	Alison	123 ABC Place	000-123-4567
Baker	Joe	234 Tree Street	000-123-4568
Loughry	Marcia	456 Forest Drive	000-123-4569

Instead of containing telephone directory information, the Active Directory database contains the names and descriptive information (called *attributes*) about objects in your Windows 2000 environment.

The term *object* can refer to a user, a group, a printer, or any other real component and its accompanying attributes. Active Directory is a database containing all the objects in your Windows 2000 environment.

Now take the telephone directory comparison a step farther. What if the phone company were to deliver your telephone book in an electronic format each year? Cool, huh? You'd receive a file or CD containing the phone book. You could sort through the information electronically to find all people with the last name of Loughry, all residents of Forest Drive, or even all residents with the first name Joe!

Active Directory has a logical structure (or hierarchy)

Now assume that the phone company sends you a statewide telephone directory each year. The phone company groups the information in this directory in a logical manner — by city name. So along with name, address, and telephone number fields, you now have another field by which you can sort your database — city (see Figure 1-2).

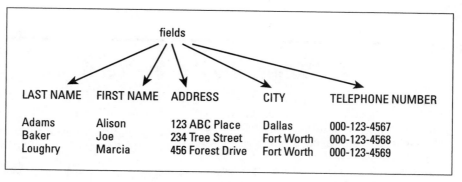

fields

LAST NAME	FIRST NAME	ADDRESS	CITY	TELEPHONE NUMBER
Adams	Alison	123 ABC Place	Dallas	000-123-4567
Baker	Joe	234 Tree Street	Fort Worth	000-123-4568
Loughry	Marcia	456 Forest Drive	Fort Worth	000-123-4569

Carrying this example still farther, you can also have an electronic phone book set up as a *countrywide* phone book that logically groups its entries first by state and then by city. Or you can have a *worldwide* phone book that logically groups data by country, by state or province, and finally by city.

This logical, top-down design (that is, moving from the largest to the smallest unit) is known as a *hierarchical* structure. Active Directory also exhibits a hierarchical structure.

You can customize Active Directory (it's extensible)

Much as you see in the electronic phone book example in the preceding section, Active Directory also exhibits a *logical* structure. As you can with an electronic phone book, you can search the Active Directory database for the objects that you want to access. Unlike the phone book, however, you can customize the Active Directory database to include additional objects and object attributes that you deem important. This feature makes Active Directory *extensible,* which means that you can add to it.

I get into the more technical aspects of the Active Directory database architecture and how to modify the database in later chapters. For now, you need to know only the following simple facts about Active Directory:

✔ Active Directory is a database containing all the objects in your Windows 2000 environment.

✔ Active Directory has a logical structure (or hierarchy).

✔ You can customize (or extend) Active Directory to include the additional objects and attributes you define.

Where did it come from?

Although you may begin to think so before you're through, Microsoft didn't introduce Active Directory just to make its certification tests harder and your life more stressful. Active Directory actually derives from a standard known as *X.500*. The X.500 standard is a set of recommendations for designers of directory services to ensure that the products of various vendors can work together. These are the X.500 protocols:

✔ Directory Access Protocol (DAP)

✔ Directory System Protocol (DSP)

✔ Directory Information Shadowing Protocol (DISP)

✔ Directory Operational Binding Management Protocol (DOP)

Active Directory, however, actually uses the Lightweight Directory Access Protocol (LDAP), Version 3, to access the directory database instead of using any of the preceding X.500 protocols. So although Active Directory is X.500 *compatible,* meaning that it can work with other X.500-based directory services, it's not X.500 *compliant,* which means that it doesn't strictly adhere to all the specifications of X.500.

Getting Hip to Active Directory Lingo

Experience shows that new terminology often accompanies new technologies, and Active Directory is no exception. Although most of the terms that you use in describing the system may seem familiar, they take on new meaning in relation to Active Directory. So before beginning to plan and implement Active Directory, you need to master its new language.

The building blocks of Active Directory

First, be aware that Active Directory embodies both a *physical* and a *logical* structure. The *physical structure* encompasses the network configuration, network devices, and network bandwidth. The *logical structure* is conceptual; it aims to match the Active Directory configuration to the business processes of a corporation or organization. In the best logical structures, Active Directory resources are structured for the way employees work, not to simplify construction of the network.

If you logically organize the components within the Active Directory, the actual physical structure of the network becomes inconsequential to the end users. If user JoeB wants to print to a printer named A5, for example, he no longer needs to know which server hosts the printer or in which domain the print server resides. In Active Directory, he simply pulls up an Active Directory list of all available printers and chooses printer A5.

Although you may think that this process sounds too good to be true, you need to keep in mind that this new functionality doesn't quite configure itself! You, the system administrator, must first design the logical structure of your organization's Active Directory, matching its structure to how employees interact within the organization. Chapters 4 through 6 in this book help you to plan and implement, but first you must become familiar with the individual components that you use for planning the physical and logical structures.

Domain

In Windows 2000, Microsoft defines a *domain* as a security boundary or an administrative boundary, which means that all the users within a domain function under the same security policy and user-account policy. If you want to assign different policies to some users, those users belong in a separate domain.

JohnB, for example, is a regular user in the Sales department who must change his password every 30 days. SueD, on the other hand, is a user in the Treasury department who has access to sensitive information and therefore must change her password every 14 days. The two departments, Sales and Treasury, have different user-account policy settings. Because you assign user-account policies according to domain, users in these two departments belong in separate domains.

The term *domain* takes on a different meaning in Windows 2000 than it had in Windows NT. In Windows 2000, a domain is a group of resources that shares common security and administrative boundaries. The geographic location of resources isn't of primary importance. In Windows NT, domains usually consist of either resources that are grouped geographically or user accounts (all users and groups for an organization) that are not necessarily grouped geographically.

Here are some other important characteristics of a Windows 2000 domain:

✔ A Windows 2000 domain has at least one *domain controller*. A domain controller is a server that authenticates (validates the password and ID of) users seeking access to the domain.

✔ A domain's directory database *replicates* between all domain controllers in the domain. Replication is the exchange of updated database information among domain controllers so that all the domain controllers contain identical database information.

✔ A single domain can form a *tree,* which you learn about in the following section.

In the design process for the logical structure of an Active Directory database, you use a triangle in the design flowchart to represent a domain (see Figure 1-3).

Figure 1-3:
The symbol that you use to represent a domain when drawing a design flowchart.

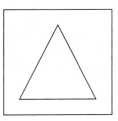

Another reason to consider defining an additional domain is to keep replication traffic local — confined among domain controllers connected by a local area network (LAN). The transmission speed between domain controllers in a LAN is much faster than it is between domain controllers at a distance that are connected by a slower, wide area network (WAN). The exchange of updated database information among domain controllers during replication causes additional traffic that can clog the network and result in slower response times. So by keeping your replication local, you can keep replication time to a minimum and ensure that the network lines are available for other traffic. (I talk more about defining domains in Chapter 4.)

Tree

A *tree* is a hierarchical grouping of domains within the same namespace. A namespace is a logically structured naming convention in which all objects are connected in an unbroken sequence. (I talk more about namespaces later in this chapter and in Chapter 3.) As you design an Active Directory tree, you begin with the topmost domain, which oddly enough is known as the *root* (or *parent*) domain. Subdomains (sometimes called *child* domains) branch downward from the root, as shown in Figure 1-4. Supposedly, if you turn your logical structure drawing upside down, it resembles a tree — hence the name. (Go on — turn the book upside down and look for the image of a tree in Figure 1-4!)

Regardless of whether you actually see a tree when you turn the book upside down, the term *tree* is one that you use often in discussing directory services. And the arboricultural (it's a real word — honest!) terminology doesn't stop there — as you'll discover as you find out more about Active Directory.

As you add domains to an Active Directory tree, you automatically create *transitive* trust relationships. Transitive trusts extend the relationship between two trusted domains to any other domains that those two domains trust. These trusts are bidirectional and enable users in one domain to access resources in the other domain. In an Active Directory tree, all domains are connected through transitive trusts, so a user in one domain can access any other domain in the tree.

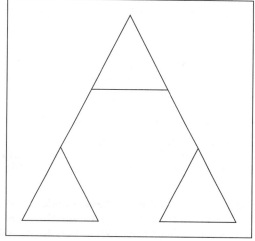

Figure 1-4:
A tree diagram in Active Directory.

You can also link trees or forests through *explicit,* or one-way, trusts. By creating an explicit trust between Tree A and Tree B, for example, you can specify that users from Tree A can access resources in Tree B, but users in Tree B cannot access resources in Tree A.

Forest

A *forest* is a logical grouping of trees that you join together in a transitive trust relationship, as shown in Figure 1-5. A forest has the following characteristics:

- ✔ Each tree in a forest has a distinct namespace.
- ✔ The trees in a forest share the same schema and global catalog. (I discuss schema and global catalog a little later in this chapter.)

Chapter 4 helps you to determine when to create a tree and when to create a forest.

Organizational unit (OU)

An *organizational unit* (or OU) is nothing more than a logical container within a domain. You use it to store similar objects so that they're in a convenient location for administration and access. Here are some of the objects that you store in an OU:

✔ Printers

✔ File shares (a folder located anywhere on the network that has been designated as *shared* so that others can access it)

✔ Users

✔ Groups (a grouping of users that can be jointly administered)

✔ Applications

As you plan your Active Directory structure, you also plan the logical structure of the OUs within each domain. Keep the following points in mind as you become familiar with OUs:

✔ You can *nest* OUs within each other to create a hierarchical structure.

✔ Each domain can have its own hierarchy of OUs, or the OU hierarchy can be identical in each domain. You cannot, however, extend an OU across domains. OUs are always completely contained within a single domain.

✔ Structure OUs to correspond with the business practices of your company. Earlier in the chapter, I talked about matching the logical structure to the way employees work. OUs can help you to organize network resources so that they're easy to locate and to manage.

✔ Traditionally, you use a circle to represent an OU in a logical design diagram.

Figure 1-5:
A diagram
of an Active
Directory
forest.

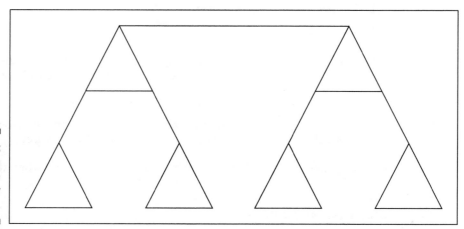

An OU model needs to reflect the administrative model of the organization. A company with centralized administrative support is more likely to implement an OU hierarchy that's similar in all domains. But a company with distributed administration is more likely to have OUs that differ from domain to domain.

A domain that you name West, for example, represents your company's western region of the United States. This domain includes OUs that you name California, Washington, and Oregon, as shown in Figure 1-6. The California OU contains two nested OUs that you name San Francisco and San Diego. The Washington OU contains objects that you organize in OUs that you further name Tacoma and Seattle. To ease administration by keeping things similar, the East domain follows the same conventions used in the West domain.

If you want, you can further organize the city OUs so that San Francisco, San Diego, Tacoma, and Seattle each contain nested OUs for user objects and printer objects.

Figure 1-6:
Nested organizational units (OUs) in Active Directory.

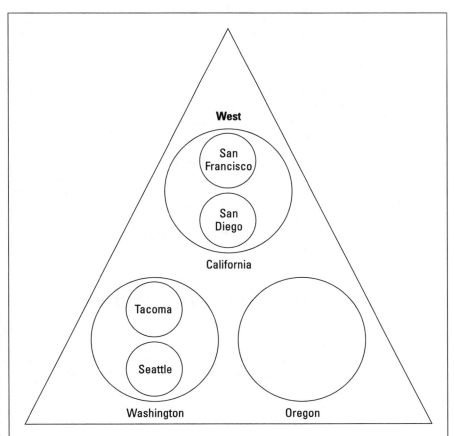

Object

An *object* is any component within your Windows 2000 environment. (I talked briefly about objects in the section "Active Directory Is a Database" earlier in this chapter.) A printer, a user, and a group, for example, are all objects. All objects contain descriptive information known as attributes.

Site

A *site* is a grouping of IP subnets connected by high-speed or high-bandwidth links. Sites are part of your network's physical topology (or physical shape), and each site can contain domain controllers from one or more domains.

During your planning stages for implementing Active Directory, you define a site topology for your environment. You use sites to optimize a network's bandwidth by controlling replication and logon authentication traffic. (Chapter 13 tells you how to use sites to control traffic.)

By dividing the network into sites, you can limit the amount of replicated Active Directory data that you must send across slow WAN links. Whereas domain controllers within a single site exchange uncompressed data because they are connected by fast links, domain controllers spread across different sites exchange compressed data to minimize traffic.

I devote Chapter 13 to a discussion of controlling replication traffic. But for now, just be aware that replication occurs whenever the domain controllers within a domain exchange directory database information. Updates or additions to the database trigger replication between domain controllers within a site.

You also use sites as authentication boundaries for network clients. Although any domain controller throughout the domain can authenticate a user, designating any but the closest one to do so isn't always the most efficient use of the network. After you specify your site boundaries, the closest available domain controller within the client's site authenticates a client logon. This setup minimizes authentication traffic on the network and speeds response time for the client.

The Active Directory schema

Along with the basic Active Directory components that I discuss in the preceding sections, you must also become familiar with the Active Directory *schema*. The schema contains definitions of all object classes (or object categories) and attributes that you can store in the directory.

All about OIDs

Object Identifiers are dotted decimal numbers that the American National Standards Institute (ANSI) assigns to each object class and attribute. ANSI assigns a specific root identifier to a U.S. corporation or organization, and the corporation then assigns variations of its root identifier to the objects and attributes that it creates. For example, Microsoft's OID is 1.3.6.1.4.1.311, which maps to the following path:

```
iso.org.dod.internet.private.
    enterprise.microsoft
```

At the time that you install Active Directory, you also install a base schema by default. This schema contains the object-class definitions and attributes of all components available in Windows 2000. As your directory tree grows, you can extend or modify the schema by adding or altering classes and attributes as follows:

- ✔ You can create a new object class.
- ✔ You can create a new attribute.
- ✔ You can modify an object class.
- ✔ You can modify an attribute.
- ✔ You can disable an object class.
- ✔ You can disable an attribute.

(In Chapter 13, I show you how to do all the schema modifications shown in the preceding list.)

Remember that, by definition, an object must have defining attributes; each object has *required attributes* and *optional attributes*. Among the required attributes of any object are the following:

- ✔ Name
- ✔ Object Identifier (OID) (see the sidebar)
- ✔ List of required attributes
- ✔ List of optional attributes

Doesn't it seem odd that a list of *optional* attributes is a *required* attribute for an object?

Not just anyone can modify the directory schema. Only members of the Schema Administrators group can do so. The Schema Administrators group is a built-in group installed by default when you initially install Active Directory. The group is preconfigured with the appropriate privileges for performing particular tasks. As system administrator, you can assign particular users to this group by adding their user IDs to the group. (See Chapter 11 for the details on adding users to groups.)

Limit the number of administrators in your organization's Schema Administrators group to protect yourself against unintended results! Every organization should have a precise change-control policy that governs changes to the directory schema. The schema affects an entire forest, so any change is replicated to every domain in the forest. The potential for disaster is huge! Chapter 10 offers suggestions for developing a change-control policy.

The global catalog

Another new component of Windows 2000 is the *global catalog*. The global catalog is a searchable index that enables users to locate network objects without needing to know their domain locations. It is a partial replica of the Active Directory, containing all objects in the directory but not all of an object's attributes.

The global catalog enables searches among trees in a forest. You can also use it to speed lengthy searches within a single tree. By default, the global catalog doesn't contain all the attributes of every object. The default global catalog configuration includes only those attributes that you're most likely to use for a search, such as a user's first or last name. Similarly, you can search the global catalog for all *color* printers instead of browsing through all the printers on the network.

You can add attributes to (or remove them from) the global catalog. But remember that the catalog replicates among all the global catalog servers in the forest. If you add attributes to the global catalog, you increase the amount of replication traffic on the network.

The default schema settings determine which object attributes appear in the global catalog. All objects appear in the global catalog, but only a small subset of the objects' attributes are included. To add additional attributes to the global catalog, you have to modify the schema. (See Chapter 13 for additional information on modifying the schema.)

By default, the first domain controller that you create in a forest becomes the global catalog server. If the environment consists of multiple sites, you can optimize network traffic by creating a global catalog server in each site.

The global catalog is a service that runs on domain controllers. You manage the service using the Active Directory Sites and Services snap-in for the Microsoft Management Console (MMC). The MMC is a Windows 2000 Server system file that you access by choosing Run from the Start menu and typing **mmc**. From within MMC, open the Console menu and choose Add/Remove Snap-in; then choose AD Sites and Services from the list that appears.

The DNS namespace

DNS (Domain Name Service) is the predominant name-resolution service on the Internet, so Microsoft chose to use DNS to translate host names to IP addresses in the Active Directory service. The DNS *namespace* is the single most important requirement for a successful Active Directory implementation, and the two are tightly interwoven. If you don't plan the DNS namespace appropriately, your Active Directory service is difficult to administer and doesn't adequately serve the user community.

A thorough understanding of DNS and of TCP/IP is essential for planning and implementing Windows 2000 and Active Directory. A good source of information is *MCSE TCP/IP For Dummies* by Cameron Brandon (published by IDG Books Worldwide, Inc.).

As you discover when you get to Chapter 3, you must plan the DNS namespace before you can design the Active Directory. You use the DNS namespace design that you create (or one that already exists for your organization) to design a domain namespace for Active Directory.

If you're not using the Microsoft DNS service, you must use another DNS service that's compliant with RFC 2136 and RFC 2052.

Because It's Good for You: The Benefits of Active Directory

I don't know about you, but whenever Mom told me to eat my vegetables because "they're good for you," I still wasn't particularly motivated. I needed to know more about what that broccoli was actually going to do for me.

So maybe, like me with my vegetables, you need to hear about the real benefits you'll ultimately realize if you bite the bullet now and make the management and design changes required by Windows 2000 and Active Directory.

Active Directory offers appealing features for administrators and end users alike, as the following list describes:

- ✔ Ease of management because of the centralized nature of the Active Directory database.

- ✔ Enhanced scalability (it can get lots bigger!) that enables the Active Directory database to hold millions of objects without altering the administrative model.

- ✔ A searchable catalog that enables you to quickly and easily search network resources. The network becomes less intrusive, enabling users to concentrate on their work instead of on their tools.

- ✔ Consolidation of domain controller roles. You no longer need primary domain controllers (PDCs) and backup domain controllers (BDCs); instead, Active Directory relies on domain controllers (DCs).

I encourage you to follow through all the planning and testing steps that I present in this book. With the right preparation, Active Directory can offer tremendous advantages for both you and your organization.

Chapter 2

Doing Your Active Directory Homework

In This Chapter

▶ Analyzing your current architecture and infrastructure

▶ Gathering requirements

▶ Figuring out what you need

▶ Installing versus upgrading

Do you ever use a shopping mall directory to locate a store? If so, what two things do you do before you figure out how to reach that store? Probably the following:

✔ Locate your destination

✔ Identify your current location (the "you-are-here" dot)

You follow these same two steps whenever you use a roadmap to take a trip. The point is that you must know where you're starting from before you can begin your travels.

Similarly, before you begin designing an Active Directory structure for your environment, you need to identify your starting point. After you define and document the current environment, you can move on to planning and implementing. In this chapter, I show you how to begin preparing a plan for your Active Directory implementation.

Beginning at the . . . Well, Beginning!

Few of you are going to start out with no network or infrastructure in place. So before you begin migrating to Windows 2000 and Active Directory, you must create a plan that enables you to maximize the network and equipment you already have. Furthermore, you must make sure that the plan accommodates both the needs of users and your organization's future business direction. And then you must consider the desires of the IT director and the CFO, who usually want to reduce hardware expenditures and lower administrative costs.

Whew! You have a lot of planning to do. Fortunately, you can do several things to make the planning phase easier. By completing the steps in the remainder of this chapter, you define your current location and locate your starting point. From there, you move easily into planning your Active Directory tree because, by that point, the answers are right at your fingertips.

 I doubt that you're going to be planning and implementing Windows 2000 and Active Directory all by yourself. After you create all the documents that I list in this chapter, I recommend that you produce a project notebook for each member of your project team. The notebook should contain logical structure diagrams (Chapter 4), physical topology diagrams (Chapter 5), and all the documentation on your current architecture from this chapter.

Reviewing your current architecture

The first step in getting ready to install Active Directory is to review and document your current network architecture. In Chapters 8 and 9, I help you determine the migration strategy for various operating systems and architectures. But first you must identify the architecture that's currently in place so that you can later determine which migration strategy is right for your situation.

The output (or homework) resulting from this review is a logical architecture document that includes the following components:

 ✔ A diagram of the current architecture

 ✔ A profile of servers and their roles

 ✔ A listing of services running on each server

The goal of compiling this logical architecture document is to provide a complete picture of the existing environment, including the servers and services, so that you can appropriately plan your Windows 2000 implementation. If you currently have an NT 4.0 environment, for example, you diagram the domain model, identify the servers and their roles, and create a list of services running on each server. In Figure 2-1, I show an example of a logical diagram for a single-master domain model. (If the term *single-master domain model* is unfamiliar to you, don't even worry about that right now. I discuss the various domain models in Chapter 7.)

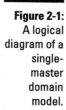

Figure 2-1:
A logical
diagram of a
single-
master
domain
model.

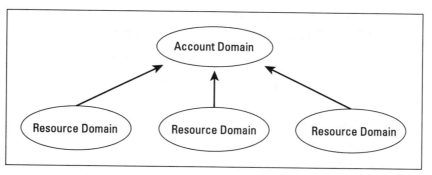

Next, you need to create a listing of all the servers in all the domains on your network. The more information that you include in this preparatory document, the less time you can expect to spend hunting for the information during the planning process.

Finally, you need to document every service that's running on every server. For example, DNS, DHCP, and WINS are all services that could be running on your servers. You can integrate this information into your list of servers, or you can prepare a separate document for it. Just be sure that you have documented all this information before moving on to the planning phase.

You don't want any big surprises turning up for the deployment team when they arrive to migrate the server to Windows 2000! I once showed up at a site expecting to find 8 NT 4.0 servers. Instead, I found 14 servers and a combination of operating systems: NT 3.51, NT 4.0, Banyan Vines, and NetWare. Needless to say, I wasn't prepared to migrate those servers.

This preparation document is going to get a lot of use! During the planning phase, you use it to plan the Active Directory tree and to identify the Windows 2000 features and services that you need to implement. Later, you use the document to determine a migration strategy and migration order for your Windows 2000 migration. Finally, you use it as a guide during the implementation phase to make sure that the deployment team has a complete profile of each server you are migrating to Windows 2000.

Analyzing network diagrams

Your next task is to locate and analyze the diagrams of your network infrastructure. Somewhere around the office, you have a diagram. It was created at the time that you (or whoever came before you) put the network in place, and it may or may not be up to date. If you can't find the network diagram, you need to create one. If the existing diagram is outdated, you need to change it. You can't plan an effective Active Directory structure without an accurate picture of the current network.

At a minimum, the network diagram needs to include information about the following characteristics and features:

- ✔ Physical locations of your company's offices (cities and countries)
- ✔ Bandwidth capacity between locations
- ✔ IP addresses of network devices
- ✔ Routers
- ✔ Switches
- ✔ Hubs
- ✔ Servers
- ✔ Firewalls

In a very large enterprise, network diagrams often fill several pages. In such a case, you want to make your first diagram a big-picture view without a great deal of detail. Figure 2-2 shows this simplified type of diagram for a company with three locations on their WAN. Subsequent pages then contain the details for specific locations or portions of the network. (In Chapter 5, I explain more about creating a network diagram.)

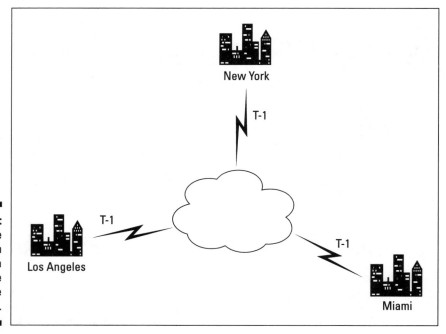

Figure 2-2:
A sample diagram showing a big-picture view of the network.

If you're the lucky one who gets to create a network diagram, take heart. I include evaluation versions of Visio Professional 5.0 and Visio Enterprise 5.0 on the CD-ROM that you find in the back of this book. You can use Visio for creating your physical and logical network diagrams. In fact, I used Visio 5.0 to create all the original diagrams for this book.

Taking stock: Inventorying your hardware and software

You need to inventory all the hardware and installed software on the network to determine whether your equipment meets the Windows 2000 Server system requirements. This software inventory helps you to determine whether you can upgrade each server, or if you must do a fresh install on each one.

Include the following items in your hardware inventory:

- Vendor name and model number
- Processor type
- Memory
- Disk capacity
- Disk subsystem
- Disk configuration
- File system
- Network card make and model
- Other installed devices

Include the following items in your inventory of server software:

- Operating system version
- Service packs, patches, and hot fixes
- Application software
- Services
- Drivers

A *hot fix* is a software "patch" to fix a software problem. Software vendors distribute these to clients who have an urgent need for a solution to a particular problem and can't wait for the next service pack or version to be distributed.

Documenting current DNS services

If your current environment doesn't include DNS services, your documenting is easy! But DNS is a necessary component for Active Directory, so you do have to include it in your planning. If you're not currently using a DNS service, I recommend that you implement Microsoft's DNS service.

If you use DNS already, you first need to determine whether the existing DNS service meets the requirements of Active Directory.

To correctly integrate with Active Directory, the DNS service must comply with RFC 2052 and RFC 2136 standards. RFC 2052 describes the Service Location resource records. RFC 2136 describes dynamic updates.

Microsoft doesn't insist that you implement its own DNS product. Microsoft does, however, tout its capability of storing DNS information in the Active Directory database so that replication becomes more efficient. A third-party DNS product can't store information within Active Directory (shrewd planning by Microsoft), so the network is burdened with additional replication traffic.

Regardless of whose product you're using, however, you still need to document the existing DNS entries. You may want to create a diagram similar to the one shown in Figure 2-3 to help you visualize the DNS hierarchy.

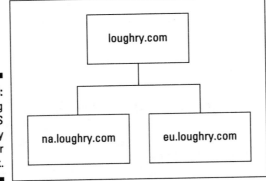

Figure 2-3:
Diagramming the DNS hierarchy of your network.

In Chapter 3, I talk at length about DNS. But if you aren't familiar with DNS or just want a refresher, check out *MCSE TCP/IP For Dummies* by Cameron Brandon (published by IDG Books Worldwide, Inc.).

Analyzing the administrative model

What type of administrative model is currently in place? Remember that Active Directory enables you to delegate administrative authority for specific branches of the tree. To plan the new tree appropriately, you need to understand what's already in place.

Perhaps your organization relies strictly on centralized administration and has only a small number of system administrators with equivalent levels of privilege. More likely, as various departments or divisions brought domains and servers on-line, you needed to distribute authority among additional administrators. All this information goes into your documentation.

You may notice that I rely on conceptual views quite a bit, and this area is no exception. I suggest that you draw a diagram representing your NetWare Directory Service (NDS) tree or Windows NT domain model and indicate the administrative boundaries on the diagram. In Figure 2-4, for example, the one-way trust relationships show that domain administrators in the Corporate Account domain can administer all four domains. Yet the domain administrators of the regional domains can administer only within their regions. The fact that the arrows are pointing in a single direction illustrates that the trust relationships work only in that direction. Capturing these administrative boundaries from the existing environment in your diagram is important so that you can plan domains and organizational units in the Active Directory tree accordingly.

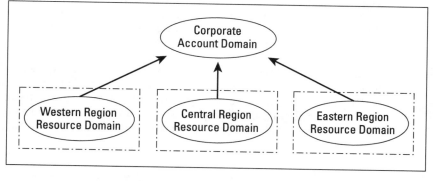

Figure 2-4:
Documenting a Windows NT administrative model.

Gathering standards documents

Most organizations put a variety of standards in place within their information technology (IT) department. These standards can include any of the following categories:

✔ Naming standards for users, groups, servers, and domains

✔ Hardware standards for servers, desktops, and network devices

✔ Protocol standards

✔ Network addressing standards

✔ Application standards

✔ Security standards

Document and gather all these IT standards. You obviously need the naming standards and security standards as you construct the Active Directory structure. The other standards you use in determining what equipment and applications from your current environment are suitable for Windows 2000.

At this point, if you have worked your way through all the preceding sections of this chapter, you have a notebook (or a pile of paper!) that provides a complete snapshot of the existing infrastructure, including administrative details and corporate standards. Now that you have a clear idea of where you're starting from, the following sections help you determine where you're going!

Know Thyself: Identifying Your Goals

Before you begin designing the Active Directory and implementing Windows 2000, it's a very good idea to make sure that the project team's direction is in step with that of the corporation as a whole. After all, if the company is going in one direction and your team is going in another, the project is likely to fail. This section provides you with a couple pulse points to check before you go any farther with your planning.

You may consider these points elementary. But if you've never before designed or planned at the enterprise level, you need to be aware that these are the things that many people tend to overlook in their zeal to implement a new system. Skipping these steps costs you money in the long run and may mean the difference between a successful project and an embarrassing failure.

Identifying the corporate direction

Make sure that you know the corporate direction. Does the company plan to diversify or to concentrate on existing business? Does it plan to open new offices or to centralize in fewer locations? Obviously, you need to know which scenario to plan for.

A good way to gather this information is to obtain a copy of the company's business plan. Most of the time, you find that a company plans at least five years out. Knowing the plans for the next two or more years enables you to plan for appropriate network and server capacity.

Getting the boss's viewpoint

Well, the viewpoint of the boss is right in line with the corporate direction, right? Not always true — the budget may determine the real direction.

Before you begin planning, sit down with the IT manager or director to determine her mission. Perhaps you discover that the company has charged the IT manager with reducing administrative costs by 50 percent. That fact certainly determines how you plan your directory tree! Or maybe you discover that she plans to consolidate hardware to more effectively use existing equipment. Again, that information is going to profoundly affect how you design and implement.

Gathering user requirements

Last, but not least, is the task of polling your user community to determine what it needs from the network and network services. Some project teams hold a meeting and invite a representative from each department. Some send out questionnaires that ask each user to describe how he uses his PC in completing his work. But the best way to gather user requirements is to use a combination of both methods.

First, send an e-mail directing users to a Web page that explains the anticipated changes. Have them complete a survey that captures their use of network resources. Find out what capabilities they need that the current network doesn't offer. If your project includes desktop upgrades, have them fill out a station review so that you obtain an inventory of their hardware and software. Finally, schedule a meeting with a representative from each department to discuss special needs and concerns.

"Unplug it and see who screams" is *not* a method of administration that I recommend! By meeting with the users in advance, you often uncover resources that the IT department isn't aware of and doesn't support. Nevertheless, someone screams if the resource goes down. Finding out up front enables you to plan for those requirements — and to prevent a black mark on your project-satisfaction survey.

Documenting requirements

After you gather requirements from all areas of the corporation, divide the combined requirements into the following three categories:

- ✔ Must-haves
- ✔ Nice-to-haves (but not a requirement)
- ✔ Icing on the cake

Begin with the must-have category and determine which features of Windows 2000 and Active Directory fulfill those requirements. Then work through the remaining categories, adding services where feasible and affordable.

I like to create a chart that compares user requirements against the services or features that the new environment can provide. Such a chart makes a good slide for presenting to the boss, as well as a good checklist at the end of the project.

Full Steam Ahead!

You're almost done with the prep work. I guarantee that you're going to like this section because this is where you begin actually working with Windows 2000 Server.

After you compile a complete inventory of your existing servers, you next need to determine whether the existing equipment is suitable for Windows 2000, as well as which version of Windows 2000 Server your network requires. You also need to determine the best way to migrate your servers to Windows 2000 — by an installation or an upgrade. An *installation* takes place if you load Windows 2000 Server onto a partition that doesn't currently hold an operating system (OS). (This procedure is sometimes known as a *fresh build*.) An *upgrade* takes place if you load Windows 2000 Server over an existing operating system, overwriting the previous OS's system files in the process.

Microsoft recommends that you upgrade domain controllers first, beginning with the PDC (primary domain controller). You can upgrade a member server to Windows 2000 Server before upgrading your domain controllers, but I prefer to upgrade the more complex servers first. If you find that you must upgrade a member server before upgrading the domain controllers, you can make the member server a standalone server and join it to a domain at a later time. Or you can let it peacefully coexist with the Windows NT servers in the domain.

Windows 2000 Server is not as restrictive in determining server roles during installation as is Windows NT. You can promote a Windows 2000 member server to a domain controller. You can also demote a domain controller to a member server or a standalone server. You can make all these role changes happen without reinstalling the operating system.

Those pesky system requirements

Whether you install or upgrade, the hardware must meet the Windows 2000 Server system requirements and appear on the Windows 2000 Server Hardware Compatibility List (HCL). The Windows 2000 Server CD contains a copy of the HCL, but the most current version is always on the Microsoft Web site at www.microsoft.com. Table 2-1 lists the system requirements for Windows 2000 Server.

Table 2-1	System Requirements for Windows 2000 Server	
Component	**Minimum**	**Recommended**
Monitor	VGA or higher	
Processor	P166	P-II 300
Memory	64MB	128MB
Disk space	850MB	1.2GB

Windows 2000 Server supports up to two processors. Windows 2000 Advanced Server supports up to four processors. If you plan to *install* a server with three or four processors, you must purchase Windows 2000 Advanced Server. But if you *upgrade* a multiprocessor server from Windows NT 4.0 and that server already supports up to four processors, Windows 2000 Server can support all four of those processors. Notice that the discrepancy between the system requirements depends on whether you're installing or upgrading. Odd!

Review the hardware inventory you created earlier, matching the hardware and software for each server against the HCL and system requirements. Highlight any equipment that's not on the HCL and any servers that don't meet the system requirements. You need to either upgrade or replace those components that don't meet all Windows 2000 Server requirements.

If your equipment doesn't appear on the HCL, contact the hardware vendor to see whether it's recently been tested for use with Windows 2000 Server.

The big decision: Upgrading versus starting over

Installing or upgrading — each option has its advantages and disadvantages, and everyone has a preference. You should already have a list of all servers, their roles, and the services running on each server. Use the list to decide which servers require a fresh install of Windows 2000 and which are good candidates for an upgrade.

Always create a full backup of the server before beginning any upgrade or additions. Then verify the backup by reloading some of the data. This extra step takes a few more minutes, but it's well worth the effort in the long run. If the backup tape is faulty, you could lose a lot of valuable data — and possibly your job.

Upgrading

Obviously, if the current operating system is anything but Windows NT, you must install Windows 2000 Server from scratch. But if the current operating system is Windows NT Server 3.51 or 4.0, you can either install a new build of Windows 2000 Server or upgrade the existing version of Windows NT Server.

You can't upgrade Windows NT Server version 3.5 to Windows 2000 Server. Nor can you upgrade Windows NT 4.0 Server Enterprise Edition to Windows 2000 Server. You can upgrade the Enterprise Edition of NT 4.0 only to Windows 2000 Advanced Server. Make sure that you buy the right product.

Upgrading a server has the following two distinct advantages:

- ✔ You don't need to reinstall all your applications.
- ✔ You don't need to re-create users, groups, and permissions.

In a large enterprise, reinstalling applications and re-creating objects and permissions is time-consuming. Reinstalling and re-creating can also leave too great a margin for error!

You must upgrade each of your existing servers to one of the following three server roles in Windows 2000:

- ✔ Domain controller
- ✔ Member server
- ✔ Standalone server

Windows 2000 no longer has separate roles for the primary domain controller (PDC) and backup domain controller (BDC). Instead, you simply have domain controllers (DCs). The function of member servers is the same as under Windows NT. Standalone servers do not belong to a domain.

As you can see from Table 2-2, Windows 2000 Server Setup directs you to take the following upgrade paths:

- Upgrade a PDC to a domain controller.
- Upgrade a BDC to either a domain controller or a member server.
- Upgrade a member server to either a member server or a standalone server (not a member of a domain).
- Upgrade a standalone server to either a standalone server or a member server.

An X in a column in Table 2-2 means that the server listed to the left can become the type of server indicated by the column heading when you run Setup to upgrade a server.

Table 2-2	Upgrade Paths in Windows 2000 Server Setup		
NT Server Role	*DC*	*Member Server*	*Standalone Server*
PDC	x		
BDC	x	x	
Member server		x	x
Standalone server		x	x

Windows NT places strict parameters around server roles. You determine the role of each server at installation, and other than promoting or demoting a domain controller, you can't change the server's role without reinstalling the operating system. You also can't move domain controllers to different domains without reinstalling the operating system. Unless you know exactly what you're doing, you quickly become very good at reinstalling!

But Windows 2000 Server is much more flexible than NT. As I mention earlier in this section, servers can change roles. But you can also move domain controllers to different domains. You can even rename domains without reinstalling the operating system. Active Directory is purposely flexible so that the structure can change as the business model changes. Imagine!

Starting fresh

Most experienced system administrators have horror stories of unexplainable phenomena on servers that they upgraded from NT 3.51 to NT 4.0. (None of them have ever *seen* the ghosts, yet they know that they're there!) Many feel that a fresh build is the only way to avoid conflicting drivers and mismatched system files. If you can afford the time it takes to reinstall applications and re-create users and permissions, a fresh install may prove to be your best choice.

When you install Windows 2000 Server, you discover that a multitude of optional services and features are available. The options that you install depend on the role the server plays and the services that you choose to provide on the network. Make sure that you know all the following information before you begin the installation so that you select the correct options:

- ✔ Server role
- ✔ Server name
- ✔ IP addressing information
- ✔ Partition sizes
- ✔ File system
- ✔ Domain or workgroup name
- ✔ Additional services your users require

Thinking about dual-booting? (Give that idea the boot!)

Dual-booting refers to the process of installing two operating systems on the same server. Each time you restart the server, you can choose which operating system to use. To be honest, I can think of few circumstances that require a server to dual-boot. Dual-booting is more common on workstations, desktops, and laptops if the user has applications that run only on a certain operating system.

Sometimes an administrator creates a dual-boot configuration if she is concerned about a system crash during an upgrade. The administrator leaves the former operating system in place so that she can still boot the server if a crash occurs. But because Windows 2000 enables you to boot in *safe mode* (starting the server using only basic drivers), creating a dual-boot configuration gains you little, and it adds a lot of complexity.

The biggest problem with dual-booting on a server is the choice of file system to use: FAT, FAT32, or NTFS. In case you identify a need to dual-boot your server, be aware that you face a significant compatibility issue between the NTFS file systems in Windows NT 4.0 and Windows 2000. NTFS in Windows 2000 has enhanced features that aren't available if you're booting under NT 4.0. Although FAT or FAT32 are better choices for sharing files between different operating systems, they offer little or no file security.

Think carefully before taking on the challenge of dual-booting a server. It could prove to be much more trouble than it's worth.

Pulling it all together

By now, you may realize that I have a fetish for documentation — particularly when the documentation concerns migrating servers and data. But, hey — experience is a painful teacher! It's taught me to leave little to chance. That's why I work from charts and checklists as often as possible. And that's why I suggest that you document and organize all the information that I discuss in this chapter.

Some of the information that you gather while planning for Active Directory and Windows 2000 may surprise you. You're likely to uncover services and resources that you weren't aware of before your inventory. Rest assured, however, that the planning and forethought that you put into implementing Active Directory is certain to pay off!

Active Directory is an exciting technology, but it's also very complex. Through implementing Active Directory, you alter the way that you manage and use the network — a potentially expensive proposition, and one that deserves to be treated with care.

Part II
Planning and Building Your First Model

The 5th Wave   By Rich Tennant

IT WAS THE LAST TIME EMILY SERVED ALPHABET SOUP TO HER WORD PUZZLE PLAYING HUSBAND.

Event viewer... NDS tree... Net BIOS...

Obsessive... fanatical... fixated...Ooo-compulsive...

In this part . . .

Active Directory is a very new animal and requires special accommodations. In this part of the book, you find out how to create a logical directory structure that makes network resources more accessible to users and more efficient for you to manage. Then you step right along to creating the physical structure, which optimizes network resources and bandwidth. You measure bandwidth, diagram network resources, and plan for essential services. Finally, you get to create and configure a test model of an Active Directory tree.

Chapter 3

Playing the Name Game

*I*n introducing Active Directory in Windows 2000, Microsoft also presents us with a newly important role for DNS. In past versions of Windows NT, DNS played a secondary role in name resolution while WINS took center stage. But although the Windows Internet Naming Service (WINS) is still around for backward compatibility, DNS is now the star of the show!

DNS is a huge topic, with numerous books devoted to its concepts and implementation. In this chapter, I cover some DNS basics that directly relate to implementing and managing Active Directory. I also tell you more about another new Microsoft technology: Dynamic DNS.

Integrating DNS and Active Directory

Active Directory can't exist without DNS, which provides its underlying namespace. Before you begin designing an Active Directory tree, you must first define a DNS namespace. Now that DNS is assuming such vital importance, you need to understand certain aspects of DNS.

Essential DNS

Simply put, DNS (Domain Name Service) is a name-resolution service. A network client searching for a host uses DNS to resolve the host's name to its IP address. In simple (really simple!) terms, the process goes something as follows:

1. A network client transmits a message to a DNS server, asking for the IP address that matches a given host name.

2. The DNS server searches its DNS database for the host name and locates the IP address that corresponds to the host name.

3. The DNS server returns a message containing the IP address to the network client.

4. The network client then directs a message to the desired host by using the appropriate IP address.

If you need more information about DNS client and server interaction, see *MCSE TCP/IP For Dummies* by Cameron Brandon (published by IDG Books Worldwide, Inc.).

In its simplest form (are you seeing a simple pattern emerging?), an entry in the DNS database table looks something like the following example:

```
L01.corp.com   IN   A   10.50.4.41
```

This entry is known as a *resource record*. The preceding example matches the IP address `10.50.4.41` to a server with the name `L01` in the `corp.com` domain. A *DNS table* consists of a listing of resource records similar to this example.

Identifying resource records

DNS resource records define more than just names and IP addresses. Various types of resource records identify servers, domains, zones, and services. For example, a resource record identifying a *canonical name* (an alias or nickname) for a server would look like the following:

```
exchange   IN   CNAME   10.50.4.48
```

I list the most common types of resource records in Table 3-1.

Table 3-1	Common Types of Resource Records
Type	*Purpose*
A	*Address* resource records match an IP address to a host name.
CNAME	*Canonical name* resource records associate a nickname to a host name.
MX	*Mail exchange* resource records identify mail servers for the specified domain.
NS	*Name server* resource records identify servers (other than the SOA server) that contain zone information files.
PTR	*Pointer* resource records match a host name to a given IP address. Note that this is the opposite of an A record, which matches an IP address to the supplied host name.
SOA	*Start of authority* resource records specify which server contains the zone file for a domain.
SRV	*Service* resource records identify servers that provide special services to the domain.

An SRV record identifies Active Directory servers within a domain. Before a network client can query the Active Directory database, it must first locate an Active Directory server. SRV records in the DNS database identify those servers. The network client can then query an identified Active Directory server for information about domain resources such as users, printers, and network file shares.

SRV (service) records hold particular importance in Active Directory. Active Directory is dependent on a DNS implementation that supports SRV resource records (as RFC 2052 defines). If your current DNS doesn't support SRV records, change quickly to one that does!

Introducing LDAP

Network clients use *Lightweight Directory Access Protocol* (LDAP) to query the Active Directory database.

RFCs 1777 and 2251 define LDAP. It's based on the X.500 Directory Access Protocol (DAP) but is more efficient and widely implemented.

Understanding RFCs

You no doubt are noticing the frequent sprinklings of the abbreviation RFC throughout this book. A Request for Comments, or RFC, is a document that proposes a new Internet specification or protocol. The Internet Engineering Task Force (IETF) publishes these documents. The IETF is an organization of international participants with an interest in the operation of the Internet. Additional information about the IETF is available at the following Web site:

```
www.ietf.org
```

An author submits RFCs to the IETF as *Internet Drafts*. After approval by the IETF, an Internet Draft becomes an RFC, and the IETF publishes it. By assuring that products adhere to the standards of a particular RFC, vendors ensure interoperability between products.

Windows 2000 introduces a great deal of new technology, so referencing the RFCs on which the technologies are based is a common practice. Following are some important RFCs that relate to Windows 2000 and Active Directory:

- RFC 1777, LDAP version 2
- RFC 1779, LDAP naming conventions
- RFC 1823, LDAP API
- RFC 2052, SRV records
- RFC 2136, Dynamic DNS
- RFC 2247, LDAP naming conventions
- RFC 2251, LDAP version 3

You can find these RFCs on the IETF Web site that I listed earlier in this sidebar.

Don't worry too much about remembering the RFC number associated with a particular technology. (I usually mark those by using the Technical Stuff icon, which means, "Here are the specifics, in case you want to know.") The only two that you may hear mentioned frequently in relation to Active Directory are RFC 2052 and RFC 2136.

The LDAP standards define the following:

- How a client accesses directory service database information
- How a directory service stores the directory information
- How a directory service names the directory objects

Active Directory has a *schema* that defines the object classes and attributes of information that you store in the database. LDAP defines the object classes and attributes. By default, the Active Directory schema contains a base set of objects and the attributes for those objects. You can add to the schema additional objects and attributes that the LDAP standard defines. (In Chapter 13, I tell you how to modify the basic schema.)

The more objects and attributes that you store in the Active Directory database, the larger it becomes. Think carefully about the consequences of replicating this additional information across your network.

LDAP also governs how you name objects within the Active Directory. These naming conventions sometimes look complex, but they actually are hierarchical and map directly to the domain namespace.

Including Dynamic DNS (DDNS)

Another noteworthy addition to Microsoft's DNS is Dynamic DNS, or DDNS (defined in RFC 2136). DDNS enables hosts to write (or register) their own records to the DNS database.

This is similar to the way that WINS lets a computer register a NetBIOS name with the WINS database. But WINS isn't included (or needed) in native mode Windows 2000 implementations. Because Active Directory is dependent on DNS, Microsoft made its DNS service dynamic so that administrators don't need to continually update DNS records.

WINS is still available for backward compatibility with Windows NT 3.51 and 4.0 servers in your domains. When you operate with Windows 2000 servers and NT 3.51 or 4.0 servers in the same domain, you are in *mixed mode*. When all domain servers run Windows 2000, you change to *native mode*. (See Chapter 8 to find out the details of changing to native mode.)

Mixed mode and native mode pertain only to the domain controllers in your domains. A domain can run in native mode and still accommodate Windows 95/98 or Windows NT 3.51 and 4.0 clients.

Although DDNS is not an absolute requirement for Active Directory, I highly recommend it. Without it, administrators must manually type in all the records — a time-consuming, exacting, and tedious task. Sounds like another good reason to use the Microsoft DNS service, doesn't it?

Creating a Domain Namespace

Because you base an Active Directory logical structure on a DNS namespace, you must design the namespace before planning the logical structure. The *namespace* naming convention is hierarchical (logically structured) and contiguous, which means that the objects are connected in an unbroken sequence. All the names within a namespace share the same root domain.

If your root domain is `XYZcorp.com`, for example, all the objects in your namespace share the root domain `XYZcorp.com` as the rightmost name in their fully qualified domain name. That `L01.sales.XYZcorp.com` and `prt1.hr.XYZcorp.com` share the same namespace should, therefore, be pretty obvious.

Begin the process of creating a namespace by choosing a name for your root domain. You want the name to adequately represent your entire organization, yet be brief. Remember that the more layers (or child domains) you include in the namespace, the longer the domain name, and the more characters you have to type. You can't change this name without rebuilding DNS and Active Directory, so make sure that this name displays the following characteristics:

- ✔ The domain name is appropriate for long-term use.
- ✔ The domain name follows DNS naming conventions (as the following paragraph describes).
- ✔ The domain name isn't in use elsewhere on the Internet.
- ✔ The domain name is registered (by your organization) with the correct Internet authority.

Domain names can contain a maximum of 255 characters. Each level of the name can be a maximum of 63 characters, and you insert a period (.) between the levels to separate them. You read the domain name from right to left to determine the hierarchical structure of the namespace. The rightmost name is the top (or root) domain. Allowable characters for DNS names are *0* through *9*, *A* through *Z*, *a* through *z*, and the hyphen character (-). You cannot use any other symbols or special characters in a DNS name.

In the United States, the highest-level domain in a namespace must be one of the top-level Internet organization domains listed in Table 3-2. Outside the United States, a three-character country code represents each country. (See Appendix C for a complete list of these country codes.) Within the top-level domains, a governing agency or party is responsible for assigning second-level domain names. In the United States, an organization known as the InterNIC assigns, or registers, domain names.

Contact the InterNIC at `www.internic.org` to register a domain name. The InterNIC Web site includes a tool that tests a proposed domain name to see whether it's already in use on the Internet. You may need to try several iterations of your chosen domain name before finding one that isn't currently in use.

Don't assume that your chosen domain name is available even after you use the testing tool on the InterNIC Web site. Wait until you receive verification from InterNIC that it's actually registering the domain name to your organization or company before you create your namespace. Remember: You can't change this name without rebuilding DNS and Active Directory!

Table 3-2	Top-Level Internet Domain Names
Domain Name	*Use*
com	Commercial
edu	Educational
gov	U.S. government
mil	U.S. military
net	Networking
org	Not-for-profit organizations

Looking back at my previous example, XYZcorp.com, and reading from right to left: com is the top-level name, XYZcorp is the second-level name that you assign to the company, and sales and hr are each a child domain of XYZcorp. The hierarchy of this namespace is shown in Figure 3-1.

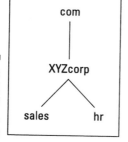

Figure 3-1:
Hierarchical
structure of
XYZcorp.com.

The Internet has been around for a while now, so your organization or company probably has a domain name already. Documenting and diagramming your DNS namespace is important so that you can plan your Active Directory tree (or forest) according to your namespace. In discussing your organization's namespace, refer to the assigned second-level domain name as your root domain.

Implementing Microsoft DNS: You will be assimilated!

If you already have a registered domain name for your company or organization but your DNS implementation doesn't support RFC 2052 and RFC 2136, you have the following two choices:

✔ Migrate to an RFC 2052-compliant version of DNS, such as Microsoft DNS.

✔ Implement Microsoft DNS as a child domain of your assigned root domain.

The SRV records that RFC 2052 details are an absolute requirement if your DNS implementation is to support Active Directory. Dynamic DNS (DDNS), defined in RFC 2136, is not a requirement, but it is strongly recommended. Without DDNS, you're forced to manually enter all the DNS records into the database.

Migrating to a new DNS service can be tedious and time-consuming, so the second option is probably your best choice. In using this option, you create a child domain that contains all the objects in your proposed Active Directory namespace. What you are doing is integrating Microsoft DNS into an existing DNS namespace. So although the child domain where Microsoft DNS is added isn't the root of the total namespace, it functions as the root of the Microsoft DNS namespace. Active Directory recognizes only the portion of the namespace running Microsoft DNS in the Active Directory database; but because all the Windows 2000 elements are within this namespace, that's okay. Using my earlier example again, you can see that I created a child domain to XYZcorp called ad (see Figure 3-2).

Figure 3-2:
Active Directory sees *ad* as the root domain for objects in this scenario.

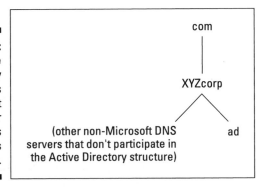

Notice that if you decide *not* to implement Microsoft DNS and to implement some other DNS that's compliant with RFC 2052, you still face another "gotcha." Microsoft DNS saves its data within the Active Directory database. Other DNS implementations can't do that. (As they say on *Star Trek*, "You *will* be assimilated!")

Using Microsoft DNS and integrating DNS data in the Active Directory tree provide the following advantages:

✔ Fault tolerance

✔ More efficient replication traffic

Microsoft DNS optimizes replication traffic by storing DNS data within the Active Directory database. Thus the DNS data replicates along with the Active Directory data. Other DNS versions can't store their data within Active Directory and, therefore, require DNS replication on the network as well. With both Active Directory and DNS replicating updates on your network, you'll see lots of extra traffic. So storing DNS data in the Active Directory database is much more efficient and provides fault tolerance because the information is available from every domain controller.

Selecting internal and external domain names

Another consideration in designing your namespace is whether you want your organization's external domain name — the one that fronts to the Internet — to be the same as the internal domain name. If you don't have an Internet connection and don't plan to obtain one, you don't need to be concerned with an external name.

Choosing a different external domain name offers the advantage of clearly delineating public resources from private corporate resources. But if you use a different external domain name, your e-mail addresses aren't the same as your logon IDs.

If you choose different internal and external names for the root domain, make sure that you register both names with InterNIC or the appropriate governing authority. If another company has already registered the internal name and you try to access an internal resource from outside your firewall, you're not going to reach the correct destination!

Conversely, the primary advantage of using the same name for internal and external root domains is that e-mail names and logon IDs are identical. This arrangement requires some extra proxy configuration but is in common use.

Some pointers about efficient DNS design

I throw a lot of DNS information at you in this chapter. As a review, keep the following guiding principles in mind as you design your namespace:

 ✔ Keep the domain structure shallow for efficient navigation.

 ✔ Follow the standard DNS naming conventions.

 ✔ Choose short domain names wherever possible; long names are tedious to type.

 ✔ Make sure that the root domain name is stable — you can't change it easily.

Active Directory Naming Conventions

Windows 2000 and Active Directory are based on a variety of standards and protocols that follow certain naming conventions. Before I introduce you to implementing and migrating to Active Directory, you need to understand the terms — or names — used to describe various directory objects. They're used in many of the installation wizards and help files, and they can be quite confusing if you don't have them straight.

Fully qualified domain name

A *fully qualified domain name* (FQDN) is the entire path leading to a network object. For example, user JoeB is located in the West domain in a tree named corp.com. JoeB's FQDN is

```
joeb.west.corp.com
```

Similarly, a printer located in the same tree and domain might look like this:

```
prt1.west.corp.com
```

A computer called Host1, located in the Accounting domain of the xyz.com tree, would have a FQDN of

```
host1.accounting.xyz.com
```

Using the FQDN you can always identify the exact location of an object in the namespace.

Distinguished name

A *distinguished name* (DN) is an X.500-based naming convention. Distinguished names use some very odd abbreviations:

DC   domain component
OU   organizational unit
CN   common name

These abbreviations are combined in a specific order, from left to right, to describe the exact path leading to an object. Domain components are listed first, followed by organizational units, and then common names.

If you apply distinguished names to the examples I used for FQDNs in the preceding section, here are the results:

```
DC=com,DC=corp,DC=west,CN=Users,CN=JoeB
```

```
DC=com,DC=corp,DC=west,CN=Printers,CN=Prt1
```

```
DC=com,DC=xyz,DC=accounting,CN=Computers,CN=Host1
```

Relative distinguished name

A *relative distinguished name* (RDN) is also an X.500-based convention. Think of an RDN as a subset of the distinguished name convention. A relative distinguished name is the portion of the name that is an object attribute. (See Chapter 13 for more information on object attributes.)

For example, in the following distinguished name

```
DC=com,DC=corp,DC=west,CN=Users,CN=JoeB
```

JoeB is the relative distinguished name.

Similarly, Host1 is the relative distinguished name of

```
DC=com,DC=xyz,DC=accounting,CN=Computers,CN=Host1
```

Relative distinguished names are sometimes called *relative* names.

User principal name

A *user principal name* (UPN) is the name usually recognized as an e-mail address. It consists of the user's logon name and the domain name where the user object is located.

For example, user JoeB located in the domain xyz.com has the user principal name

```
JoeB@xyz.com
```

Similarly, user John Doe (logon name JohnD) located in domain corp.com has the user principal name

```
JohnD@corp.com
```

Globally unique identifier

LDAP uses the globally unique identifier (GUID) to search for objects in Active Directory. It's a 128-bit unique number assigned to a specific object when the object is created. The GUID never changes. Directory objects can be renamed, but the GUID remains the same. This makes it ideal for searching for objects in Active Directory because even though the object's name may change, the GUID is always consistent.

Chapter 4

Creating a Logical Structure

. . . .

In This Chapter

▶ Creating trees and forests

▶ Defining domain boundaries

▶ Determining your structural model

▶ Designing an OU hierarchy

▶ Delegating administrative privileges

. . . .

*B*efore you begin implementing an Active Directory structure on your network, take the time to draw it out on paper first. Stare at it, rearrange it, poke holes in it, and generally abuse it. That's right! Cause all the damage you can while the design is still on paper.

In this chapter, I show you how to design and organize an Active Directory tree or forest. The decisions that you make right now, in the design phase of your Active Directory structure, have a huge impact on your work life. These decisions affect the complexity and cost of managing your network for a long time to come. Make sure that you create a tree or forest that makes your job easier — not harder!

Planting a Tree or a Forest?

Your first decision in designing an Active Directory structure is deciding whether you need one tree or multiple trees. The easiest way to determine how many trees to design is to consult your DNS namespace. All objects in an active directory tree must share the namespace. If your organization has more than one namespace, you need more than one tree.

Within Active Directory, each object has an X.500-based distinguished name. (See Chapter 3 for more information on distinguished names.) This distinguished name creates a path from the object to the root domain at the top of the tree. If all the objects in your planned tree can extend from the same root domain name, you can create a single tree. Figure 4-1 shows a corporation with a single namespace.

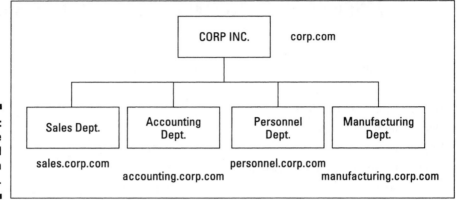

Figure 4-1:
A namespace contained within a single tree.

To put it simply, you create a forest only if you need to use more than one namespace. If you require more than one namespace because you require more than one naming structure, you need to plan an additional tree for each namespace. Figure 4-2 shows a corporate structure with two parallel divisions. Each division has different name requirements, which means that you must plan a separate tree for each division.

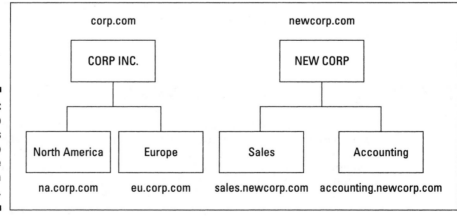

Figure 4-2:
Two namespaces require two separate trees (a forest).

Think of the differences between a tree and a forest in the following way:

- ✔ A tree is a logical grouping of domains within the same namespace.
- ✔ A forest is a logical grouping of trees that a transitive trust relationship joins together. Each tree in a forest has a distinct namespace.

Trees within a forest share the following common characteristics:

- ✔ The same schema
- ✔ The same global catalog

Defining Domains: If One Isn't Enough

A domain is the cornerstone that you lay whenever you create trees and forests. Regardless of whether you design a tree or a forest, the starting point is always the *root domain*. The root domain is the first domain that you create in your Active Directory structure, and it sits at the top of your diagram.

The root domain of your tree, similar to any other domain, is a grouping of resources built on the following components:

- ✔ Domain controllers
- ✔ Security policies (see Chapter 10 for more information)
- ✔ Administrative policies (see Chapter 11 for more information)

For many small and medium-sized companies, a single root domain with a structured OU model, as shown in Figure 4-3, provides sufficient flexibility for an Active Directory tree. If this is your situation, congratulations! You can move right along to the section "Organizing with OUs: Containers for Your Trees," later in this chapter. Life is good.

But larger companies, companies with complex organization charts, and companies with multiple sites often find that a single domain isn't suitable. If you suspect that your organization falls into one of these three situations, read on.

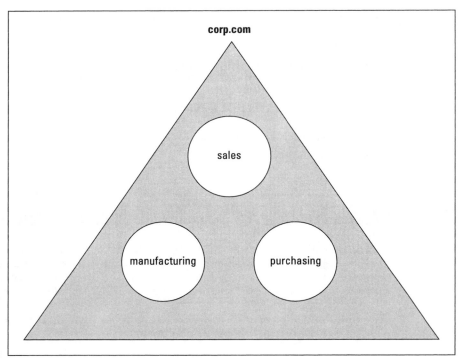

Less is more!

A tree can consist of a single domain, and this configuration is highly desirable! Whenever possible, you want to limit your design to a single domain that you can organize and administer through OUs.

But reality seldom follows best practice. (There's always a catch, isn't there?) More times than not, a single domain just isn't possible. After you specify a root domain, consider the following justifications for creating additional (child) domains:

- ✔ Your organization uses slow WAN-link connections, and you need to limit replication traffic across those links.
- ✔ Your organization has varying security needs that you can't accommodate within a single domain.
- ✔ Your organization has distinct political or organizational factions that require separate *administrative boundaries,* which means that specific domains are controlled by different groups of administrators.

✔ Your organization is very large, and additional domains provide for future growth and also ease administrative burdens.

✔ Your organization spans international boundaries, and multiple domains enable you to separate corporate resources according to those boundaries.

✔ Your organization is migrating from an NT model with multiple domains.

Unfortunately, I have found that the most common reason for a corporation to require additional domains is to accommodate politically polarized groups who refuse to share the same sandbox. That statement may not sound quite so harsh if you consider the substantial expense that accommodating such turf wars involves.

Microsoft recommends that you keep your Active Directory tree shallow. Remember that, within domains, you also have an OU hierarchy. (For more information about the OU hierarchy, see the section "Organizing with OUs: Containers for Your Trees," later in this chapter.) Between the tree hierarchy and the OU hierarchy, you may introduce significant complexity if you design too many levels. Each added domain or OU level decreases performance on your network. After you progress beyond five levels deep in domains or OUs, you begin to see a significant decrease in system performance.

A good rule to keep in mind is to limit the depth of domains in a tree to a maximum of three. Two is preferable. One is optimal.

Recognizing the divine order of things

The key to designing an efficient Active Directory is to base the structure of the tree on the structure of your company. Start with a copy of your current corporate organization chart. Identify the root domain by determining the highest-level organizational group on the chart. The name of the root domain must always match the first level of the namespace. If you determine that you have separate namespaces and need more than one tree, work through designing one tree at a time.

After you name a root domain, you can't change the name without completely rebuilding the Active Directory tree. So make sure that you thoroughly think through your domain name before you begin building your tree!

Use a triangle to represent a domain as you draw an Active Directory diagram. In your drawing, leave room under the root domain for the lines that represent the trust relationships. Figure 4-4 shows an Active Directory diagram with lines representing the automatic trust relationships between the domains in the tree.

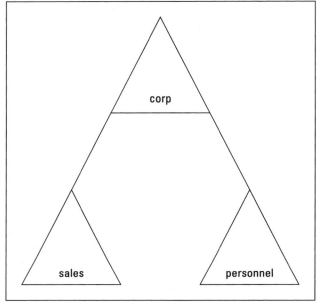

Figure 4-4:
An Active
Directory
diagram
showing
domains
and trust
relationships
between
domains.

Remember that, in Windows 2000, trusts are bidirectional and transitive. The trust relationship is passed along to all other domains connected by transitive trusts. A domain added beneath the `sales` or `personnel` domain in Figure 4-4, for example, automatically trusts the `corp` domain, which is the root domain.

If your company doesn't have an organization chart on which you can base your design, you must create your own structure. Most Active Directory structures follow either a geographic or functional model, as the following sections explain.

Geographic modeling

One popular method for designing an Active Directory structure is to use a *geographic model.* If your organization is structured along international boundaries, this model is the one to use.

Look at the organization chart in Figure 4-5. This corporation structures itself along international boundaries. Administrative functions within one location function separately from those in other locations. You can efficiently manage this company by using a geographically modeled structure. The corresponding domain structure is shown in Figure 4-6.

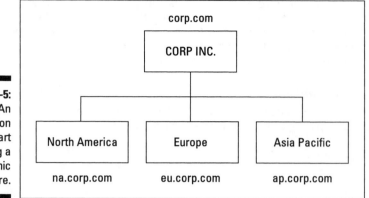

Figure 4-5:
An
organization
chart
displaying a
geographic
structure.

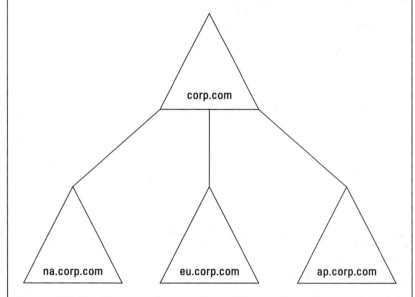

Figure 4-6:
A domain
tree
displaying a
geographic
model.

Geographically bounded domains don't necessarily dictate a decentralized administrative model. Although decentralized administration is common in a geographic model, a centralized — even remote — IT department can still manage multiple domains.

In the domain tree shown in Figure 4-6, I name the domains according to world regions. To keep the fully qualified domain names short, I abbreviate Europe as eu, North America as na, and the Asia Pacific region as ap. But many times, you need to be more precise. In such cases, I suggest that you use the three-character country codes that the International Standards Organization (ISO) specifies (see Table C-1 in Appendix C) or the two-character U.S. state codes that the U.S. Postal Service defines (see Table C-2 in Appendix C).

Functional modeling

A *functional model* adapts to a variety of organization charts. Use it to group domains according to the following business models:

- ✔ Department
- ✔ Division
- ✔ Project

If you believe that a functional model is best for your organization, choose one of these three categories and define the child domains accordingly. Creating additional domains that reflect departments and divisions is quite common. Creating a domain based on a project, however, is less common because projects are seldom permanent. Domains should be stable. If you try to implement a project-based domain structure at a company where projects change frequently, you're creating an administrative nightmare.

Don't get in the habit of creating domains for resources that just don't fit anywhere else. If you find yourself considering this approach, the resources in question are more appropriately suited to an OU.

In most cases, you'll find that your situation calls for either a geographic or division-based (functional) model. Both of these models tend toward stability. As you see in the following section, these models are also suitable when you are defining OUs.

Organizing with OUs: Containers for Your Trees

An *organizational unit* — or *OU* — is a logical container that you use to arrange groups of objects for convenient administration and access. You contain OUs within a domain. They can't span multiple domains nor can they contain objects from other domains.

OUs can contain the following items:

- ✔ Users
- ✔ Groups

> ✔ Printers
>
> ✔ Computers
>
> ✔ Network file shares
>
> ✔ Nested OUs

Generally, OUs are an efficient way to organize corporate resources because, like domains, you can arrange them hierarchically and they can accommodate various organizational models. An OU can easily assume the role of a resource domain but without the expense of additional hardware.

But you can have too much of a good thing! Make sure that you minimize the depth of your OU structure. The deeper the overall Active Directory structure, the more performance degradation you experience. Try to limit the OU structure to a maximum of three layers deep.

Creating a structure

Just as you examine your organization's policies and business model before you define domains, you should do the same before defining an OU structure. Although you can vary the OU hierarchy from domain to domain, doing so isn't a good idea. Ideally, you should make the OU hierarchy consistent and easy to understand. Varying the structure from domain to domain is certain to generate lots of help desk calls as users try to locate resources.

The following list suggests some OU models that you want to consider for your Active Directory structure:

> ✔ Administrative
>
> ✔ Cost-center
>
> ✔ Project
>
> ✔ Division/department
>
> ✔ Geographic
>
> ✔ Object

The models that most people commonly adopt are administrative, division/department, and object. The object model, as shown in Figure 4-7, is very appealing. Think how easily you can manage changes to large numbers of similar objects! Cost-center and project-based OU models tend to be less stable. Projects and cost centers come and go; as they do, the administrative burden increases as the administrator must add and remove OUs.

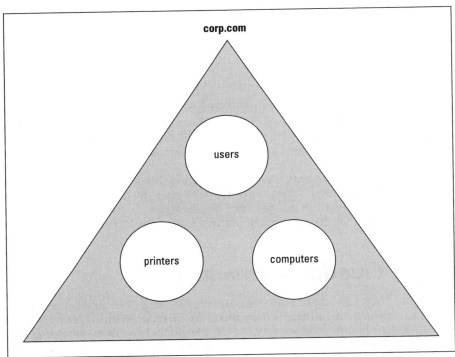

Figure 4-7:
An example of an object-based OU model.

corp.com

users

printers

computers

Planning for delegating administration

In contrast to domains, which set administrative boundaries, OUs provide opportunities for distributed administrative authority. At the OU level, you can specify an administrator's rights to create new user or group accounts, to create or modify specific objects, and to grant access permissions to container objects. You can even control whether users can see an OU!

If your organization already has a recognizable administrative model, you can map the appropriate administrative roles to the OU structure. But in many cases, administrative roles within an organization aren't clearly defined. Instead, they evolve over time, and you have no discernable model to follow. In such a case, answer the following series of questions as you create each new OU to help you plan how to delegate the appropriate level of authority:

- ✔ How are people going to use the OU?
- ✔ Who is going to administer the OU?
- ✔ What level of rights does the OU administrator require?

In Chapters 10 and 11, I get into the specifics of security and of managing users and groups. For now, during the planning phase, your concern is more with planning where and how you will delegate administrative privileges than with managing Active Directory objects.

Ideally, the administrative model is the most important factor in determining how your logical structure takes shape. For each OU, ask the question "Who is going to administer this OU?" Sometimes you have highly specialized engineering teams who prefer to administer their own users and resources. You place their resources in an OU or OU structure and then assign the appropriate administrator to the role. Frequently, you see administrative privileges assigned according to geographic location. For example, administrators in the Asia Pacific region might have administrative control over resources in their region of the world, whereas U.S.-based administrators have control over North American resources.

Consider the skill level and job role of each member of your administrative team as you decide who will have administrative authority over each OU. A help desk could be given password reset privileges over an OU containing users; highly skilled system administrators could be assigned to the schema administrator and enterprise administrator roles; and a department supervisor could be given administrative authority over a specific share. Be sure to assign privileges that are appropriate to the role. (See Chapter 11 for details on how to assign privileges.)

Planning your logical Active Directory structure requires such attention to detail. In the following sidebar, I've provided a checklist to help you through this planning.

Logical design checklist

Planning comes before implementing! Be sure that you complete the following steps before you create domains and OUs:

1. Using the DNS namespace, identify and name the root domain.

2. Determine whether a tree or a forest is appropriate for your organization.

3. Determine whether you need additional domains.

4. Consult your company's organization chart to decide which domain model is best for your needs and whether you need additional child domains.

5. Analyze the business models and processes in your organization to determine which OU model is best for your needs.

6. Determine who is to administer each OU.

7. Decide what administrative privileges OU administrators require.

8. Create a diagram for your logical Active Directory structure that shows the domains and OUs required for your organization. For assistance in this process, review the diagrams I provided in this chapter.

Effectively planning administrative authority requires a certain level of security and administration knowledge. For more detailed information on these subjects, check out *Windows 2000 Server For Dummies* by Ed Tittel (with Mary Madden and James Michael Stewart), published by IDG Books Worldwide, Inc.

Chapter 5

Getting Physical

In This Chapter

▶ Mapping your existing infrastructure

▶ Designing a physical structure

▶ Determining available bandwidth

▶ Planning your site topology

*T*he topics that I discuss in previous chapters deal with the logical Active Directory structure. The logical structure attempts to match the Active Directory design to an organization's business model and processes. In this chapter, I discuss the physical aspects of Active Directory.

If you've sketched out a logical structure design (as I suggest in Chapter 4), you've taken the first steps in matching your proposed Active Directory design to your organization's business model. If you're building a network from scratch, you have the luxury of matching the network design to the logical design. In most cases, however, the network infrastructure is already in place, so you face the challenge of adapting the logical design to the existing network.

In this chapter, I tell you how to map your existing network infrastructure and how to adapt your logical Active Directory (AD) structure to suit the network. I also walk you through planning domain controllers, global catalog servers, and sites.

Mapping the Network Infrastructure

To adjust the logical AD structure to accommodate the limitations of a physical network, you first need to know what the network looks like. If you have a current network diagram, you're in luck! But double-check and make sure that the diagram is accurate. I often find that minor updates to the network don't appear in such a diagram.

If you're starting out without a diagram, don't panic. You may need to indulge in a bit of research, but you can usually create an accurate diagram from scratch. Actually, you may find that you need to create more than one diagram. The CD-ROM that accompanies this book contains evaluation versions of Visio Professional 5.0 and Visio Enterprise 5.0, tools that can prove quite useful in documenting your network. I used Visio Professional 5.0 to create the originals of the diagrams used in this book. If you don't want to begin your diagram from scratch, my Visio drawings are also included on the CD.

If you need help in getting up to speed with Visio 5.0, check out *Visio 5 For Dummies* by Debbie Walkowski (published by IDG Books Worldwide, Inc.).

A complete set of network diagrams indicates the following elements:

- ✔ Geographic locations of your organization
- ✔ Servers
- ✔ Routers
- ✔ Switches
- ✔ Links
- ✔ Link speeds
- ✔ Subnets
- ✔ Network services in use (WINS, DHCP, and so on)
- ✔ Number of users in each geographic location

Let the drawing begin!

First, you need to create a high-level diagram. How do you get started? You can begin with a map — a campus map, state map, U.S. map, world map, floor plan — whatever you need to represent your organization's physical locations. In my examples, I use a U.S. map provided in Visio to reduce the complexity of the examples. Feel free to use whichever map is appropriate for your diagram.

Next, plot the locations of each branch office or other company location on the map. The map isn't really the focus of the drawing, but rather serves as a point of reference for the network diagram, so I usually gray out the map itself so that it appears as a faint background. Figure 5-1 shows major locations in Los Angeles, Dallas, Chicago, and New York. The approximate number of users at each location also appears on the map. Keeping these numbers at the forefront is helpful while you're planning for network traffic patterns.

Figure 5-1:
Plotting your
corporate
office
locations.

Documenting links and link speed

Your diagram is beginning to take shape. Now you add the WAN links
between the sites. If you don't have an old diagram from which to work, however, and you don't have any other documentation, how do you determine
the links and link speeds? I suggest that you contact your service provider
and ask for this information. They can tell you what links exist and the speed
of each link. In Figure 5-2, my diagram shows the links and link speeds
between each of the branch offices.

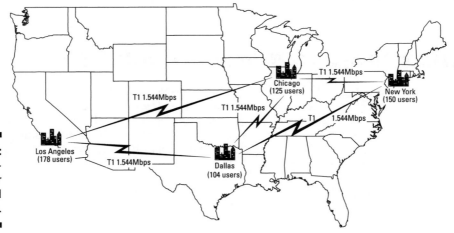

Figure 5-2:
Document-
ing your
links and
link speeds.

Wow! Now you have a useful document. But what does it actually tell you? Right now, it tells you only how your branch offices link together. Some administrators may assume that, with a relatively low number of users and a T1 link between each site, you have plenty of bandwidth. Some things that the drawing doesn't tell, however, are how people use those links, what network services add traffic to the links, and at what intervals traffic passes through the links. Clearly, you still have some work to do.

Allowing for network services

How the user community uses the network and what network services they use has a huge effect on available bandwidth. You need to know what network services are in place at each location, as well as the configurations of those services. If the Los Angeles office and the New York office use WINS servers, for example, users at the other two offices must traverse the network for name-resolution services. Similarly, you need to know the location of the access point to the Internet. Do all users access it through a single office, or are multiple access points available?

You also need to know what type of work takes place in each office location. Office staffs are typically less demanding of the network than are engineers and system administrators. And graphic designers are more demanding than office staffers. Try to obtain a good understanding of how your organization uses its network resources. For example, you can contact the manager at each branch office and discuss the work done by her group. Or you can take a survey of the applications employees use at each site. You also need to determine where they store data (local or remote servers) and whether they exchange or share data with employees at other locations.

Measuring Available Bandwidth

Knowing link speeds is valuable information, but it's still not the only measurement that you need. You also must know how much *available bandwidth* you have. *Bandwidth* refers to the amount of data that you can transmit across a communications channel in a particular amount of time, usually one second. *Available bandwidth* is the amount of bandwidth that's actually available for use. So, in other words

```
Total bandwidth - normal network traffic = available bandwidth
```

WAN links are costly, and expanding the pipe isn't always an affordable solution if you're overutilizing links. Network and system architects are generally responsible for making sure that network resources are configured correctly and that everyone uses these resources appropriately. Fortunately, several network and protocol analyzer tools are available that enable you to determine the current utilization of the network. After you determine what resources people are using, determining what's still available is simple math.

EtherPeek and TokenPeek (both by AGGroup) are available on the CD-ROM included with this book. These products capture network packets so that you can measure traffic. Other tools, such as the Microsoft Performance Monitor, enable you to measure traffic on a particular segment but don't actually capture the packets.

To correctly measure available bandwidth, take traffic readings on every segment at periodic intervals. Analyzing several days worth of traffic is best — preferably, an entire week. This amount of data gives you a good view of network traffic patterns and peak traffic times. You can then use this information to identify over- or underutilized links, to correct bottlenecks, and to optimize network traffic.

After you gather available bandwidth data, add the information to your network diagram. As you can see in Figure 5-3, the link between Los Angeles and Chicago has an average available bandwidth of 40 percent. That means that most of the time, 40 percent of the link is available for additional traffic; the remaining 60 percent is handling existing traffic.

Figure 5-3:
Adding
average
available
bandwidth
percentages
to your
diagram.

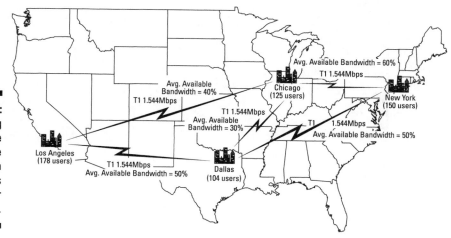

Microsoft Network Monitor

In Windows 2000 Server, Microsoft provides a partial version of its own traffic-capturing tool, Network Monitor. I strongly suggest, however, that you bite the bullet and purchase the Microsoft Systems Management Server (SMS) to use in conjunction with Windows 2000 Server. SMS includes a complete version of Network Monitor. The partial version of Network Monitor included with Windows 2000 Server captures packets on the local segment only. In many cases, however, you need to capture packets on remote segments, and the full version of the tool included with SMS enables you to do that. Figure 5-4 shows a capture taking place in Network Monitor; Figure 5-5 shows the data after it has been captured.

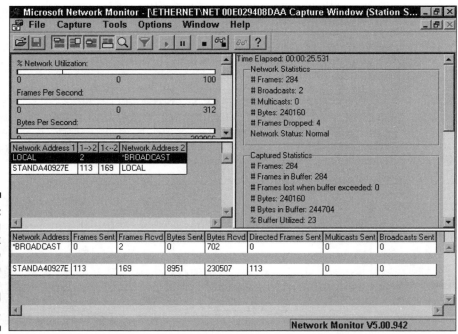

Figure 5-4: Using Network Monitor to capture traffic on a local segment.

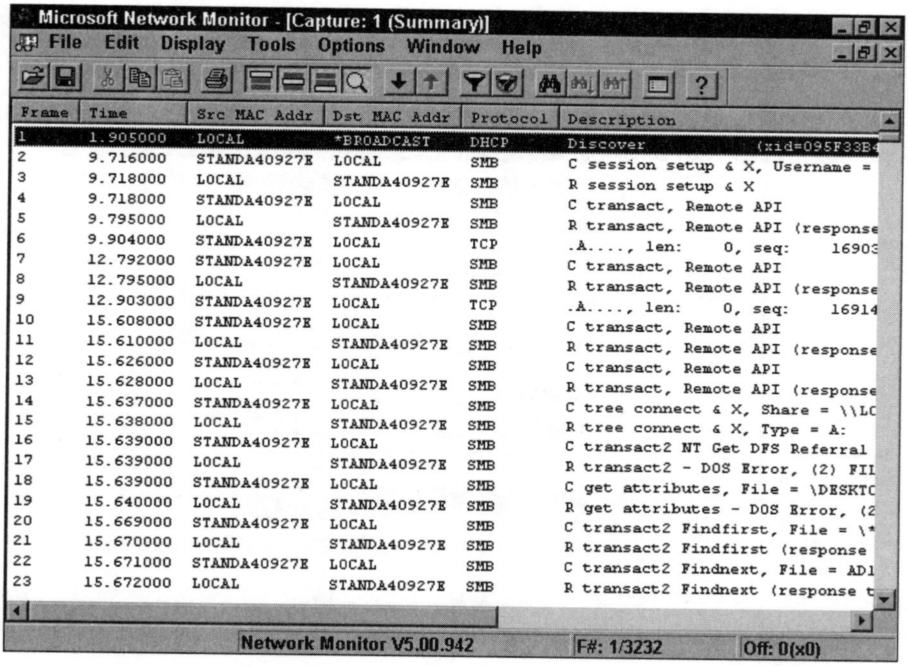

Frame	Time	Src MAC Addr	Dst MAC Addr	Protocol	Description
1	1.905000	LOCAL	*BROADCAST	DHCP	Discover (xid=095F33B
2	9.716000	STANDA40927E	LOCAL	SMB	C session setup & X, Username =
3	9.718000	LOCAL	STANDA40927E	SMB	R session setup & X
4	9.718000	STANDA40927E	LOCAL	SMB	C transact, Remote API
5	9.795000	LOCAL	STANDA40927E	SMB	R transact, Remote API (response
6	9.904000	STANDA40927E	LOCAL	TCP	.A...., len: 0, seq: 16903
7	12.792000	STANDA40927E	LOCAL	SMB	C transact, Remote API
8	12.795000	LOCAL	STANDA40927E	SMB	R transact, Remote API (response
9	12.903000	STANDA40927E	LOCAL	TCP	.A...., len: 0, seq: 16914
10	15.608000	STANDA40927E	LOCAL	SMB	C transact, Remote API
11	15.610000	LOCAL	STANDA40927E	SMB	R transact, Remote API (response
12	15.626000	STANDA40927E	LOCAL	SMB	C transact, Remote API
13	15.628000	LOCAL	STANDA40927E	SMB	R transact, Remote API (response
14	15.637000	STANDA40927E	LOCAL	SMB	C tree connect & X, Share = \\LC
15	15.638000	LOCAL	STANDA40927E	SMB	R tree connect & X, Type = A:
16	15.639000	STANDA40927E	LOCAL	SMB	C transact2 NT Get DFS Referral
17	15.639000	LOCAL	STANDA40927E	SMB	R transact2 - DOS Error, (2) FIL
18	15.639000	STANDA40927E	LOCAL	SMB	C get attributes, File = \DESKTC
19	15.640000	LOCAL	STANDA40927E	SMB	R get attributes - DOS Error, (2
20	15.669000	STANDA40927E	LOCAL	SMB	C transact2 Findfirst, File = *
21	15.670000	LOCAL	STANDA40927E	SMB	R transact2 Findfirst (response
22	15.671000	STANDA40927E	LOCAL	SMB	C transact2 Findnext, File = ADI
23	15.672000	LOCAL	STANDA40927E	SMB	R transact2 Findnext (response t

Figure 5-5: Viewing captured packets using Network Monitor.

EtherPeek and NetSense for EtherPeek

EtherPeek is another good packet-capturing tool. As does Network Monitor, EtherPeek captures network packets so that you can review and analyze traffic patterns and network utilization. Figure 5-6 shows an analysis of data captured using EtherPeek. This analysis indicates that almost 30 percent of the traffic on this network segment is HTTP (or Web) traffic, and another 20 percent is IPX (NetWare) traffic.

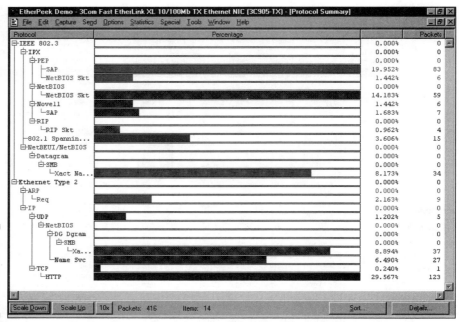

Figure 5-6:
Analyzing
network
traffic using
EtherPeek.

If you want some help analyzing and interpreting the EtherPeek packet capture, NetSense for EtherPeek can give you a hand. As you can see in Figure 5-7, I used NetSense to create a protocol chart that shows the protocol distribution of the broadcast packets from the EtherPeek packet capture. The protocol chart makes it very clear that 45 percent of my broadcast traffic is IP traffic, whereas 9 percent is IPX traffic. An additional 45 percent is broadcast traffic from other protocols — something I should investigate if broadcast traffic is too high on my network.

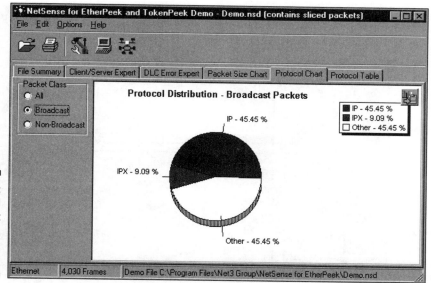

Figure 5-7:
A protocol
chart that
I created
by using
NetSense.

Using the same information that I generated in Figure 5-7, I selected the Peer
Map icon (which resembles a network symbol) from the NetSense toolbar.
Figure 5-8 shows the resulting peer map of the traffic from the EtherPeek
packet capture. This chart shows exactly what kind of network traffic is pass-
ing between two network resources. For example, I can see that the user at
address 204.72.198.91 exchanges TCP traffic with www.geocities.com. This
information is useful to you in determining how your network resources are
being used. Looking at similar information from your own network tells
where heavy traffic patterns exist.

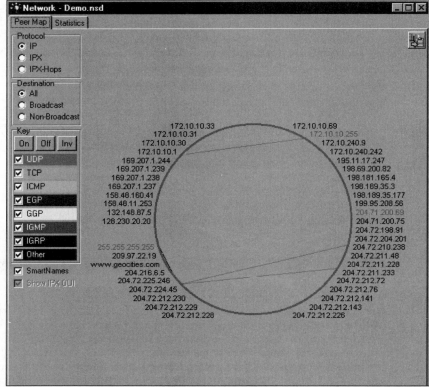

Figure 5-8:
A NetSense
Peer Map
showing
traffic
patterns
between IP
addresses
on the
network.

Next, I returned to the NetSense screen and clicked the Station Peer Map icon
(which resembles a computer) to create a station map, shown in Figure 5-9.
The station map displays protocol traffic between hardware addresses
instead of IP address. I find this information valuable because it shows me
the type of devices that are communicating. Looking at the map in Figure 5-9,
I see that a Cisco device at address 05F5C0 is a central point for IPX on my
network. I can also see that IPX traffic and IP traffic are segregated to specific
portions of my network.

These tools are quite useful in determining the flow of traffic on your network, as well as the available bandwidth. When I'm analyzing the traffic on a
client's system, I often find that the actual traffic patterns are much different
than what the network administrator expects.

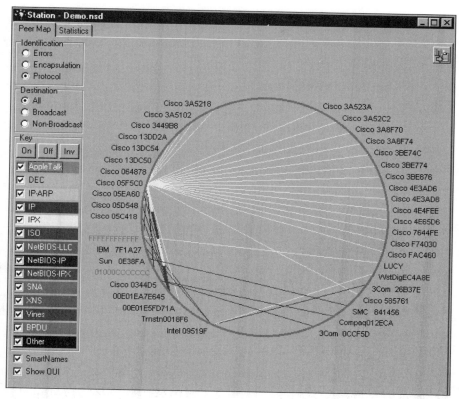

Figure 5-9:
A NetSense
Station Map
showing
traffic
patterns on
the network.

Designing a Site Topology

After you have a representative diagram of the network, you can start planning Active Directory sites. A *site* is a grouping of subnets connected to one
another by high-speed links (preferably LANs). You use these sites to help
control replication and authentication traffic on the network. Sites help con-
fine replication and authentication traffic to local devices so that unnecessary
traffic doesn't cross the WAN. They're not Active Directory objects, so you
don't see them in the AD database. You can view or create sites using the
Active Directory Sites and Services tool from the Administrative Tools menu.
(To access the Administrative Tools menu, choose Start⇨Programs⇨
Administrative Tools.)

Although the logical structure that you create in Chapter 4 helps users to locate resources easily, it doesn't take the network into account. By defining sites based on the network infrastructure, you can segregate authentication and replication traffic so that it doesn't traverse WAN links. This configuration leads to better response time for user logons and also helps optimize costly WAN utilization.

A site can contain computers from more than one domain. (In turn, a domain can span a number of different sites.) The purpose of a site is to physically group computers for optimum network traffic. Client computers use the site information to locate the nearest domain controller. System administrators use sites to limit, and therefore optimize, replication traffic on the network.

To determine the best locations for your organization's sites, look at the network diagram that you create in the section "Mapping the Network Infrastructure" earlier in this chapter. In the example that I've been using in this chapter, I show four sites — Los Angeles, Dallas, Chicago, and New York (see Figure 5-10) — in which my organization has branch offices. Your situation may be more complex, and you may need to define more than one site within a geographic location. Remember to group only subnets connected by fast links. Otherwise, you risk exposing users to slow logon authentication, and you introduce unnecessary replication traffic on your WAN links.

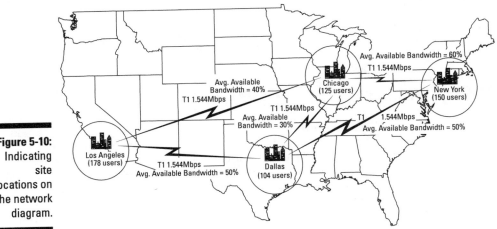

Figure 5-10:
Indicating
site
locations on
the network
diagram.

Chapter 6

Building a Test Model

*W*indows 2000 and Active Directory are radical changes from the familiar Windows NT 4.0 world. I'm certain that you wouldn't consider introducing any new technology without first testing it in a lab setting, and Active Directory is no exception. (If you like living dangerously, however, go ahead and try implementing Active Directory without testing it first.)

Here, then, is where I quit doing all the talking. In this chapter, you build a test model of a domain, install Active Directory, and create Active Directory objects (users, groups, and printers). Working from the plans and diagrams that you create in Chapters 2 through 5, I walk you through the steps for building a test model of Active Directory. And I include lots of screen shots so that you don't have trouble following along.

Using the Installation Wizard

If you've been running Windows NT 4.0 Server, you may remember back to when you installed it. As you ran Setup, you specified whether your server was a PDC (primary domain controller), BDC (backup domain controller), or member server. Windows NT 4.0 enabled you to promote a BDC to a PDC, but it didn't enable you to promote a member server to a BDC or PDC.

Windows 2000 is refreshingly flexible in regard to domain controllers — you run the Active Directory Installation Wizard on any Windows 2000 Server to promote it to a domain controller. You can also run the wizard to return a domain controller to a member server or to a standalone server role.

But before you run the wizard and install Active Directory, make sure that you complete the following preparations:

- ✔ Install Windows 2000 Server with at least one NTFS (NT file system) partition.
- ✔ Configure the IP address, subnet mask, DNS server address, and default gateway on the server.

If you need help installing Windows 2000 and configuring your network settings or DNS, refer to *Windows 2000 Server For Dummies* by Ed Tittel (with Mary Madden and James Michael Stewart), published by IDG Books Worldwide, Inc.

Remember that Active Directory is dependent on DNS, so if you already have a DNS service in your environment, you must configure DNS before running the Active Directory Installation Wizard. After you confirm that you correctly configured the server and that DNS is functioning correctly, you can install Active Directory on the server.

Follow these steps to have the installation wizard guide you through the process of installing Active Directory:

1. **Click the Start button and choose <u>R</u>un from the Start menu.**

2. **In the <u>O</u>pen text box of the Run dialog box that appears, type** dcpromo.

   The installation wizard opens with the Welcome screen, as shown in Figure 6-1. Read the text on each screen — Microsoft provides concise explanations for each step of the wizard. As you see on this screen, the installation wizard installs Active Directory services onto this server, which makes the server a Windows 2000 domain controller.

3. **Click <u>N</u>ext.**

   The Domain Controller Type screen appears (see Figure 6-2). You don't do anything elaborate to create the first domain (the root domain) in the Active Directory tree. The installation wizard prompts you to choose one of the following two roles for this domain controller:

   - Domain controller for a new domain

   - Additional domain controller for an existing domain

4. **Click the <u>D</u>omain Controller for a New Domain option button because you're configuring the first domain controller in the root domain.**

   Notice that this option creates a new child domain, a new domain tree, or a new forest.

Figure 6-1:
The initial
Welcome
screen of
the Active
Directory
Installation
Wizard.

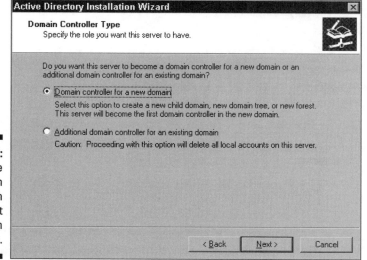

Figure 6-2:
Create the
first domain
controller in
the root
domain
here.

Look at the second option in Figure 6-2, which adds an additional
domain controller to an existing domain. Notice the Caution sentence —
if you choose this option, it deletes all local accounts on the server. The
server is becoming a domain controller, so this option removes local
accounts.

5. Click Next.

On the Create Tree or Child Domain screen, shown in Figure 6-3, you find specific choices for configuring either a new domain tree or a child domain in an existing tree. Again, make sure that you read the text on these screens. Microsoft makes the process simple by providing such clear instructions.

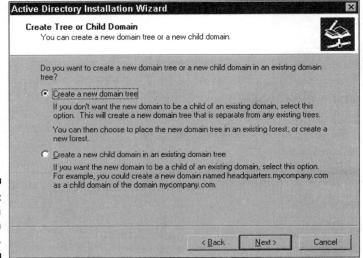

Active Directory Installation Wizard

Create Tree or Child Domain
You can create a new domain tree or a new child domain.

Do you want to create a new domain tree or a new child domain in an existing domain tree?

○ Create a new domain tree

If you don't want the new domain to be a child of an existing domain, select this option. This will create a new domain tree that is separate from any existing trees.

You can then choose to place the new domain tree in an existing forest, or create a new forest.

○ Create a new child domain in an existing domain tree

If you want the new domain to be a child of an existing domain, select this option. For example, you could create a new domain named headquarters.mycompany.com as a child domain of the domain mycompany.com.

< Back   Next >   Cancel

Figure 6-3:
Create a
new domain
tree here.

6. Choose Create a New Domain Tree because you're creating your first model.

7. Click Next.

The Create or Join Forest screen gives you even more choices (see Figure 6-4). At this point, you specify whether the new domain tree you're creating belongs in a new forest or in an existing forest.

8. Choose the Create a New Forest of Domain Trees option button.

As you can see, the wizard tells you that this option is correct if you're creating the first domain in your organization. (Could Microsoft make this process any easier?)

9. Click Next.

The New Domain Name screen appears, as shown in Figure 6-5, and asks you to specify a name for the new domain.

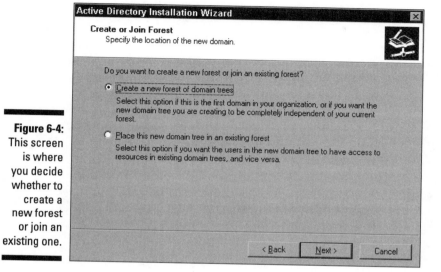

Figure 6-4:
This screen
is where
you decide
whether to
create a
new forest
or join an
existing one.

Figure 6-5:
Name your
root domain
here.

10. **Type the name of your top-level domain in the Full DNS Name for New Domain text box.**

Remember that this domain is your root domain. Consult your DNS hierarchy document and type the domain from your diagram. You can see in Figure 6-5 that I'm naming my root domain `loughry.com`.

11. Click Next.

The NetBIOS Domain Name screen appears, as shown in Figure 6-6.

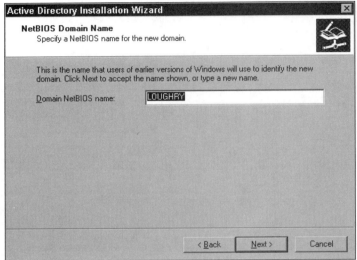

12. Type a NetBIOS domain name in the Domain NetBIOS Name text box.

By default, the wizard suggests the leftmost part of the DNS domain name as the NetBIOS name. You can use the suggested name or type a different name.

Computers running earlier versions of Windows, such as Windows NT 3.51, Windows NT 4.0, and Windows 95/98, use the domain name that you specify on this screen. NetBIOS domain names are necessary until you're in native mode with all clients running Windows 2000 Professional. Notice that I enter LOUGHRY for my domain name.

The next two screens enable you to specify where you want to locate the Active Directory database, the database log files, and the Sysvol folder.

13. Click Next.

The Database and Log Locations screen appears. The default storage location for the Active Directory database is in the following directory:

```
C:\WINNT\NTDS
```

14. Leave the default text or type a new path in the Database Location text box.

Next, the wizard asks you where you want to store the Active Directory log. As you can see in Figure 6-7, Microsoft provides a performance hint at the top of the screen, suggesting that you store the database file and the Active Directory log on separate hard disks. If you have only one NTFS partition, however, the wizard defaults to the same path for both files, which is the case in Figure 6-7.

Figure 6-7:
Insert the paths for where you want to store the Active Directory database and log files.

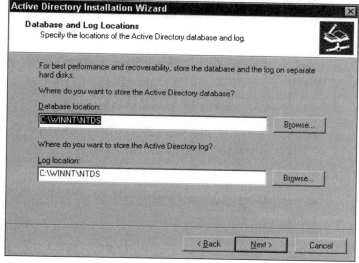

In my example, because of the absence of another hard drive, the wizard defaults to storing both the database and log files in the same location.

15. **If you want to store the log file on a separate hard disk or in a different location, type a new path; otherwise, leave the default text in the Log Location text box.**

In my example, because of the absence of another hard drive, the wizard defaults to storing both the database and log files in the same location.

A common practice in configuring database servers is to store the log files on a separate disk from the database file. Microsoft recommends this storage method when you configure Exchange Server, SQL Server, and other database-based applications as well, because this method provides superior system performance.

16. **Click Next.**

The Shared System Volume screen appears, as shown in Figure 6-8. The Sysvol folder holds the domain's public files and replicates to all domain controllers within a domain. Notice that you must store the Sysvol folder on an NTFS 5 volume!

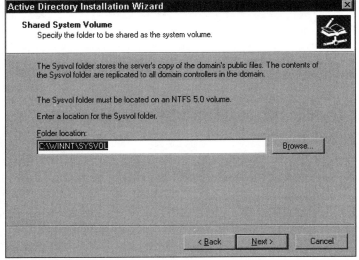

Figure 6-8:
On this
screen, you
specify the
location of
the Sysvol
folder.

The Sysvol folder resides in the following default location:

```
C:\WINNT\SYSVOL
```

17. Leave the default text or type a new path in the Folder Location text box.

18. Click Next.

A dialog box similar to the one shown in Figure 6-9 may appear. Don't panic! This message is telling you one of the following two things:

- You configured DNS incorrectly if you configured an existing DNS service prior to running the Active Directory Installation Wizard.

- You didn't configure DNS prior to running the Active Directory Installation Wizard.

If you attempted to configure DNS services before running the Active Directory Installation Wizard, this message is saying that you got it wrong. Remember that Active Directory is dependent on DNS. You can't proceed past this point until you correctly install DNS. But don't despair — continue to Step 19.

19. Click OK.

Voilà! As you can see in Figure 6-10, the installation wizard oh-so-nicely asks, "Want me to configure and install a DNS server for ya?" (Okay, okay, I paraphrased a little!)

Figure 6-9:
This warning message may appear, indicating that you didn't install DNS or that you configured it incorrectly.

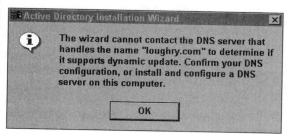

Figure 6-10:
The helpful wizard now offers to configure DNS for your domain.

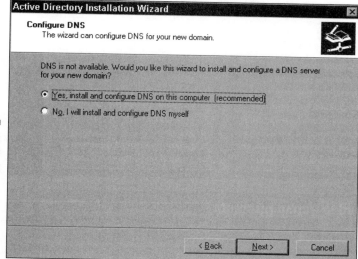

Well sure, that's fine with me! (After all, I want to continue with this installation example.)

20. **Click the Yes, Install and Configure DNS on This Computer option button to have the wizard install and configure a DNS server.**

    If you click No, the wizard ends because you can't install Active Directory without a properly configured DNS server.

21. Click Next.

The Permissions screen appears, as shown in Figure 6-11. Beginning with this screen, the Active Directory Installation Wizard takes care of some final, miscellaneous questions. This screen asks whether you want to set permissions to be compatible to pre–Windows 2000 servers or compatible to Windows 2000 servers only.

22. For this example, click the Permissions Compatible with Pre–Windows 2000 Servers option button.

If Windows NT 4.0 users aren't going to be accessing the domain, choose the Permissions Compatible Only with Windows 2000 Servers option.

Figure 6-11:
On this screen, you specify Windows 2000 permissions to network resources or pre–Windows 2000 permissions to the network.

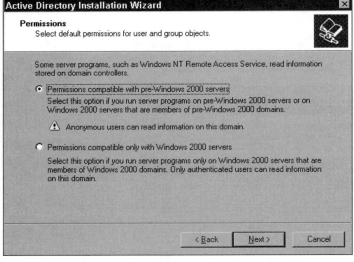

23. Click Next.

The Directory Services Restore Mode Administrator Password screen (whew, that's a long one!) appears, as shown in Figure 6-12.

24. Type the password for the Administrator account.

This password is the one you use if you need to start the computer in Directory Services Restore Mode to restore the directory from a backup or to compact the directory database. (Chapter 14 covers both of these circumstances.)

25. Click Next.

And — finally — the wizard's Summary screen appears, as shown in Figure 6-13. This screen displays all the options you selected while running the installation wizard. Review these choices carefully. Use the Back button if you need to make any changes.

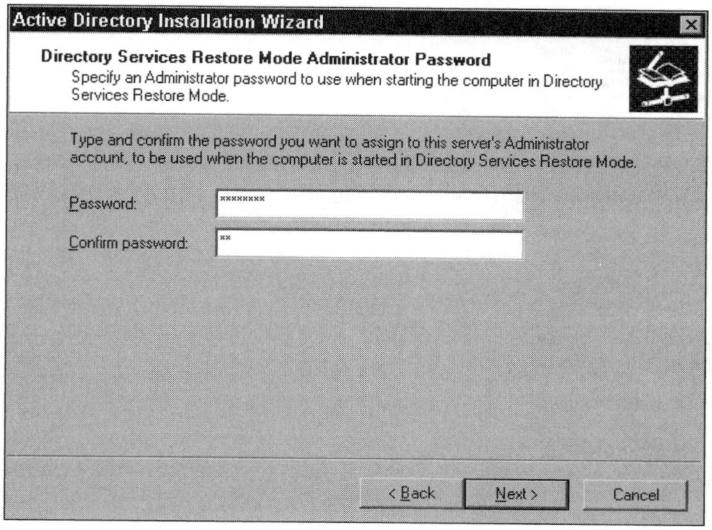

Figure 6-12:
Specify an
Administrator
password
here.

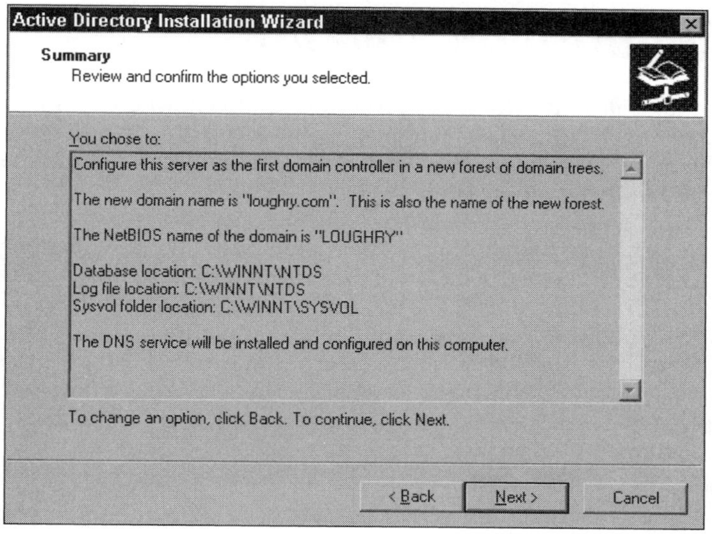

Figure 6-13:
Review all
your
installation
choices on
the
Summary
screen.

26. When you're comfortable with your choices, click Next.

Watch the messages in the dialog box while the wizard configures Active Directory. After the configuration is complete, the Finish button appears at the bottom of the screen (see Figure 6-14).

27. Click Finish to complete your installation of Active Directory.

Figure 6-14:
The final
Active
Directory
Installation
Wizard
screen.

Adding Additional Domains

If your logical Active Directory structure (that I showed you how to create in Chapter 4) calls for multiple domains, now is the time to add them. Begin by adding child domains to the tree that you created during the installation process in the preceding section.

Adding a child domain is simple: Start the Active Directory Installation Wizard on a Windows 2000 server that you want to promote to a domain controller in the child domain. (Refer to the directions provided in the preceding section if you need help with running the installation wizard.) After you reach the Create Tree or Child Domain screen, as shown in Figure 6-15, select the Create a New Child Domain in an Existing Domain Tree option button. Then complete the rest of the installation wizard as you did while installing the root domain.

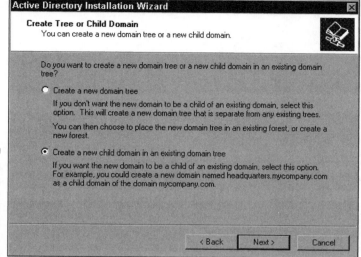

Figure 6-15:
Use this
screen to
add a child
domain to
your tree.

Creating Organizational Units

Remember that best practice dictates that you limit your trees to as few domains as possible. Organizational units offer a good alternative to domains, and in many cases, you can use them in place of child domains. So you may choose to have a tree that consists of only one domain. After you add all the domains to your tree that you want, you can start adding OUs. (Refer to Chapter 4 if you need a refresher on when to use OUs versus domains.)

Creating an OU is a fairly simple process. Follow these steps:

1. **From the Start menu, choose Programs⇨Administrative Tools⇨ Active Directory Users and Computers (see Figure 6-16).**

   The AD Users and Computers tool appears.

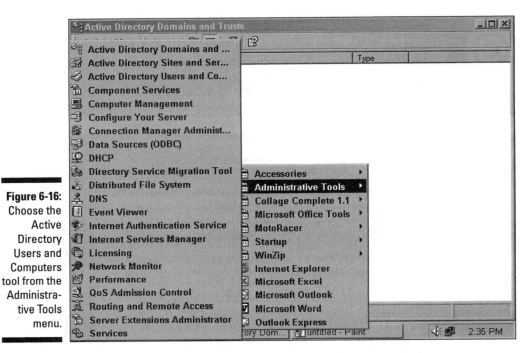

Figure 6-16:
Choose the
Active
Directory
Users and
Computers
tool from the
Administra-
tive Tools
menu.

The AD Users and Computers tool is a Microsoft Management Console (MMC) snap-in. It replaces the User Manager for Domains tool that you used in Windows NT.

2. **From the leftmost pane of AD Users and Computers, click to select the domain to which you want to add an OU.**

3. **Choose Action⇨New⇨Organizational Unit (see Figure 6-17).**

   Notice that the Action menu is actually located at the left end of the tool-bar, rather than on the menu bar.

4. **Type the name of the new OU in the Name text box of the New Object - Organizational Unit dialog box that appears (see Figure 6-18).**

   Remember to use short names for your OUs. In Figure 6-18, you can see that I'm adding an OU that I call AP to the loughry.com/ domain. If you look closely at the area of the figure behind the dialog box, you can see that I previously added two other domains that I named NOAM and EU.

5. **Click OK to close the dialog box.**

That's all there is to it!

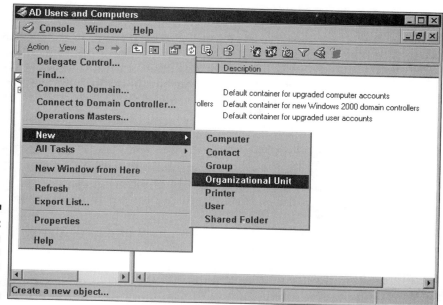

Figure 6-17:
You add an OU from the Action menu.

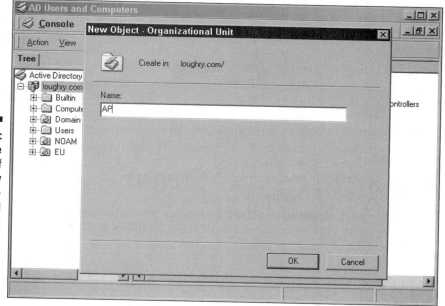

Figure 6-18:
In the Name text box of the New Object - Organizational Unit dialog box, type a short name for the new OU.

You can nest OUs within OUs to further organize your Active Directory. Simply select the parent OU and follow the procedure that I use in the preceding steps. But what if you make a mistake? For this example, I created an OU that I called NOAM in which I decided to nest three additional domains. But I inadvertently used city names instead of state names as I named the OUs. Not a problem! Simply select the offending OU, right-click, choose Rename from the pop-up menu that appears (see Figure 6-19), and type a new name for the OU.

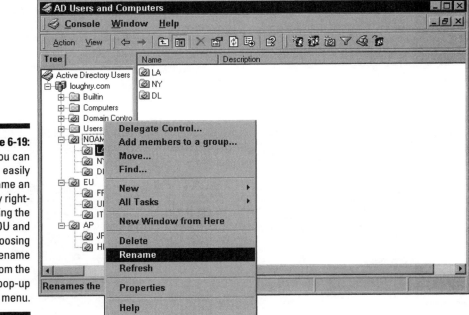

Figure 6-19: You can easily rename an OU by right-clicking the OU and choosing Rename from the pop-up menu.

Creating Users and Groups

After you finish adding OUs, you're ready to define users and groups. This process is as simple as the steps that you follow to create an OU.

Adding a user to your OU

Adding a user is as easy as adding an OU. Follow these steps:

1. **In AD Users and Computers, select the OU into which you want to place the user.**

Refer to Step 1 of the preceding section if you need help in getting to the AD Users and Computers screen.

2. From the toolbar, choose Action⇨New⇨User.

The New Object - User screen appears, as shown in Figure 6-20.

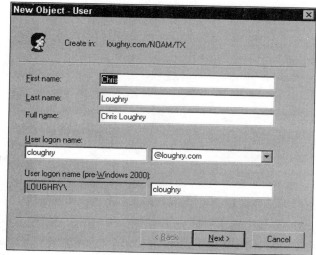

Figure 6-20:
You use this
screen to
add a new
user.

3. Type the user information in the appropriate text boxes.

4. Click Next.

On the screen that appears, you specify the user's password and password settings (see Figure 6-21). If you used Windows NT in the past, the user screens should look very familiar.

5. Type the user's password, type it again to confirm the password, and choose the appropriate password settings.

6. Click Next.

On the Summary screen, review the user information you entered to ensure that everything is correct. (If you see a mistake, simply use the Back button to return to the correct screen and fix the mistake. Then use the Next button to return to the Summary screen.)

7. Click Finish.

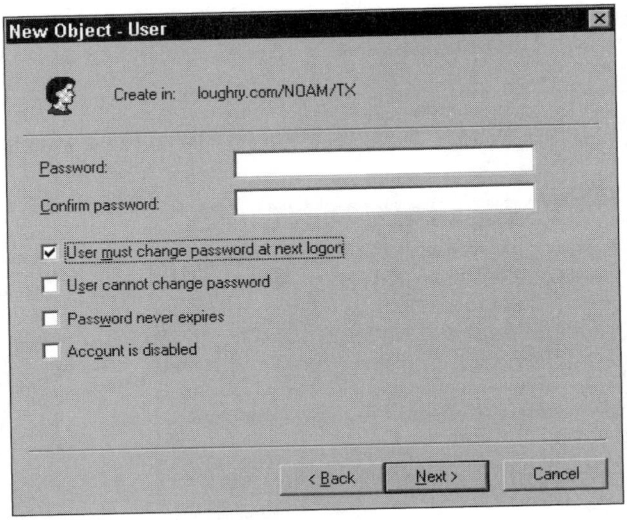

Figure 6-21:
Set a user's
password
on this
screen.

Adding a group to your OU

Creating a group pretty much follows the same steps that you use for creating a user. Look back at your logical structure diagram (the one that you created in Chapter 4) to make sure that you're adding objects in the correct hierarchy. Using the AD Users and Computers snap-in, select the OU to which you want to add a new group and choose Action⇨New⇨Group to open the New Object - Group dialog box. Then just fill in the appropriate text boxes and click the OK button. In Figure 6-22, you can see that I'm creating the group ACC within the OU that I call NOAM.

You use a similar process to add computers to the domain. Just choose Action⇨New⇨Computer to open the New Object - Computer dialog box; then name your new computer object in the Computer Name text box (see Figure 6-23).

I think you get the idea. Adding objects is quite straightforward. I encourage you to continue adding objects to the domain and experiment with the options and settings. Later, in Chapter 11, I cover user and group administration. You get plenty of practice before going live in a production domain!

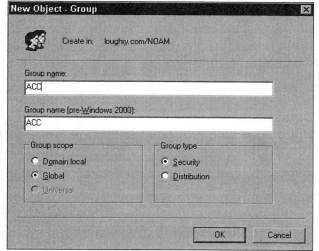

Figure 6-22:
Name your
new group
in the New
Object -
Group
dialog box.

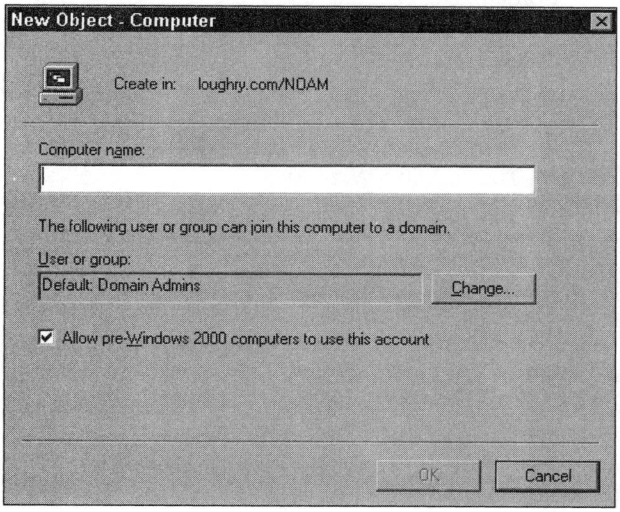

Figure 6-23:
Give your
new com-
puter object
a name in
the New
Object -
Computer
dialog box.

Demoting Domain Controllers

This section seems to offer a good opportunity to talk about demoting domain controllers by using the Active Directory Installation Wizard. If this is your only domain, and the domain controller is the final DC in the domain, you can also use the wizard to remove Active Directory from your network (if you ever have a need to do so).

If you use it to remove Active Directory, shouldn't you call it a *De*-installation Wizard?

Start the installation wizard by choosing Start⇨Run and typing **dcpromo** in the Run dialog box that appears.

As you can see in Figure 6-24, Active Directory is already installed on the server, so the wizard tells you that you can use the wizard only to remove Active Directory from the server. If you want to remove this test installation at this time, click Next. As you see in Figure 6-25, if the domain controller is the last DC in the domain, the domain is completely removed and ceases to exist.

Figure 6-24: Start the Active Directory Installation Wizard to demote a domain controller.

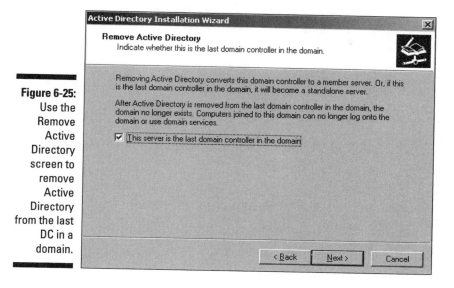

Figure 6-25:
Use the
Remove
Active
Directory
screen to
remove
Active
Directory
from the last
DC in a
domain.

After the wizard finishes (see Figure 6-26), Active Directory is gone from the server, and you can click the Finish button to end the wizard.

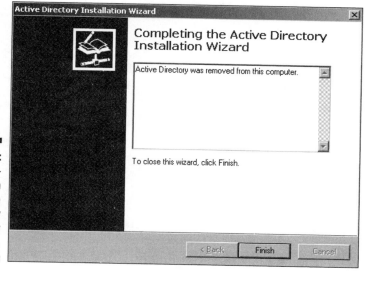

Figure 6-26:
The de-
installation
of Active
Directory
is now
complete.

Part III
Migrating to Active Directory

The 5th Wave   By Rich Tennant

BEAL & WASP
DATABASE
CONSULTANTS

"Your database is beyond repair, but before I tell you our backup recommendation, let me ask you a question. How many index cards do you think will fit on the walls of your computer room?"

In this part . . .

These chapters of the book prepare you to make the transition from your current system to Active Directory. I review the NT domain models and provide strategies for converting them to an Active Directory tree. I also do a little comparing, helping you understand some distinctions between the old models and the new. And finally, I offer some suggestions for those of you migrating from Novell, UNIX, and Banyan's StreetTalk.

Chapter 7

Comparing Windows NT to Windows 2000

● ●

In This Chapter

▶ Exploring Windows NT domain models and Windows 2000 domain trees

▶ Relating NT trust relationships to Windows 2000 trust relationships

▶ Understanding domain controllers and replication in Windows 2000

● ●

I expect many of you to base your Windows 2000 knowledge on what you already know about Windows NT. But although many of the terms are the same, the function of the components may differ between the two operating systems. Domains, trusts, and domain controllers all work differently in Windows 2000 than they do in Windows NT. Synchronization and directory replication differ as well.

In this chapter, I show you how the components of Windows 2000 differ from those of Windows NT. You need to understand these distinctions so that you can efficiently migrate an existing Windows NT environment to Windows 2000 and Active Directory. You also need to know the differences so that you can correctly design and manage Active Directory.

Comparing NT Domain Models to Windows 2000 Domain Trees

You probably picked up a little about Windows NT 3.51 or 4.0 at some point in the past. If so, you may be familiar with the concept of grouping users and servers into domains. Grouping resources in this fashion offers several advantages, including the following:

✔ A single login grants access to all resources within the domain.

✔ Administration becomes easier because user accounts exist in the domain rather than on each server.

> ✔ Resource administration becomes easier because domain policies manage groups of resources instead of each resource requiring individual administration.

You can group Windows NT domains into one of the following four administrative models:

> ✔ Single domain
>
> ✔ Single-master domain
>
> ✔ Multiple-master domain
>
> ✔ Complete trust

Although these models offer a great degree of flexibility in administration, they also add complexity and cost to the network. Hardware costs can become significant because each domain requires a primary domain controller (PDC) and (unless you live dangerously) a backup domain controller (BDC). Administratively, multiple domains usually lead to multiple trust relationships and additional groups. The more domains that you have, the more complex administration becomes.

On the surface, the answer to the problems introduced by multiple domains would seem to be a single domain. A single domain is great for a small environment, but sometimes it can't accommodate all the objects that you find in a large enterprise. Users, groups, printers, servers, and computer accounts can number into the thousands in a large enterprise. So in many cases, multiple domains become necessary.

In addition, corporate politics often force the creation of additional domains. You commonly find divisions or groups within a company that refuse to give control of their resources to a centralized administrative group. In fact, this situation is so common that corporate politics frequently become the deciding factor in selecting a Windows NT domain model.

Single domain model

The Windows NT *single domain* model, as shown in Figure 7-1, is the easiest to administer. In this model, all servers, users, and other resources reside within one domain. The domain contains a single PDC and one or more BDCs, depending on the size of the domain and its geographic makeup.

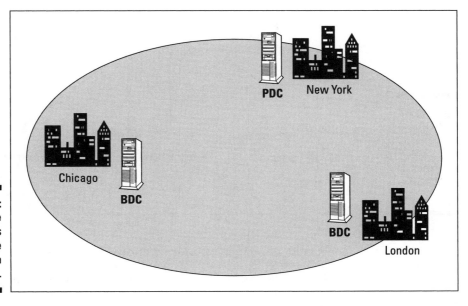

Figure 7-1:
The
Windows
NT single
domain
model.

By design, a single domain can contain servers that span the globe, connected by various LAN or WAN links. But in practice, you're best off limiting a single domain to locations that connect to one another via high-speed WAN links. Slow WAN links can lead to domain controllers that don't replicate properly, resulting in out-of-synch directories between the servers. This situation creates the potential for saturating slower WAN links with replication and authentication traffic, leaving little or no bandwidth available for transporting data.

Single-master domain model

The *single-master domain* model is suitable for all but the very largest organizations. This model groups user accounts and groups into one domain, usually known as the *account domain,* and groups printers and servers into *resource domains,* as shown in Figure 7-2. One-way trust relationships (illustrated by the arrows pointing from the trusting domain to the trusted domain) enable users in the account domain to access resources in the resource domain, subject to access rights, of course. It's kind of like a printer in the resource domain is saying "I'm a printer, and I trust you to authenticate the users who access my resources."

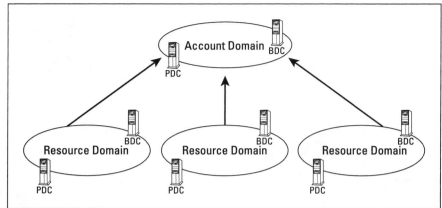

Figure 7-2:
The single-master domain model in Windows NT.

This domain model adapts to centralized or distributed administration. A central administrative group can manage the user accounts, leaving management of the resource domains to local administrators. Or you can administer all the domains centrally. Large corporations that desire centralized administration usually adopt the single-master domain model.

Multiple-master domain model

The *multiple-master domain* model is very similar to the single-master model. The usual configuration consists of two account domains and multiple resource domains (see Figure 7-3). The resource domains trust the account domains, meaning that there is a one-way trust relationship between them, and both account domains trust each other.

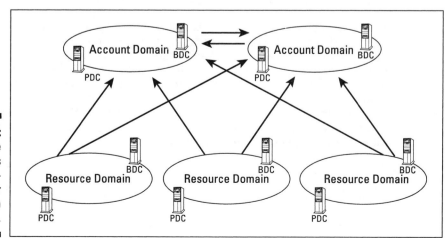

Figure 7-3:
The Windows NT multiple-master domain model.

The multiple-master domain model is perfect for megacorporations with large numbers of users. International companies that practice "follow the sun" administration frequently use this model. Under this kind of administration, administrators in the first account domain work their shift and then hand off responsibility to the administrators in the second account domain.

Complete-trust model

The *complete-trust* model is an administrator's nightmare because you have to administer every single trust relationship! As shown in Figure 7-4, every domain in the complete-trust model trusts every other domain. After you have more than three or four domains, administration of all the trusts becomes very time-consuming.

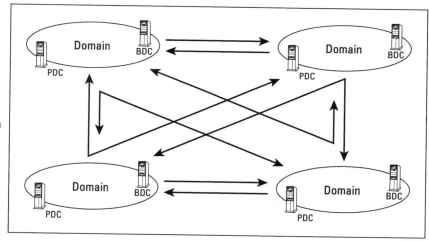

Figure 7-4:
The complete-trust model in Windows NT.

This model is sometimes known as the *full-mesh* model; but in my mind, it's the full-*mess* model! This domain model is usually the result when a corporation employs a totally decentralized administration or if disparate corporate divisions never learn to play well with others.

Windows 2000 domain trees

In Windows 2000, Microsoft endeavors to retain the advantages that domains provide and to simultaneously remove some of their limitations. Domains are still a primary unit of administration in Windows 2000, but they hold a much larger number of objects than in Windows NT.

Furthermore, you can delegate administrative authority over organizational units within a domain to different administrative groups in Windows 2000. A domain tree can easily consist of a single domain, yet still accommodate a decentralized administration. Figure 7-5 shows a domain tree with organizational units.

You can successfully migrate each of the four Windows NT domain models to a Windows 2000 domain tree. Chapter 8 steps you through the process of migrating each model.

One final thing to keep in mind regarding domains in Windows NT and Windows 2000 is that you usually create Windows NT domains for administrative reasons, whereas you create Windows 2000 domains to optimize network traffic.

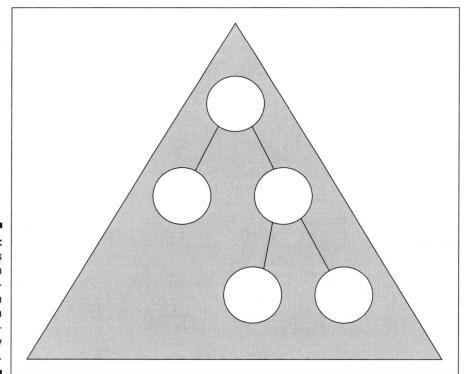

Figure 7-5:
A Windows 2000 domain tree populated with OUs, which are represented by the circles.

Contrasting NT Trusts and Windows 2000 Trusts

As I touched on in the preceding section, Windows NT joins separate domains into an administrative model through *trust relationships,* or *trusts.* A Windows NT trust relationship enables users in one domain to access resources in another domain without merging administrative control of the two domains. NT administrators create trust relationships between specific domains — they don't exist by default if you create multiple domains. Figure 7-6 shows a one-way trust relationship in which users in Domain A can access resources in Domain B.

Figure 7-6:
A Windows NT one-way trust relationship.

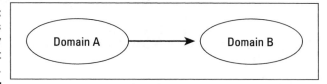

Windows NT trust relationships are *one-way* only, meaning that the trust works in only one direction. One domain, the *trusted* domain, holds the users who require access. The second, or *trusting* domain, holds resources that the users in the trusted domain want to access. If you want both domains to trust each other, that situation requires a second trust relationship. Figure 7-7 illustrates a two-way Windows NT trust relationship.

Figure 7-7:
A Windows NT two-way trust relationship.

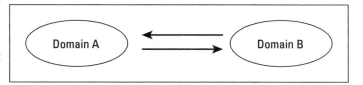

After you go beyond two domains, trust relationships can get a little sticky. Windows NT trust relationships are *nontransitive* — that is, they apply only to two specific domains and don't extend to additional domains trusted by either of these first two domains. Look at the Windows NT trust relationships shown in Figure 7-8. Domain A trusts Domain B. Domain B trusts Domain C. Does this imply that Domain A also trusts Domain C? No!

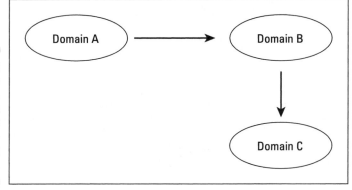

Figure 7-8:
In this
relationship,
Domain A
does not
automati-
cally trust
Domain C.

Because Windows NT trust relationships are nontransitive, the trust between Domains A and B is explicit to those domains and Domain C doesn't inherit that trust just because B then trusts C. In this scenario, you need to provide Domain A with a specific trust relationship with Domain C if you want such a relationship to exist between these two domains.

But in Windows 2000, trust relationships work much differently than in Windows NT. In Windows 2000, you group domains together hierarchically (don't worry — I can't say it either) in domain trees. Each time that you add a domain to the tree, you automatically add a default trust relationship as well. These trusts are two-way trusts that are *transitive,* meaning that the trust relationships between domains are transferable to other domains.

Look at the domain tree shown in Figure 7-9. Domain A is the root domain of the tree. It's also the parent domain to Domain B. (Domain B is a child domain to Domain A.) Adding Domain B to the tree automatically creates a two-way, transitive trust relationship between Domain B and its parent, Domain A. This situation is known as a *parent-child* trust relationship.

Now look at Figure 7-10. You add Domain C here as a child to Domain B. Again, you create a default trust relationship between Domains B and C. Does this configuration mean that Domain A now trusts Domain C? Yes!

In Windows 2000, default two-way trusts exist between all domains in a tree. All domains in a tree trust all the other domains in the tree.

The administrator doesn't need to manage these default trust relationships. Windows 2000 creates them by default, and they're automatically two-way and transitive. They don't add administrative burden.

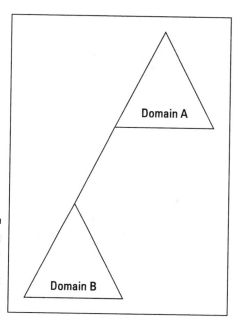

Figure 7-9:
A Windows 2000 parent-child trust relationship.

What kind of trust relationships exist between trees in a forest? I'm glad you asked! As shown in Figure 7-11, domain trees in a forest are joined together through two-way transitive trusts. Because the trusts are transitive, users in one tree can access resources in another, and vice-versa. You create the trust relationship by default as you add the second tree to the forest. Microsoft refers to the trust relationship between trees in a forest as a *tree-root* trust relationship.

To shorten the path between domains in the same forest, administrators can create *cross-link* trust relationships. These relationships are manually created transitive trusts. Because a cross-link trust connects two domains directly, this type of link is sometimes used in a large enterprise to speed response times.

One-way, nontransitive trusts didn't go away in Windows 2000. They're still available if you need to create them. As shown in Figure 7-12, you can create a trust relationship to access resources in a domain outside a tree or forest. This setup is known as an *external* trust relationship. Administrators can also create external trust relationships between other Windows 2000 domain trees and forests or between a Windows 2000 domain and a Windows NT domain. External trusts are always one-way, nontransitive trusts.

To create a trust, follow these steps:

1. **Using the Active Directory Domains and Trusts utility (located on the Administrative Tools menu), right-click the domain for which you want to create a trust, and choose Properties from the pop-up menu.**

2. **In the Properties dialog box, click the Trusts tab.**

3. **Click the Add button adjacent to either the Domains Trusted By This Domain or the Domains That Trust This Domain option (the option you choose depends on the direction of the trust you are creating).**

   Depending on which option you choose in Step 3, either the Add Trusted Domain or Add Trusting Domain dialog box appears.

4. **Type the name of the domain in the Trusted (or Trusting) Domain text box; then type a password for the trust between the two domains in the Password box. In the Confirm Password box, type the password again.**

5. **Click OK to close the Add Trusted (or Trusting) Domain dialog box; then click OK once more to close the Properties dialog box and return to the Active Directory Domains and Trusts utility.**

   You should now see the trust displayed in the Active Directory Domains and Trusts window.

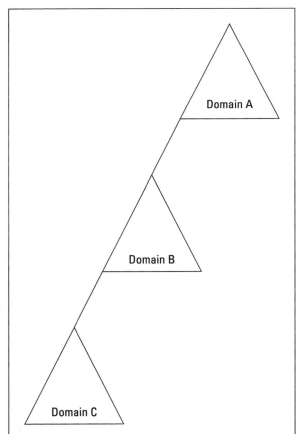

Figure 7-10:
Windows
2000
domains
trust all
other
domains in
that tree.

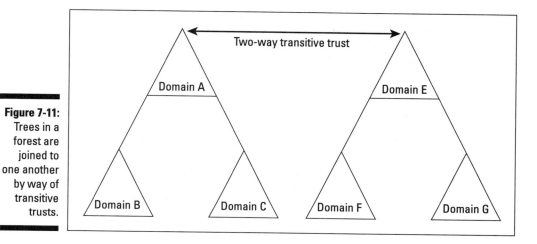

Figure 7-11:
Trees in a
forest are
joined to
one another
by way of
transitive
trusts.

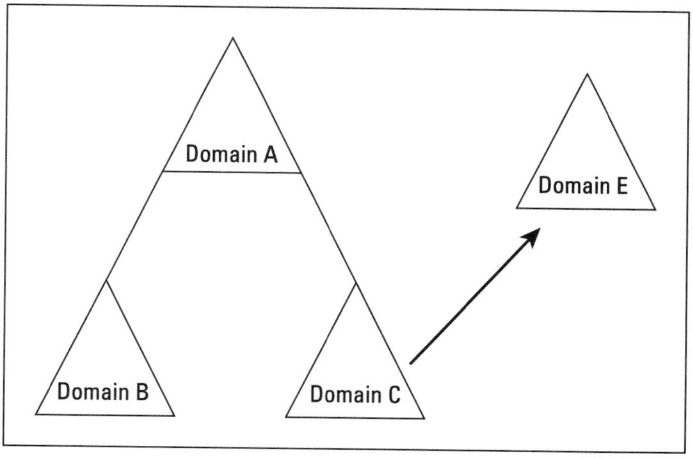

Figure 7-12:
An external
trust
between
two domain
trees.

Replicating versus Synchronizing

In Windows NT, each domain contains a PDC and at least one BDC for *fault tolerance,* which provides for redundant components in case of a system outage. In the case of Windows NT, a BDC provides domain controller functions if the PDC crashes. The PDC holds the master database of users, groups, and objects, and you make all changes to the database on the PDC. At periodic intervals, the PDC sends the database to all BDCs in the domain. In Windows NT terminology, whenever the PDC sends this information to the BDCs, it is *synchronizing* the database.

Windows 2000 Server, however, doesn't distinguish between *primary* and *backup* domain controllers. Instead, they're known simply as *domain controllers,* or DCs. Because you don't specify a primary controller, all DCs maintain a full copy of the domain directory database. You can make changes to the database on any DC. Active Directory then *replicates* the database changes to all other DCs in the domain.

Notice the distinction in terminology in referring to database updates in Windows NT and in Windows 2000: Windows NT refers to *synchronizing,* whereas Windows 2000 refers to *replicating.* Replication is an important topic in Windows 2000 and generates some new terminology of its own. In Chapter 12, I explain the ins and outs of controlling replication, a process that can make or break your network. For now, just know that in the Windows 2000 world, *replicating* refers to updating the domain directory databases.

Chapter 8

Migrating from NT 3.51 and 4.0

In This Chapter

▶ Identifying supported upgrade paths

▶ Devising a backout plan

▶ Choosing a migration model

▶ Upgrading domain controllers

▶ Upgrading member servers

*I*f you're running a Windows NT 3.51 or 4.0 server, you're probably planning to upgrade to Windows 2000 sometime in the future. Whether the time is imminent or still a ways down the road — as we say in Texas — you need a plan for moving from your existing NT domain model to a new Windows 2000 environment.

In this chapter, I discuss the upgrade paths to Windows 2000 Server and Active Directory that Microsoft supports. I include specific migration strategies for each of the four NT domain models: single domain, single-master domain, multiple-master domain, and complete trust. So this chapter truly includes something for everyone!

Preparing to Upgrade

Before migrating any of your servers, follow these preparatory suggestions to ensure that your upgrades go smoothly.

✔ Decide in which order you're migrating the servers (which one to migrate first, second, third, and so on).

✔ Identify which operating systems you're upgrading.

✔ Double-check to make sure that the system meets all hardware requirements.

✔ Prepare a backout plan in case something goes wrong during the migration. (See the section "Backing Out Gracefully," later in this chapter.)

✔ Gather your supplies (naming standards, software, manuals, logical diagrams, and so on).

Supported upgrade paths

You can take several paths to Windows 2000 Server and Active Directory, but the following are the only two that Microsoft supports:

✔ Windows NT 3.51 to Windows 2000

✔ Windows NT 4.0 to Windows 2000

In saying that NT 3.51 and 4.0 are *supported* upgrade paths, I mean that Microsoft supports licensed users of NT 3.51 and 4.0 who upgrade to Windows 2000. Microsoft devised and tested upgrade strategies for these products and assists you if they don't work. If you call Microsoft technical support for assistance on these upgrades, they'll help you troubleshoot. On unsupported upgrades, you're on your own.

Upgrading from NT 3.1 or 3.5

NT 3.51 and 4.0 servers aren't the only Microsoft servers still running out there. Some of you may want to move from earlier NT products, such as NT 3.1 or 3.5, to Windows 2000. You can indeed make this upgrade; it just takes a little more effort.

Follow these general steps to upgrade from NT 3.1 or 3.5:

1. **Make sure that your server hardware meets the Windows 2000 Server hardware requirements, as shown in Table 8-1.**

2. **Upgrade the server to either NT 3.51 or NT 4.0.**

3. **Upgrade to Windows 2000.**

Verifying hardware requirements

Before you run the Windows 2000 Setup program, make sure that your hardware meets the Windows 2000 Server hardware requirements, as shown in Table 8-1.

Table 8-1	Hardware Requirements for Windows 2000 Server
Component	*Requirement*
Processor	Pentium 166 Mhz or higher
Memory	64MB required; 128MB recommended
Hard Disk	1.2GB required on the boot partition; 2GB or more recommended
Video	VGA or higher video card and monitor
Hardware	Must be on the Windows 2000 Hardware Compatibility List.

The Windows 2000 Hardware Compatibility List (HCL) mentioned in Table 8-1 is a list of equipment that has passed Microsoft's standards for compatibility.

Although Microsoft recommends 128MB of RAM for Windows 2000 Server, I don't believe that amount is sufficient for domain controllers that run the Active Directory Service. Having 256MB of RAM provides much better performance, and I recommend it as the minimum amount for domain controllers.

Backing out gracefully!

After you verify that your hardware meets the minimum requirements, you want to devise a backout plan in case something goes wrong. (Sometimes you find that you don't have all the software you need, or sometimes a piece of hardware malfunctions.) All system administrators know that they need to follow change-control processes, but surprisingly few actually do so — which is a very good way to ensure an unplanned job change!

Ideally, your organization is using a standard change-control process that details the work plan and the backout steps necessary to return the server to production condition. Figure 8-1 shows a change-control form that you can adapt for your organization.

The purpose of the change control process is to make sure that changes to the network are

✔ Planned

✔ Tested

✔ Documented

✔ Communicated to all affected users

✔ Recoverable

Change Control Form
(Attach documented plan and backout plan to this form.)

Description of proposed change:

Purpose of proposed change:

Proposed maintenance window:

Network users who will be affected by this change:

Review board recommendation:
      Approved _____   Not Approved _____

Manager approval:

Figure 8-1:
A generic change-control form.

Documenting a recovery plan is just as important as testing and documenting the proposed change. Upgrades sometimes go wrong — you may even have experienced such a situation yourself at some time. But if you have a plan for returning the server to production before the problem affects users, you're doing your job properly. (Give this admin a raise!)

After you document the proposed change, have a group of your peers meet to review the plan. (This group should become a regular review board for change approvals.) Such a review makes some administrators a little nervous at first, but I think you're quickly going to find that your peers are supportive. If you've tested and documented the plan thoroughly, you've already proven that it works. And, after all, your peers may find themselves in the hot seat next time.

After a review board approves the change, specify a maintenance window and notify users of the server's unavailability during that period. If the upgrade isn't complete by a predetermined time, implement the backout plan so that the server is back in production by the end of the maintenance window.

Ensuring stability

Although your ultimate goal is migrating to Windows 2000 Server, you still have a Windows NT production domain to support for now. In case the migration doesn't go well, you need to operate under Windows NT.

Microsoft advises — and I heartily suggest — that you take a Windows NT BDC offline to preserve the existing users, groups, and policies, just in case the migration doesn't go well. Simply remove one of the BDCs from the network after making certain that it's synchronized with the PDC. If the first migration attempt proves unsuccessful, you can bring this BDC back online, promote it to PDC, and resynchronize your Windows NT domain.

 If you need a refresher on promoting Windows NT domain controllers, refer to *MCSE Windows NT Server 4 in the Enterprise For Dummies* by Ken Majors, Dave Dermon, and Jeffrey Ferris (published by IDG Books Worldwide, Inc.).

Identifying a Migration Model

Your current Windows NT domain model determines the migration strategy you use to get to Windows 2000. Identify your current domain model so that you can identify a strategy and order for upgrading each of the domains into the Active Directory tree. (See Chapter 7 if you need assistance in identifying your Windows NT domain model.)

Two of the NT domain models — single domain and single-master domain — accommodate upgrading a domain that becomes the root domain of your new Windows 2000 tree. In upgrading the multiple-master domain model or the complete-trust model, you first create a new Windows 2000 root domain and then upgrade the Windows NT domains to child domains in the tree.

Upgrading a single domain

A single Windows NT domain is relatively easy to migrate. Figure 8-2 shows the single domain model compared to the structure for the Windows 2000 tree. The NT domain becomes the root domain in the new Windows 2000 tree. (See the section "Upgrading the PDC to a Root Domain," later in this chapter, for further instructions on creating a root domain.)

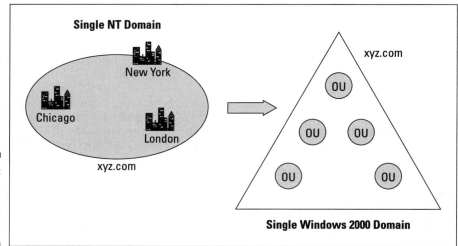

Figure 8-2:
Upgrading a single Windows NT domain.

Upgrading the single-master domain model

In upgrading the single-master domain model, the master domain becomes the root domain in the Windows 2000 tree, as shown in Figure 8-3. (See the section "Upgrading the PDC to a Root Domain," later in this chapter, for further information.) The resource domains become child domains in the tree. Use OUs to organize users and resources within the domain.

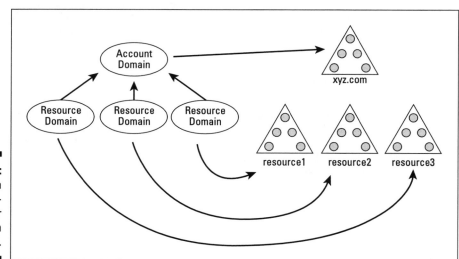

Figure 8-3:
Upgrading a single-master domain model.

Upgrading the multiple-master domain model

If you upgrade from the multiple-master domain model, you first create a new Windows 2000 root domain for your Active Directory tree. Then you migrate the Windows NT account domains as child domains in the new tree. Finally, you migrate the resource domains as child domains of the account domains.

After you upgrade all the domains, you can consolidate the account domains and the resource domains to achieve a more streamlined directory tree. Simply move the account domain objects into one domain, and move all the resource domain objects into another domain. For easy administration, you can create OUs to organize objects within the domain. (See Chapters 6 and 11 for additional information on creating OUs and managing objects.)

Figure 8-4 shows an example of how you can place the Windows NT domains into the new tree. After you migrate all the domains, use OUs to organize users and resources within the domains.

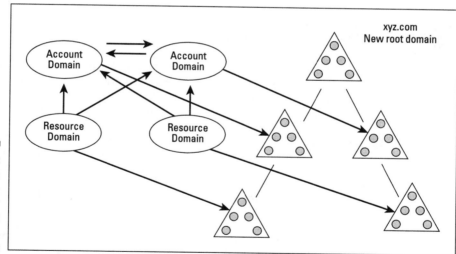

Figure 8-4:
Upgrading a multiple-master domain model.

Upgrading the complete-trust model

Before you migrate any of the Windows NT domains in a complete-trust model, you want to create a new Windows 2000 root domain for the Active Directory tree. Next, you migrate each of the Windows NT domains to the new tree as a child domain. Figure 8-5 shows how you place the domains in the tree. After you migrate all the domains, use OUs to organize users and resources within the domains.

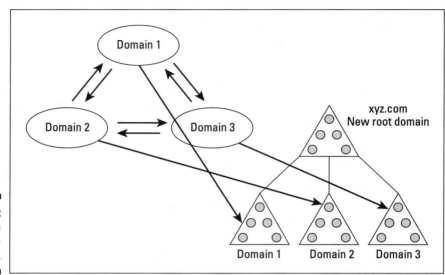

Figure 8-5:
Upgrading a
complete-
trust model.

Upgrading Servers

The first step in migrating from any of the four Windows NT domain models is to upgrade the domain controllers from Windows NT to Windows 2000 Server. The primary domain controller (PDC) contains the primary copy of the Windows NT domain database, so migrate the PDC first.

As you migrate a Windows NT PDC to a Windows 2000 domain controller, user accounts, groups, and permissions automatically migrate to the Active Directory. Remember that in Windows 2000 you have no PDCs and BDCs — only domain controllers (DCs). So as a Windows NT PDC migrates to Windows 2000, it becomes simply a DC. As the Windows NT BDCs migrate, they, too, become just DCs.

As you upgrade a domain controller to Windows 2000, the Active Directory Installation Wizard automatically begins as soon as the server reboots after the Windows 2000 installation. If, for some reason, the wizard doesn't start, run the dcpromo.exe program from the Start menu to launch the wizard.

Upgrading domain controllers

Upgrading domain controllers is a two-step process, as follows:

1. **Upgrade the server to Windows 2000 Server.**

2. **Run dcpromo.exe to promote the new Windows 2000 server to an Active Directory domain controller.**

From the following sections, choose the section that best fits your particular situation and follow the specific steps for upgrading.

If you need additional assistance installing Windows 2000, refer to *Windows 2000 Server For Dummies* by Ed Tittel (with Mary Madden and James Michael Stewart), published by IDG Books Worldwide, Inc.

Upgrading the PDC to a root domain

To migrate a Windows NT PDC to a root domain in an Active Directory tree, first install Windows 2000 Server. Then follow these steps to complete the Active Directory installation:

1. **From the Start menu, choose Run.**

2. **In the Open text box of the Run dialog box, type** dcpromo.

   The installation wizard opens with the Welcome screen, as shown in Figure 8-6.

Figure 8-6:
Launching
the Active
Directory
Installation
Wizard.

3. **Click Next.**

   The Domain Controller Type screen appears, as shown in Figure 8-7.

4. **Choose the Domain Controller for a New Domain option.**

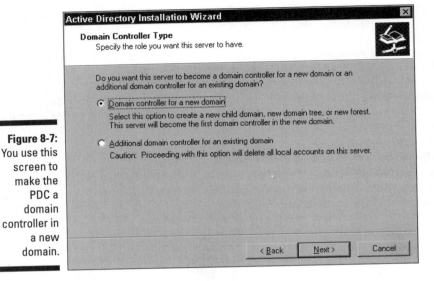

Figure 8-7:
You use this
screen to
make the
PDC a
domain
controller in
a new
domain.

5. **Click Next.**

The Create Tree or Child Domain screen appears, as shown in Figure 8-8.

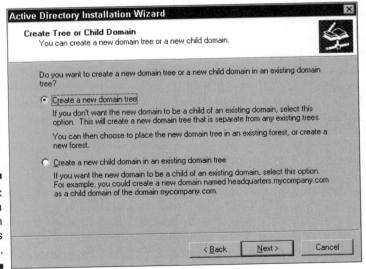

Figure 8-8:
Specify a
new domain
tree on this
screen.

6. **Choose the Create a New Domain Tree option.**

This step establishes the new domain controller as the first DC in a new domain that's forming a new Active Directory tree.

7. **Click Next.**

The Create or Join Forest screen appears, as shown in Figure 8-9.

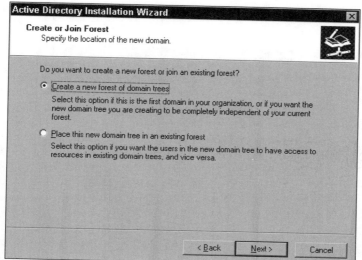

Figure 8-9:
Create a
new forest
on this
screen.

8. **Choose the Create a New Forest of Domain Trees option.**

This option establishes the domain tree as the first tree of a forest.

9. **Click Next.**

The New Domain Name screen appears, as shown in Figure 8-10.

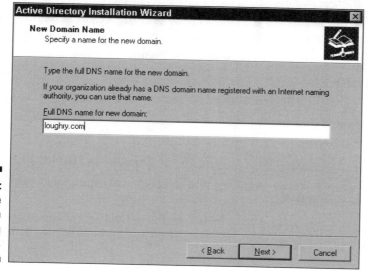

Figure 8-10:
Specify the
root domain
name on
this screen.

10. **Type the DNS root domain name for the tree in the Full DNS Name for New Domain text box.**

11. **Click Next.**

    The NetBIOS Domain Name screen appears, as shown in Figure 8-11.

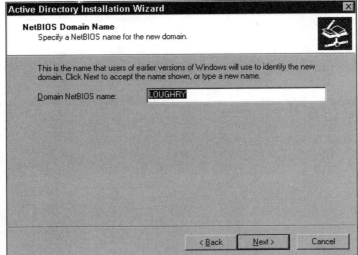

12. **Type a domain name in the Domain NetBIOS Name text box.**

13. **Click Next.**

    The Database and Log Locations screen appears, as shown in Figure 8-12.

14. **Either accept the default locations for the Active Directory database and logs or type new locations in the appropriate text boxes.**

    I recommend that you accept the default locations.

15. **Click Next.**

    The Shared System Volume screen appears, as shown in Figure 8-13.

16. **Type a location for the system folder in the Folder Location text box.**

17. **Click Next.**

    The Configure DNS screen appears, as shown in Figure 8-14.

18. **Select the appropriate option to specify whether you want the wizard to install DNS.**

    In my examples, I want to use Microsoft DNS, so I choose Yes. If you already have DNS correctly installed and configured, you won't see this screen of the wizard.

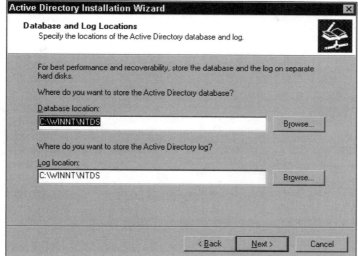

Figure 8-12:
Specify
locations for
the Active
Directory
database
and log files
on this
screen.

Figure 8-13:
Specify the
location of
the system
volume on
this screen.

19. **Click Next.**

The Permissions screen appears, as shown in Figure 8-15. This screen asks whether you want to set permissions to be compatible to pre–Windows 2000 servers or compatible to Windows 2000 servers only.

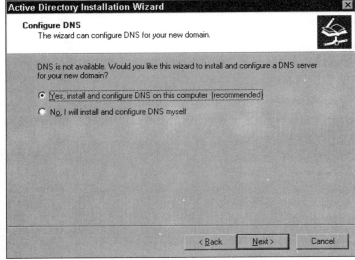

Figure 8-14:
Install and
configure
Microsoft
DNS on this
screen.

20. **Click the Permissions Compatible with Pre–Windows 2000 Servers option button.**

    If Windows NT 4.0 users aren't going to be accessing the domain, choose the Permissions Compatible Only with Windows 2000 Servers option.

21. **Click Next.**

    The Directory Services Restore Mode Administrator Password screen appears, as shown in Figure 8-16.

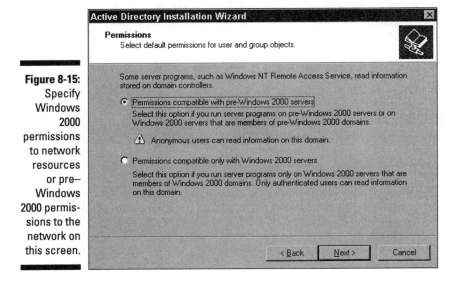

Figure 8-15:
Specify
Windows
2000
permissions
to network
resources
or pre–
Windows
2000 permis-
sions to the
network on
this screen.

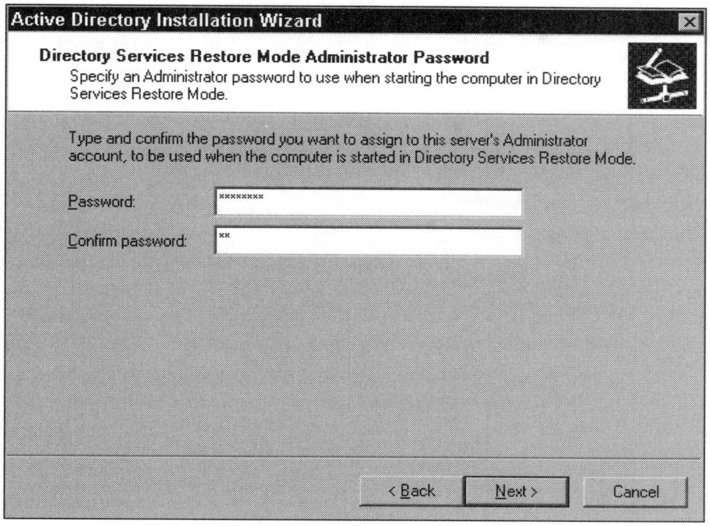

Figure 8-16:
Enter a
password
for Directory
Services
Restore
Mode on
this screen.

22. Type a password to use whenever you must start the server in Directory Services Restore Mode.

For example, you might need to start the server in Directory Services Restore mode if the Active Directory database ever becomes corrupt.

Don't lose this password! If you lose the password, you won't be able to enter Directory Services Restore mode to restore a corrupt directory database.

23. Click Next.

The Summary screen appears, as shown in Figure 8-17.

24. Verify your selections before clicking the Next button.

If any of your selections are incorrect, use the Back button to return to the appropriate screen and make corrections.

25. Click Next.

The Active Directory Installation Wizard configures Active Directory. After the configuration is complete, a Finish button appears at the bottom of the screen.

26. Click Finish to close the wizard.

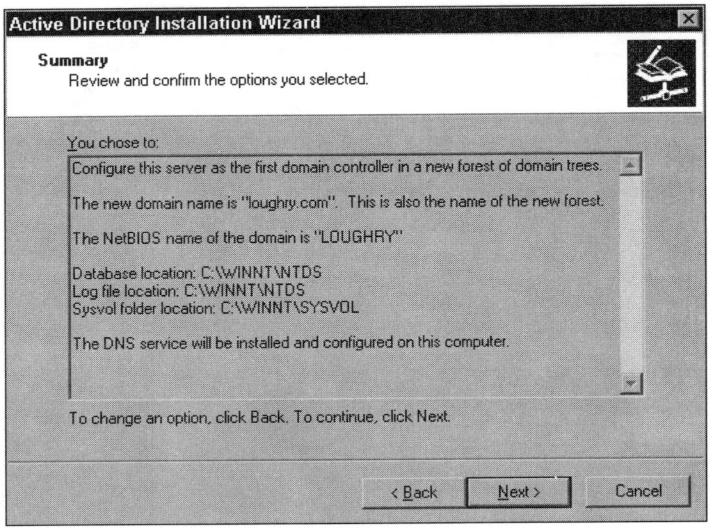

Figure 8-17:
Verify the
information
on the
Summary
screen.

Upgrading the PDC to a child domain in an existing tree

Many times, such as when you are upgrading a multiple-master or complete-trust domain model, you'll upgrade a domain PDC to create a new domain in an existing tree. The steps are very similar to those given in the preceding section. You simply choose different options on the Domain Controller Type screen of the Active Directory Installation Wizard. Follow these steps:

1. **Choose Start➪Run; then type** dcpromo **in the Run dialog box.**

   The installation wizard opens with the Welcome screen.

2. **Click Next.**

   The Domain Controller Type screen appears (refer to Figure 8-7).

3. **Choose the Domain Controller for a New Domain option.**

4. **Click Next.**

   The Create Tree or Child Domain screen appears (refer to Figure 8-8).

5. **Choose the Create a New Child Domain in an Existing Domain Tree option.**

   This step establishes the new domain controller as the first DC in a child domain in an Active Directory tree.

6. **Click Next.**

   The Create or Join Forest screen appears (refer to Figure 8-9).

   Continue the installation wizard by picking up here with Step 8 of the preceding section. As you work through the wizard, make the same choices that I describe in those steps.

Upgrading BDCs

After upgrading and migrating the Windows NT domain PDC, the next step is to upgrade and migrate the BDCs. Again, the steps are similar to upgrading a PDC. You first upgrade the BDC to Windows 2000 and then complete the Active Directory Installation Wizard. Because migrating the domain's PDC has already migrated the domain database, the BDC simply becomes an additional domain controller in an existing domain. (Or, if you choose, the BDC can become a member server in the domain.) Follow these steps:

1. **Choose Start⇨Run; then type** dcpromo **in the Run dialog box.**

   The installation wizard opens with the Welcome screen.

2. **Click Next, repeatedly, until the Additional Domain Controller or Member Server screen appears (see Figure 8-18).**

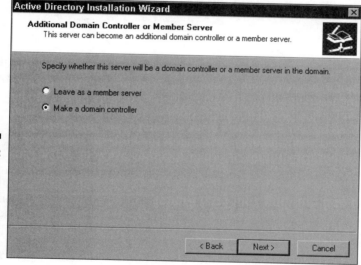

Figure 8-18:
Add an additional domain controller on this screen.

3. **Choose the Make a Domain Controller option.**

4. **Click Next.**

   The Network Credentials screen appears, as shown in Figure 8-19.

5. **In the appropriate text boxes, type the user name, password, and domain name of a valid administrator account in the domain.**

6. **Click Next.**

7. **All that's left to do is examine the summary screen. If the information is correct, click Next.**

8. **When the installation finishes, click Finish to exit the wizard.**

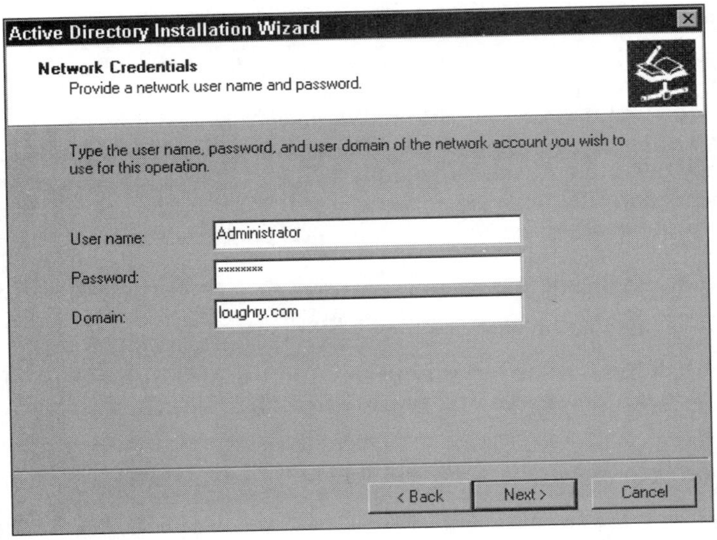

Figure 8-19:
Enter
network
credentials
in order to
add the
domain
controller to
the domain
on this
screen.

Notice that in all three of the upgrade processes that I describe in the preceding sections, all servers first became Windows 2000 Servers before becoming domain controllers.

Upgrading member servers

After you migrate all the domain controllers in a domain, you can upgrade the member servers to Windows 2000 at any time. In the meantime, the Windows NT servers continue to interact with the domain as usual. Member servers are not domain controllers, so you don't have to install Active Directory on these servers.

If you need help installing Windows 2000 Server and configuring your network settings or DNS, refer to *Windows 2000 Server For Dummies* by Ed Tittel (with Mary Madden and James Michael Stewart), published by IDG Books Worldwide, Inc.

Switching to native mode

By default, Windows 2000 domains run in *mixed mode* (a mixture of Windows NT and Windows 2000 servers) until you manually switch to *native mode*. Mixed mode enables Windows 2000 DCs to emulate Windows NT domain controllers for backward compatibility until you upgrade all the domain controllers. Native mode enables Windows 2000 domain controllers to take full advantage of Active Directory features such as transitive trust relationships, nested groups, and universal groups.

You can't change from native mode back to mixed mode! Don't switch to native mode until after you upgrade *all* the Windows NT domain controllers to Windows 2000 DCs. If you switch to native mode before upgrading all domain controllers, the Windows NT domain controllers can't participate in domain functions.

In mixed mode, you can't use all the features of Windows 2000. So after you upgrade all the domain controllers in a domain to Windows 2000 Server, you want to switch to native mode. This switch provides full Windows 2000 Server functionality and completes the migration to Windows 2000.

Switching to native mode doesn't affect client computers accessing the domain. You don't need to wait until clients upgrade to Windows 2000 Professional to switch to native mode.

To switch from mixed mode to native mode, follow these steps:

1. **Using the Active Directory Domains and Trusts screen (choose Start⇨ Programs⇨Administrative Tools⇨Active Directory Domains and Trusts), right-click the domain that you want to switch to native mode and choose Properties from the pop-up menu that appears.**

2. **On the General tab of the Properties dialog box, click the Change Mode button near the bottom of the screen (see Figure 8-20).**

3. **Click OK to close the Properties dialog box.**

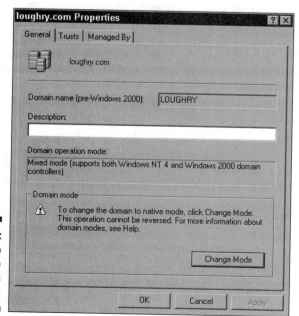

Figure 8-20:
Switch to native mode by using this dialog box.

Upgrading clients for Active Directory

If you have client computers running Windows NT 3.51 or Windows NT 4.0, you want to upgrade them to Windows 2000 Professional. Client computers running Windows 2000 Professional automatically take advantage of Active Directory services.

For Windows 95 and Windows 98 client computers to use Active Directory features, you must install the Active Directory Services Client software from the Windows 2000 Server CD. This client software requires that the client computer is running Internet Explorer 4.01 or higher with the Active Desktop feature enabled. (To enable the Active Desktop, right-click on an empty area of the desktop and choose Active Desktop⇨Enable Active Desktop.)

If the client computer isn't running the required software, the Active Directory Services Client software doesn't install.

To install the Active Directory Services Client software from the Windows 2000 Server CD, follow these steps:

1. **Choose Start⇨Run.**

2. **In the Open box of the Run dialog box that appears, type** dsclient.

   The client Setup Wizard opens.

3. **Click Next.**

4. **Read and accept the license agreement by clicking I Agree.**

   The Confirm Installation screen appears.

5. **Click Finish.**

6. **When the wizard presents the screen telling you that the installation is complete, click OK.**

7. **Choose Yes to restart the computer.**

Chapter 9

Migrating from Other Operating Systems

In This Chapter

▶ Migrating from NDS

▶ Migrating from UNIX

▶ Migrating from Banyan

*A*s you may expect, you can't upgrade servers running NetWare, UNIX, Banyan, and other operating systems to Windows 2000. For any operating system other than Windows NT, you must begin with a fresh install of Windows 2000 Server. Some utilities, however, are available to help you migrate from another directory service to Active Directory. Many of these are third-party tools, whereas others are utilities available through Microsoft.

In this chapter, I talk about migration strategies for moving from Novell, UNIX, and Banyan to Windows 2000 Active Directory.

Migrating from Novell NDS to Active Directory

Microsoft expects — or hopes — that most companies choose Active Directory instead of Novell's NDS (NetWare Directory Services). To accommodate those defecting Novell customers, Microsoft provides a utility to help with migration. Other vendors, such as Entevo and FastLane, provide migration tools as well.

A NetWare migration is a major project that you want to plan very carefully. If you read and follow the advice that I give in Chapter 2 about documenting your existing environment, you're well-prepared to plan the migration. Your migration includes the following general steps:

✔ Document the existing NetWare environment. (See Chapter 2 for instructions and suggestions.)

✔ Plan or document your DNS namespace. (Chapter 3 tells you how to plan the namespace.)

✔ Create a logical Active Directory Structure, determining where each of your current NDS containers will transfer to in the new Active Directory tree. (Chapter 4 covers designing a logical Active Directory structure.)

✔ Create a physical topology of sites so that you utilize network bandwidth effectively. (Chapter 5 tells you how to plan for the physical structure.)

✔ Build the root domain of your Active Directory tree by installing Active Directory on a Windows 2000 Server. Make sure that you install at least two domain controllers; then if one crashes, the other maintains the directory information. (Chapter 6 gives detailed instructions on installing Active Directory. If you're migrating NDS data into an existing Active Directory tree, you can skip this step because you already have domain controllers in place.)

✔ Use a migration tool to begin moving containers and objects to Active Directory. (See the following section in this chapter for details.)

✔ After you transfer the NDS data to Active Directory, migrate files to Windows 2000 servers.

Creating a logical Active Directory design from an NDS tree is sure to be a straightforward exercise for you. The underlying concepts behind the two directory services are very similar. Simply correlate the NDS containers to Active Directory domains and OUs. (Again, Chapter 4 gives instructions on creating a logical design.)

After you establish an Active Directory tree, you can begin migrating NDS directory information. In addition to the Microsoft Directory Services Migration Tool, several other third-party migration tools are available. Study the features of each carefully before selecting a tool for your migration. You can download a 30-day demo version from most vendors to test the features in a trial migration.

Directory Service Migration Tool

The Directory Service Migration Tool (DSMT) is a utility that you can use to export data from the NetWare bindery (a database file containing security information) or NDS database, store it off-line so that you can reconfigure it, and then import it into the Active Directory database. By using the DSMT, administrators can migrate users, groups, files, containers, and existing security permissions to Active Directory.

The DSMT is a powerful utility. Its capability to take a copy of a NetWare database off-line for further configuration provides a foolproof method of migrating to NT. You can perform a number of trial migrations to make sure that the directory information migrates to Active Directory in exactly the manner that you want.

Install the DSMT by using the Add/Remove Programs utility in Control Panel. Follow these steps:

1. **Choose Start⇨Settings⇨Control Panel.**

2. **Double-click the Add/Remove Programs icon.**

3. **Double-click the Add/Remove Windows Components icon.**

4. **Select Networking Services and then click the Details button.**

5. **Click the box next to Directory Service Migration Tool to place a check mark in it (see Figure 9-1).**

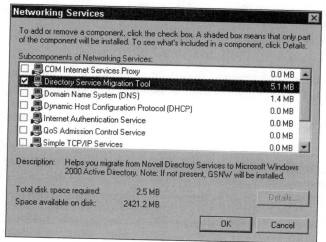

Figure 9-1:
Click the
check box
to install the
DSMT.

6. **Click OK.**

7. **After installation is complete, click Finish.**

If you haven't already installed Gateway Services for NetWare (GSNW) and NWLINK (Microsoft's version of the IPX/SPX protocol), the installation program installs them for you as it installs the DSMT.

You start the DSMT from the Administrative Tools menu, as shown in Figure 9-2. (Remember, you access the Administrative Tools menu by choosing Start⇨ Programs⇨Administrative Tools.) The DSMT is a Microsoft Management Console (MMC) snap-in, so the interface should look very familiar.

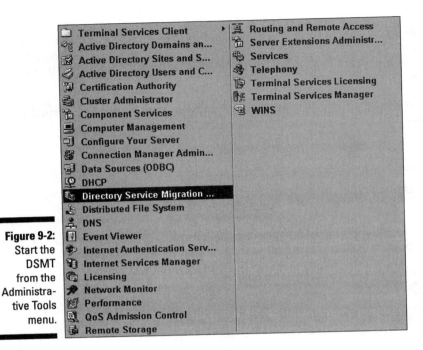

Figure 9-2:
Start the
DSMT
from the
Administra-
tive Tools
menu.

Microsoft provides sample projects so that you can practice using the tool before beginning to work with your NetWare directory data (see Figure 9-3). I advise you to explore the sample projects before you begin your own migration.

In DSMT, each migration you work on is known as a *project*. You can create any number of projects and save them to work on at a later time. Doing so is particularly helpful if you're migrating one branch of your tree at a time.

Notice in Figure 9-3 that the project name is Sample Project. The sample shows two views. A *view* is an off-line, graphical representation of the database (see Figure 9-4) that you use to manipulate the data until it looks the way you want it to for your Active Directory implementation. When you create a view, you choose which NetWare components to configure for a particular part of the migration. Then the *discover* process finds and presents all the NetWare components. You manipulate those components within the view until they appear as you want them to in Active Directory. Finally, you migrate those components to Active Directory.

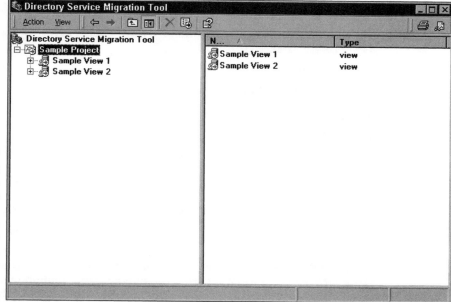

Figure 9-3:
Viewing the sample project and views in the Directory Services Migration Tool.

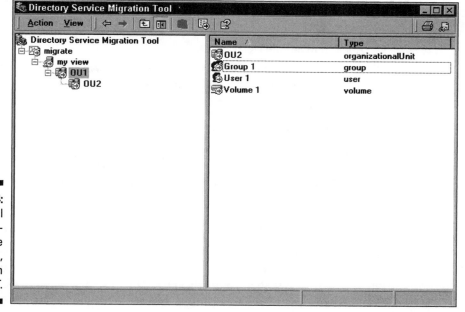

Figure 9-4:
A graphical representation of the database, created in DSMT.

To create a new project for your migration, follow these steps:

1. **Choose Start⇨Programs⇨Administrative Tools⇨Directory Service Migration Tool.**

   The DSMT opens.

2. **Choose Action⇨New⇨Project.**

3. **Type a name for the project in the Project Name text box.**

4. **Click OK.**

   The new project is now listed in the DSMT.

Creating a new view is just as easy. Follow these steps:

1. **Choose Start⇨Programs⇨Administrative Tools⇨Directory Service Migration Tool.**

   The DSMT opens.

2. **Right-click the project for which you're creating a view; then choose New⇨View from NetWare from the pop-up menu that appears.**

   This action launches the NetWare discover feature, a wizard that searches for NetWare bindery and NDS resources.

3. **Type a name for the view in the View Name text box.**

4. **Click Next.**

   A list of available NetWare resources appears.

5. **Select the resource with which you want to work in this project; then click the Add Context button. Repeat this to add additional resources.**

6. **After you finish adding NetWare resources, click Next.**

7. **Click Finish to end the wizard and move the resources to the off-line database.**

Instead of attempting to migrate the NetWare directory service on-line, use the DSMT's off-line capabilities to configure the NetWare data off-line. This practice enables you to reconfigure permissions, groups, and accounts before you add them to Active Directory. At the same time, you can keep using your NetWare directory service for production during the migration.

To modify any of the resources in the off-line database using DSMT, simply select the object, right-click it, and choose All Tasks from the pop-up menu that appears, as shown in Figure 9-5. From the All Tasks menu, you can perform the following tasks:

✔ Configure objects in Active Directory

✔ Find and replace objects

- ✔ Find and replace references to objects (if, for example, the object you're referencing isn't available in Active Directory or has a different name)
- ✔ Generate a user password
- ✔ Import an object
- ✔ Look at options for the project
- ✔ Print a copy of the tree
- ✔ Verify object dependencies

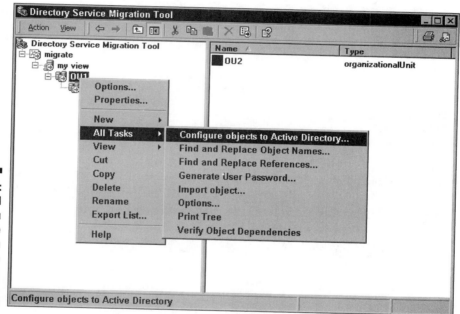

Figure 9-5:
The All Tasks menu shows the tasks you can perform by using DSMT.

The best way to migrate the NetWare directory service is to work with small portions of the tree at a time. Migrate containers and branches individually, adapting them to the new Active Directory tree or forest before bringing them on-line.

If you right-click a project in the DSMT and choose Options from the pop-up menu, you can customize many of these tasks in the Options dialog box. As Figure 9-6 shows, the dialog box offers tabs that enable you to configure the location of the off-line database, generate passwords, migrate files, and much more.

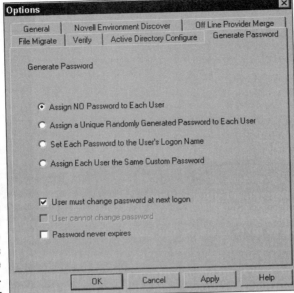

Figure 9-6:
You can configure passwords here for the NetWare accounts that you're migrating.

The default location of off-line databases is C:\Program Files\DSMigrat\Data. You can change the location on the General tab in the project's Options dialog box (see Figure 9-7).

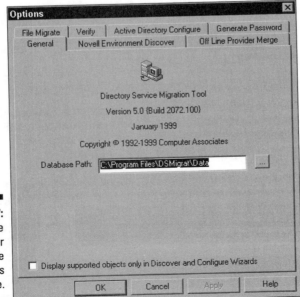

Figure 9-7:
Specify the location for the off-line databases here.

After you configure the NetWare resources to your satisfaction, you can transfer the data to Active Directory by following these steps:

1. **Within your project in the DSMT, right-click the resource you're ready to migrate and choose Task⇨Configure Object to NTDS from the pop-up menus.**

2. **Select the destination container to which you want to migrate the NetWare resources.**

3. **Click Finish.**

   The wizard runs a verification check to make sure that the migrating data is properly configured.

   Before the wizard actually writes the data to Active Directory, you get one more chance to change your mind. The wizard runs a verification check, and if the verification finishes with no errors, you can migrate the data. If you see errors, go back and reconfigure those resources; then return to Step 1 to begin the process of transferring the data to Active Directory.

4. **After the wizard finishes the verification with no errors, click the Continue button to write the data to Active Directory.**

   Your migration to Active Directory is complete.

Entevo DirectMigrate NDS and DirectMigrate 2000

DirectMigrate NDS, from Entevo Corporation, is a directory-service migration application that migrates users and files from NDS to Windows NT. It also enables you to model your NDS tree within Windows NT so that you can get a head start on migrating to Windows 2000. As an added feature, you can continue to operate your NDS production environment while your migration takes place. DirectMigrate NDS keeps track of everything. As does the Microsoft Directory Migration Tool, DirectMigrate NDS enables you to run trial migrations. This feature enables you to be sure of the configuration before migrating directory data.

DirectMigrate 2000 is another Entevo migration tool. This one enables you to migrate from Windows NT to Windows 2000. This tool is very flexible — it enables you to create an Active Directory model. Whenever you're ready, you can migrate the Windows NT environment by using the model.

A trial version of DirectMigrate 2000 is available on the CD-ROM accompanying this book.

Migrating from UNIX

You find more integration tools for UNIX and Windows 2000 than you do migration tools. Unlike Novell NDS and Banyan StreetTalk, UNIX environments don't use a dedicated directory service. Migrating from UNIX to Windows 2000 Active Directory is very straightforward — it's a completely new installation.

If you're migrating a server or servers from UNIX to Windows 2000, I suggest that you take the following actions (see Figure 9-8):

✔ Document the existing UNIX environment (see Chapter 2).

✔ Plan or document your DNS namespace (see Chapter 3).

✔ Create a logical Active Directory structure, determining where each of your current users and files will exist in the Active Directory tree (see Chapter 4).

✔ Create a physical topology of sites so that you utilize network bandwidth effectively (see Chapter 5).

✔ Build the root domain of your Active Directory tree by installing Active Directory on a Windows 2000 Server. Make sure that you install at least two domain controllers so that if one crashes, the other maintains the directory information (see Chapter 6).

✔ Create user accounts for each new user (see Chapter 11).

✔ Migrate files to Windows 2000 servers.

✔ Apply appropriate permissions to files.

Figure 9-8:
Planning a
Windows
2000 and
Active
Directory
implementa-
tion.

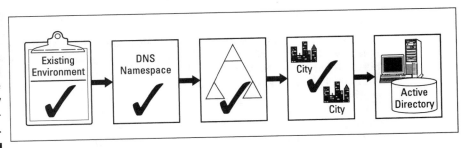

If you're migrating a large number of servers from UNIX, you may want to consider using a scripting tool such as FINAL from FastLane. By using the FINAL scripting language, you can rapidly create users and move files to their appropriate locations on Windows 2000 servers and in Active Directory. For more information, visit the FastLane Web site at www.fastlane.com.

Migrating from Banyan StreetTalk

Although no longer very popular, Banyan's StreetTalk is a very robust and stable directory service. Microsoft states that Active Directory can synchronize with StreetTalk by using the Active Directory Services Interface, but I haven't had the opportunity to test this capability.

Microsoft doesn't currently provide tools for migrating from Banyan StreetTalk to Active Directory. I keep hearing that Banyan is going to provide its own utility for migrating to Active Directory (which strikes me as sort of self-defeating), but I haven't seen any such tools yet. Before re-creating a large number of users and manually moving files, I recommend that you check out Active DMS (Directory Management Service) or FINAL (both from FastLane) to see whether either product is suitable for your migration.

So, for the present, you accomplish the task of migrating from Banyan to Windows 2000 Active Directory by freshly installing Windows 2000 and Active Directory and then populating the directory with OUs, users, and groups. For more details, see the procedure for a UNIX migration, given in the preceding section.

Part IV
Managing Active Directory

The 5th Wave   By Rich Tennant

"This part of the interview tells us whether or not you're personally suited to the job of system administrator."

In this part . . .

Now that you're living in an Active Directory world, you need to know how to manage Active Directory and its components. With all the new features of Windows 2000 and Active Directory, the tools, the tasks, and the terminology are quite different from what you're probably familiar with.

New security protocols and features lead to new ways of managing users, groups, and policies. Similarly, the introduction of Active Directory brings new administrative work — controlling replication, managing the directory database, and modifying the directory schema. The information in these chapters assists you with both day-to-day and advanced administrative tasks in Active Directory.

Chapter 10

Security

In This Chapter

▶ Understanding Kerberos

▶ Exploring authentication methods

▶ Putting group policies in place

*T*hese days, it seems that you can't go more than a week at a time without hearing of a new security vulnerability on the Internet. Operating systems, Web browsers, mail systems, Web servers — all are vulnerable to persistent intruders who want access to your company's resources.

Although attacks from outside intruders are certainly the stuff of best-selling novels, "attacks" from within are far more common. If you've been an administrator for very long, you know that even well-meaning administrators and users can make costly mistakes. Fortunately, Microsoft includes many security enhancements in Windows 2000. In this chapter, I talk about authentication, Kerberos security, and group policies.

Meet Kerberos — the Guard Dog

Kerberos Version 5, as RFC 1510 defines, is the primary security protocol in Windows 2000. (If you need a refresher on RFCs, refer to Chapter 3.) Kerberos is a distributed security protocol, which means that it enables users to access resources anywhere on the network by using a single logon.

The name *Kerberos* is certainly intimidating, isn't it? So to dispel some tension, I'd better explain it. In mythology, Kerberos (or Cerberus) was a three-headed dog who guarded the gates of Hades. The MIT (Massachusetts Institute of Technology) developers who created the Kerberos protocol back in the 1980s thought it was an appropriate name for their new security protocol. I don't know about you, but I'm reluctant to associate my network with the gates of Hades! Despite the association, Kerberos is a mature industry-standard protocol that's well-suited for distributed computing environments.

Following are the features that Kerberos brings to the Windows 2000 party:

- ✔ Faster logon authentication in a distributed computing environment
- ✔ Transitive trust relationships between domains
- ✔ Delegated (or pass-through) authentication for distributed applications
- ✔ Interoperability with non-Windows systems that use the Kerberos protocol

Token or Ticket?

Windows 2000 offers the following two domain-authentication protocols:

- ✔ NTLM
- ✔ Kerberos

Although Kerberos is the security protocol of choice, if Windows 2000 computers are operating in a mixed environment of both Windows 2000 and NT servers (as they may be for many of you), NTLM authentication is necessary for backward compatibility.

NTLM authentication

NTLM is the authentication protocol that prior versions of Windows NT use. NT stores security information in the *Security Accounts Manager (SAM)* database on the PDC before replicating it to BDCs. Each network user, computer, and group receives a unique *Security Identification Number (SID)* that distinguishes it from other objects in the network. The SID resides with the user ID in the SAM.

Similarly, each resource in the network — such as printers, files, and servers — maintains an *Access Control List (ACL)* of SIDs that can access the resource. The ACL consists of entries that detail what type of access (read-only, write, execute, and so on) the user has to the resource. These entries are known as *Access Control Entries,* or *ACEs.*

Each time that a user logs on to the domain, the system retrieves the user's security information from the SAM and encodes it in an *access token* that shows the SID and the resources the SID can access. The access token is the user's key to domain resources. Whenever a user attempts to access a domain resource, the system compares the access token to the resource's ACL. If the ACL lists adequate access privileges for the user, the system grants that user access to the resource. Figure 10-1 illustrates the NTLM authentication process.

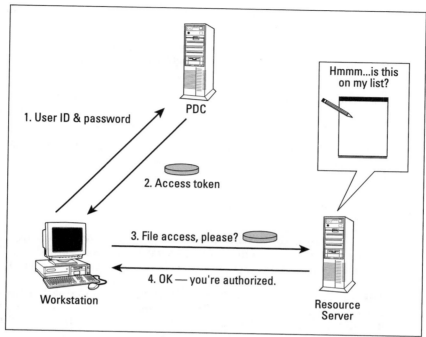

Figure 10-1:
Authentica-
ting user
logons by
using NTLM.

Client computers running Windows 95/98 (without the Directory Services Client), Windows NT, and Windows 3.1 use NTLM to authenticate user logons with a Windows NT or Windows 2000 server. Servers running Windows NT use NTLM to authenticate user logons as well.

Kerberos authentication

Kerberos is the default logon authentication protocol for Windows 2000 computers and accesses security information from the Active Directory rather than the SAM. Client computers running Windows 2000 or Windows 95/98 with the Directory Services Client software use Kerberos to authenticate with a Windows 2000 domain controller. Kerberos requires both client and server to authenticate, or logon, thus preventing an intruder from impersonating either client or server.

Kerberos is a *shared secret authentication protocol,* which means that both the client and another computer, known as the *Key Distribution Center (KDC),* know passwords. So the client and the KDC share a secret — the password. Kerberos authentication is a bit more complex than NTLM authentication. Kerberos takes the following actions to authenticate logon requests:

- A user authenticates with the KDC (which runs as a service on domain controllers).

- The KDC returns a *Ticket Granting Ticket* (or TGT) to the client. The TGT contains the user's SID and the SIDs of all groups of which the user is a member.

- The client caches the TGT until it needs to access a network resource; it then presents the TGT to the KDC and requests access to a resource server.

- The KDC returns a *Session Ticket* (ST), which contains an encrypted key code known only to itself and to the resource server.

- The client presents the ST to the resource server.

- The resource server examines the ST for a key code that is known only to the server and the KDC.

- If the key code matches the resource server's key code, the client receives access to the resource server. If the key code doesn't match the resource server's key code, the client doesn't receive access.

The theory behind this transaction is that the resource server says, "Hmm. I know and trust the KDC. The KDC must know and trust this account because it gave the account this ST. If I trust the KDC and the KDC trusts the user account, I can, therefore, trust the user account, too." Figure 10-2 illustrates the Kerberos authentication process.

Despite the added complexity of Kerberos authentication, it's faster than NTLM authentication because the client can reuse its ST tickets during a logon session. And, because Kerberos is a standard Internet protocol, Active Directory DCs (domain controllers) can authenticate clients running any operating system that uses Kerberos. Users on a network with UNIX, NetWare, MVS, IRIX, and Windows 2000 computers, therefore, can log on to any resource on the network by using a single logon.

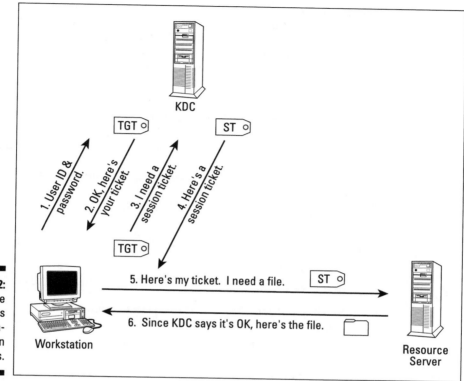

KDC

TGT ○   ST ○

1. User ID & password.

2. OK, here's your ticket.

3. I need a session ticket.

4. Here's a session ticket.

TGT ○

Figure 10-2:
The
Kerberos
authentica-
tion
process.

Workstation

5. Here's my ticket. I need a file.   ST ○

6. Since KDC says it's OK, here's the file.

Resource
Server

Implementing Group Policies

Rather than manage user accounts and access privileges individually, Microsoft invented policies to enable you to manage users and computers in bulk. You use *group policies* to configure user and computer settings for specific groups of users within a site, a domain, or an OU on the network.

Assume, for example, that you want users in a telephone order department to lock down their workstations so that no one can change the configurations. The order-center workstations are in constant use, and operators can't take orders for products if someone misconfigures the computer. As the administrator, you configure a group policy that restricts the settings that others can change on these workstations.

Similarly, assume that your company has a Research and Development unit that requires very tight security policies. The policies are too restrictive for most of your user community, so you place the R&D resources in a separate domain and apply a special group policy to that domain. This policy can enforce both user and computer settings within the domain.

Creating a group policy

Follow these steps to create a group policy for a site, a domain, or an OU:

1. **From the Start menu, choose Programs⇨Administrative Tools⇨Active Directory Users and Computers.**

   The AD Users and Computers snap-in appears.

2. **In the AD Users and Computers snap-in, right-click the desired container and choose Properties from the pop-up menu.**

3. **Click the Group Policy tab.**

4. **Click the New button.**

5. **In the Group Policy Name text box, type a name for the new group policy.**

6. **Click OK to close the Properties dialog box.**

Group policies can have a negative effect on your network. If you incorrectly configure them, they can inadvertently prevent users from logging on to the network. Plan group policies carefully and test extensively before implementing them in a production environment.

Accessing and editing a group policy

Each group policy is known as a *Group Policy Object (GPO),* and you store it in the Active Directory. You can view a GPO in either of the following two ways:

✔ View a GPO by accessing the properties of a site, a domain, or an OU, as shown in Figure 10-3. Follow these steps to access the properties:

   1. In the AD Users and Computers snap-in, select the domain or OU for the GPO that you want to view; then right-click and choose Properties from the pop-up menu.

   2. Click the Group Policy tab.

   3. Click the Edit button to access the settings of the GPO.

Figure 10-3:
Viewing the
Group
Policy
Objects for
the Austin
site.

✔ Use the Group Policy snap-in of the Microsoft Management Console (MMC) to view the settings of a GPO (see Figure 10-4) by following these steps:

1. Choose Start⇨Run and type **mmc** in the text box of the Run dialog box that appears.

   The MMC appears.

2. Choose Console⇨Add/Remove Snap-in from the MMC menu bar.

   After you choose Add/Remove Snap-in, you see a list of all the available snap-ins that can be loaded into the Microsoft Management Console.

3. From the list of snap-ins, select the Group Policy snap-in.

   A list of GPOs appears.

4. Select the GPO that you want to view.

Looking at Figure 10-4, you can see that policy settings are divided into the following two groups:

✔ **Computer Configuration settings:** These settings affect groups of computers on the network. They configure the computer desktop and apply security policies on network computers. These settings apply no matter which user logs on. Computer policies take affect right after the operating system launches.

> ✔ **User Configuration settings:** User configuration settings affect groups of users. They configure operating system and application settings, as well as security settings, logon/logoff scripts, and folder redirections. The policy settings apply to domain users no matter which computer they log on to. User policies take affect right after the user logs on.

Within these two groups of settings, the policy settings are further subdivided into the following categories:

> ✔ Software Settings
>
> ✔ Windows Settings
>
> ✔ Administrative Templates

Within the Windows Settings, as shown in Figure 10-5, you (finally!) find the Security Settings. Table 10-1 details the types of security settings configurable through a Group Policy Object.

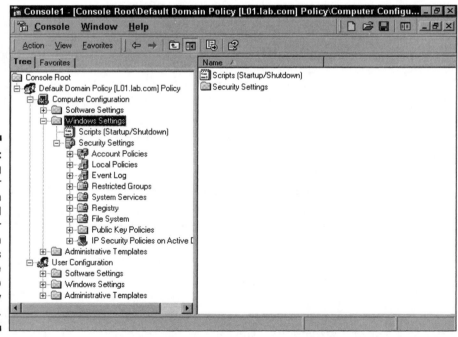

Figure 10-4:
Viewing
Computer
Configuration
settings and
User
Configuration
settings
with the
Group
Policy
snap-in.

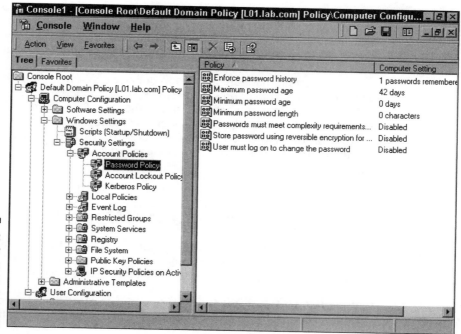

Table 10-1	GPO Security Settings
Policies	**Settings**
Account Policies	Configure password policy, account lockout policy, and Kerberos policy
Local Policies	Configure audit policies, user rights assignments, and security options
Event Log	Configures application, system, and security logs
Restricted Groups	Control group memberships for critical groups such as Administrator and Schema Administrator
System Services	Control security settings for system services
Registry	Configures security on the registry
File System	Controls security on folders
Public Key Policies	Configure trusted certificate authorities
IP Security Policies	Control IP security settings throughout the network

With the right combination of security settings, you can control and audit membership in administrative groups, restrict access to computer registries, restrict remote or local access to computers, and much more. If you use them correctly, group policies are a powerful tool for streamlining administration.

Again, make certain that you plan group policies carefully. In addition to creating an unintended effect on your network, group policies can also add significant overhead to the network and to the DCs. This additional overhead is due to the fact that Windows 2000 stores event logs in the Active Directory and replicates them to all DCs. In a large enterprise with strict audit policies, this situation results in frequent Active Directory changes — and thus frequent replication.

Disabling or deleting GPOs

You can delete or disable a GPO on a specific container (that is, a site, a domain, or an OU) by using the Group Policy tab of the container's Properties dialog box (see Figure 10-6). Just follow these steps:

1. **From the AD Users and Computers snap-in, select the desired container; then right-click and choose Properties from the pop-up menu.**

   The Properties dialog box for that container opens.

2. **Click the Group Policy tab.**

3. **Click the Options button.**

   An Options dialog box opens for that container, as shown in Figure 10-6.

4. **Click to place a check mark in the Disabled: The Group Policy Object Is Not Applied to This Container check box.**

5. **Click OK; then click Close to close the Properties dialog box.**

Figure 10-6:
Disable a
GPO on a
container by
selecting
the second
option
in this
dialog box.

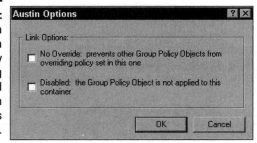

Alternatively, you can disable either the Computer Configuration settings of the GPO, the User Configuration settings, or both. Disable these settings on the General tab of the GPO's Properties (see Figure 10-7) by following these steps:

1. **From the AD Users and Computers snap-in, select the GPO; then right-click and choose Properties from the pop-up menu.**

   The Properties dialog box for that GPO opens.

2. **On the General tab, near the bottom, click either the Disable Computer Configuration Settings or Disable User Configuration Settings check box, depending on which policy settings you want to disable.**

   Clicking both check boxes disables all the GPO's settings. Check both boxes only if you want to disable all the settings of this GPO.

3. **Click OK to close the Properties dialog box.**

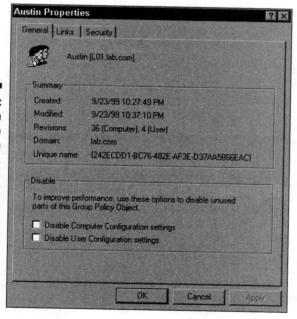

Figure 10-7:
You can disable the configuration settings of a Group Policy Object from the General tab of the Properties dialog box for that GPO.

Deleting a GPO simply unlinks the GPO from its associated container. To delete a GPO, choose the Group Policy tab of that container's Properties dialog box and click the Delete button.

Make disabling a group policy a standard practice rather than deleting it. Then if you later find that you need to reinstate the GPO, you can simply enable the GPO again.

Inheriting through GPOs

I keep cautioning you about the unintended effects of GPOs, primarily because the settings you configure through a GPO pass down to child domains and OUs — that is, the child domains and OUs inherit these settings. You can link multiple GPOs to a single container, and you can link a single GPO to more than one container. If this statement sounds confusing as you read it, think about trying to manage this confusion on your network!

If multiple GPOs affect a computer or user, the group policies apply in a specific order, as shown in the following list:

- ✔ Site
- ✔ Domain
- ✔ OU

So the user or computer's configuration is actually a composite of the GPOs that link to its site, domain, and OU. The user or computer inherits GPO configuration settings from the site, the domain, and the OU.

But what if the configuration settings in a parent container's GPO conflict with the configuration settings of the child container's GPO? In other words, what if you configure a domain GPO and an OU GPO that conflict? If the settings are compatible, both sets of configurations apply. If the settings conflict, the configuration in the OU's GPO applies. The OU settings would override the domain settings because inheritance comes into play. The specific settings for the OU override the inherited settings from the domain.

Blocking inheritance

In special circumstances, you may want to alter the inheritance of GPOs. If, for example, you want a GPO to apply to all the containers in one branch of the tree — except one — you can block the inheritance by that one container. Or, if you don't want the GPO settings of an OU to override the settings from the domain GPO, you can configure the GPO so that the OU settings don't override those of the domain.

To block policy inheritance from a parent domain, follow these steps:

1. **From the AD Users and Computers snap-in, select the desired container; then right-click and choose Properties from the pop-up menu.**

   The Properties dialog box for that container opens.

2. **Click the Group Policy tab.**

3. **Click the Block Policy Inheritance box near the bottom of the screen to put a check mark in it (see Figure 10-8).**

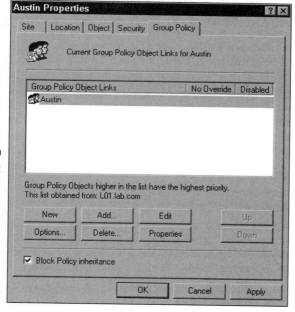

Figure 10-8:
Use the
Group
Policy tab to
block policy
inheritance
from a
parent
container.

4. **Click OK to close the Properties dialog box.**

To specify no override of policies by a child domain's GPO, follow these steps:

1. **From the AD Users and Computers snap-in, select the parent container; then right-click and choose Properties from the pop-up menu.**

   The Properties dialog box for that container opens.

2. **Click the Group Policy tab.**

3. **Click the Options button.**

   An Options dialog box opens for that container.

4. **Click the No Override: Prevents Other Group Policy Objects from Overriding Policy Set in This One box to place a check mark in it.**

   Refer to Figure 10-6 to see the No Override option in the Options dialog box.

5. **Click OK; then click Close to close the Properties dialog box.**

Chapter 11

Managing Users, Groups, and Other Objects

. . . .

In This Chapter

▶ Delegating administrative control

▶ Editing user attributes

▶ Managing Active Directory objects

▶ Creating and managing shared folders

. . . .

*U*ser and group administration is one of the more important aspects of system administration. After all, if end users can't access the appropriate network resources, the network isn't functioning correctly, is it? Because this topic is so important, I spend quite a bit of time on it. In this chapter, I discuss delegating administrative control, managing Active Directory objects, creating and managing groups, and administering group policies.

Delegating Administrative Control

If you have previous experience with Windows NT administration, you probably have eagerly awaited the opportunity to delegate administration! In the old Windows NT world, you had no way to assign password reset privileges to the help desk without also assigning more powerful administrative privileges. But Windows 2000 resolves that dilemma by introducing the capability to delegate administrative control to portions of the Active Directory tree. As with many other processes in Windows 2000, you have a wizard to help delegate control of Active Directory objects.

As part of the planning process that I describe in Chapter 4, I ask you to plan an administrative model. Your diagram illustrates how you're delegating administrative control within the tree. (If you don't have such a diagram, please see Chapter 4.) Perhaps your tree consists of several domains with different groups administering each domain. Or, as I do with my own tree, perhaps you use OUs to organize the domain and then delegate administration within the OUs. That enables you to still achieve decentralized administration but without the additional domains.

To delegate administration of an Active Directory object, simply follow these steps:

1. **From the Start menu, choose Programs⇨Administrative Tools⇨Active Directory Users and Computers.**

   The Active Directory Users and Computers snap-in appears.

2. **In the Active Directory Users and Computers snap-in, right-click the object to which you want to delegate administration.**

3. **Choose Delegate Control from the pop-up menu that appears.**

   No matter which object you're delegating control of, the procedure to start the wizard is always the same. Figure 11-1 shows the initial screen of the Delegation of Control Wizard.

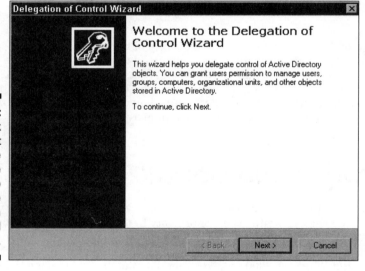

Figure 11-1:
Right-click an object and choose Delegate Control to start the Delegation of Control Wizard.

4. **Click Next.**

   The Users or Groups screen appears. This screen is where you specify the groups or users to whom you're granting control of this OU, as shown in Figure 11-2.

5. **Click the Add button, and a list of users and groups appears (see Figure 11-3).**

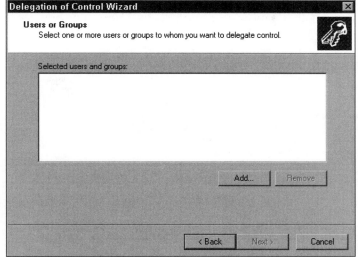

Figure 11-2:
Specify the
users and
groups who
are to
assume
control of
the object.

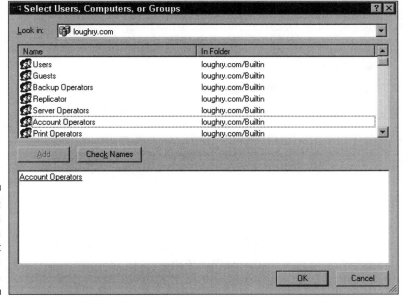

Figure 11-3:
Select users
and groups
from the list
and then
click OK.

6. **Click to select the users and groups to whom you want to delegate control of specific tasks.**

7. **Click OK.**

This action returns you to the Users or Groups screen, where you see your choices appearing in the Selected Users and Groups list, as shown in Figure 11-4.

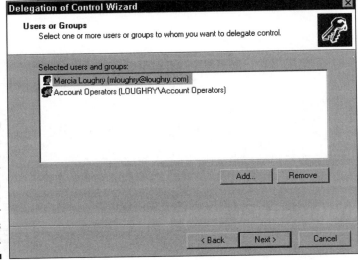

Delegation of Control Wizard

Users or Groups
Select one or more users or groups to whom you want to delegate control.

Selected users and groups:

 Marcia Loughry (mloughry@loughry.com)
 Account Operators (LOUGHRY\Account Operators)

Add...   Remove

< Back   Next >   Cancel

Figure 11-4:
Back at the
Users or
Groups
screen with
your
choices
displayed.

8. Click Next.

The Tasks to Delegate screen appears, as shown in Figure 11-5.

On this screen, you can choose which specific tasks to delegate. I'm not going to review each of the options that you can delegate because they're pretty straightforward. You can see in Figure 11-5 that I'm choosing to delegate the capability to create, delete, and manage user accounts as well as to reset passwords. So although I'm granting a user the capability to manage accounts in this OU, I'm not giving full administrative privileges to the OU nor granting privileges outside this particular container.

You can also select the second option and create custom tasks to delegate. You would select this option, for example, if you want a specific user to run scripts within this OU.

9. Click Next.

The final screen of the wizard appears, as shown in Figure 11-6. This screen summarizes your selections.

10. If the information is correct, click Finish. If you need to correct any information, click the Back button and make the changes.

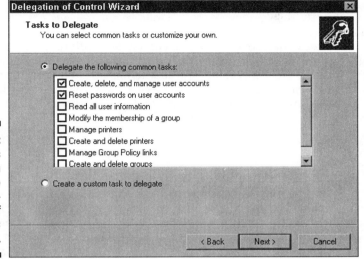

Figure 11-5:
On this screen, you delegate the administration of specific tasks.

Figure 11-6:
The final screen of the Delegation of Control Wizard summarizes your selections.

Delegating control isn't difficult, but it's something to plan carefully. If you use it correctly, delegating certain capabilities can free system administrators from a multitude of small (dare I say menial?) tasks. You can give end users administrative control over their own shared data without jeopardizing the integrity of the tree or the security of other users. Delegating administrative control is also a great way to decentralize administration by assigning authority over specific branches of the tree. Follow your organization's administrative model to determine how to delegate administration within the Active Directory tree.

Managing Users and Groups

Although I show you how to create users and groups in Chapter 6, I don't talk there about how to manage the various attributes that can describe each object. The user object, for example, has attributes for address, telephone number, e-mail address, and much more. As system administrator, you need to update and change these attributes frequently; this section explains how to do that.

The Active Directory schema defines Active Directory objects and attributes. If you populate the field for an attribute with data, the Active Directory database stores that data. You can access this stored information by performing a keyword search using an object's attribute. For example, you can search by telephone number, e-mail address, or by any other attribute. For more information on the schema, see Chapter 13.

Editing user objects

With Active Directory, you're likely to spend a good deal of time modifying user attributes. Because the Active Directory database can hold such a wide variety of user information, you can use it for e-mail information, human resources information, emergency contact information, and possibly even payroll information. Fortunately, you can edit all user information in one convenient location — the Active Directory!

From the AD Users and Computers snap-in, you can view the attributes on any user account by right-clicking the user account and choosing Properties. The Properties dialog box appears and offers you access to numerous attributes through the tabs at the top of the dialog box.

As you see in Figure 11-7, each user account can contain a great many attributes. A user's account can be almost as individualized as her personality!

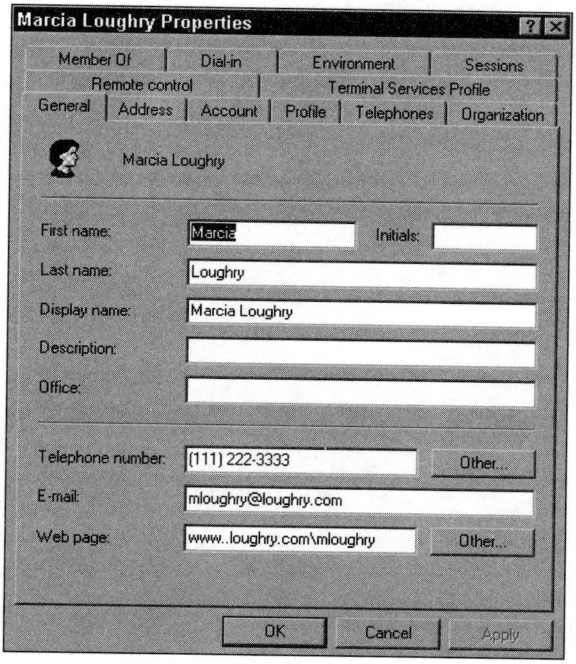

Figure 11-7:
The General
tab of a
user's
Properties
dialog box.

The information on the General Tab requires little explanation. The Display Name is the name that shows up in the tree. The Other buttons next to the Telephone Number and Web Page fields enable you to enter multiple entries in those fields.

If you click the Address tab, your screen looks like the one shown in Figure 11-8. Again, the information is self-explanatory, but you really need to become very familiar with user attributes, so please take a brief look at the text boxes available on each tab.

Marcia Loughry Properties ? X

Member Of	Dial-in	Environment	Sessions
Remote control		Terminal Services Profile	
General	Address	Account	Profile	Telephones	Organization

Street: 1212 Austin Road

P.O. Box:

City: Houston

State/province: TX

Zip/Postal Code: 75777

Country/region: UNITED STATES

OK   Cancel   Apply

Figure 11-8:
The Address
tab.

The Account tab contains a bit more detailed information about this user object, as Figure 11-9 shows. Most of this information is self-explanatory, with the possible exception of the Logon Hours and Log On To buttons, which the following list describes:

✔ **Logon Hours:** Choose this button if, as a security measure, you want to restrict the times in which a user can log on to the network.

✔ **Log On To:** Choose this button if you want to enable a user to log on to the network only from specific computers.

Although you can move around among the tabs of the Properties dialog box by clicking each tab, remember to click the Apply button if you make any changes to the information on a particular tab — before you move on to a different tab. Otherwise, when you're ready to close the Properties box, you may forget that you made changes and forget to click OK.

The Profile tab records the location of the user's profile, logon script, and home folder, as shown in Figure 11-10. The following list explains the options on this tab in more detail:

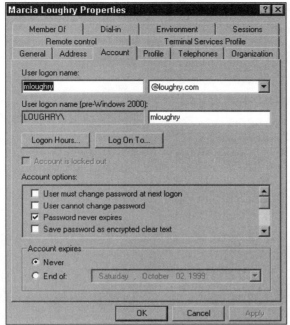

Figure 11-9:
The
Account
tab.

✔ **Profile path:** In this text box, type the local or network path to the user's profile.

A profile is a group of settings that customizes the user environment, such as desktop settings. The user's preferred settings are stored in a profile so that each time the user logs on the settings take effect.

✔ **Logon script:** In this text box, type the local or network path to the logon script.

When the user logs on to the network, the logon script runs and performs a variety of functions, such as connecting to network shares or printers.

✔ **Local path:** If the database stores the user's home directory locally, instead of on a network server, type the path here.

✔ **Connect:** In this text box, specify a drive letter for the home folder.

The home folder, also known as a *home share,* is a disk location where the user can store her personal documents.

✔ **To:** In this text box, specify the network path to the home folder.

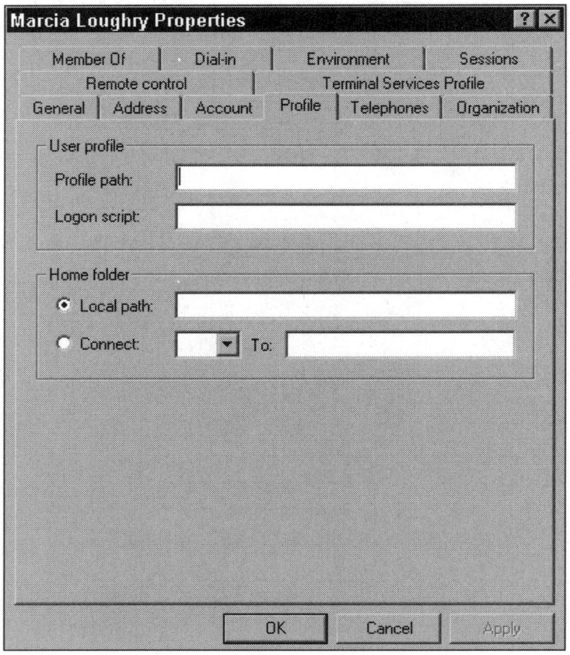

Figure 11-10:
You enter
the location
of the pro-
file, logon
script, and
home folder
on the
Profile tab.

The Telephones tab is completely self-explanatory (see Figure 11-11). Believe it or not, some users may need more fields for all their phone numbers! Just remember that if you need to enter more than one telephone number for a field, click the Other button.

The Organization tab gives you an opportunity to store job-related information about each user, as you see in Figure 11-12. Most companies currently store much of this information in a variety of separate, unsynchronized databases. You may store job titles and managers in an HR database, for example, and store e-mail information and phone numbers in an Exchange database. Because Active Directory provides a single database for the entire organization, the Organization tab is a great way to take full advantage of Active Directory!

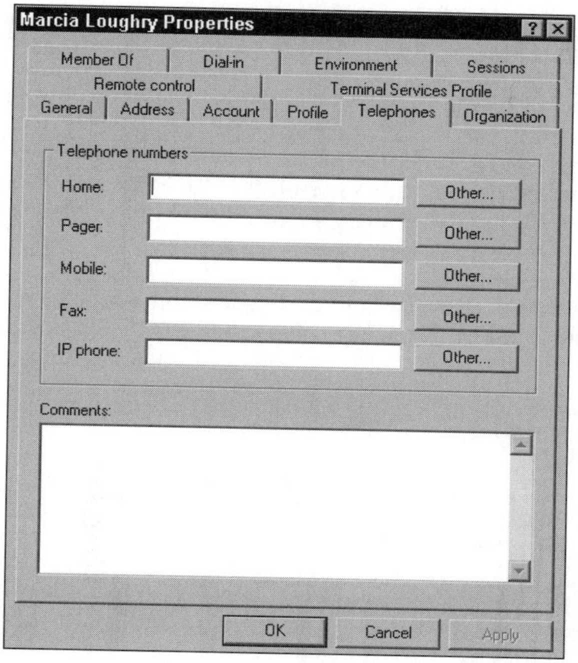

Figure 11-11:
The
Telephones
tab.

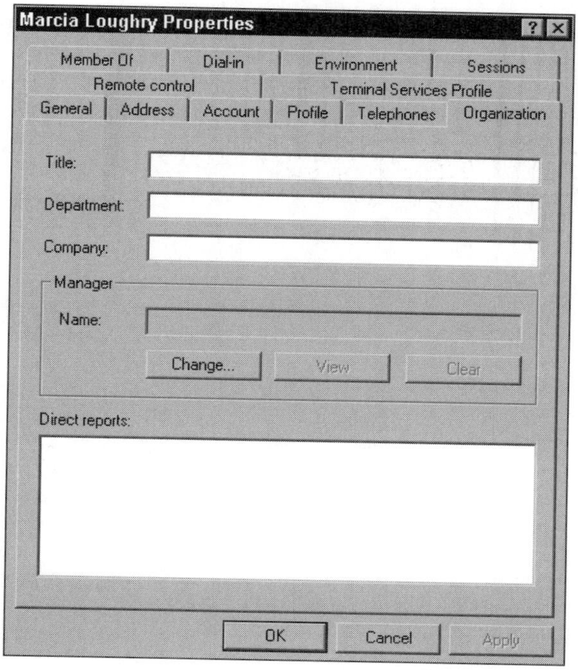

Figure 11-12:
The
Organization
tab.

If you're running Terminal Services, you also see the Remote Control tab in the Properties dialog box. (Prior to Windows 2000, Microsoft Terminal Service was a separate version of Windows NT. Microsoft has now added this thin-client function to Windows 2000 Server.) Use this tab to configure the remote-control settings for Terminal Services (see Figure 11-13). On this tab, you specify whether you can remotely control a user's Terminal Service session, whether you first need a user's permission to do so, and whether administrators can interact with the user session or simply view the user session.

If your organization isn't using Terminal Services, you don't see the Remote Control tab or the Terminal Services Profile tab in the dialog box.

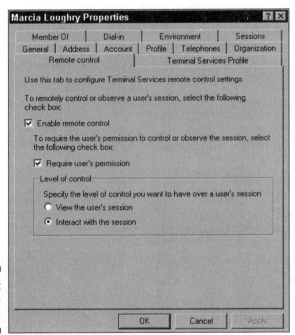

Figure 11-13:
The Remote
Control tab.

The Terminal Services Profile tab (see Figure 11-14) is very similar to the Profile tab shown in Figure 11-10. On this screen, however, the settings that you specify apply to Terminal Services. By removing the check mark from the Allow Logon to Terminal Server check box, you prevent a user from using Terminal Services.

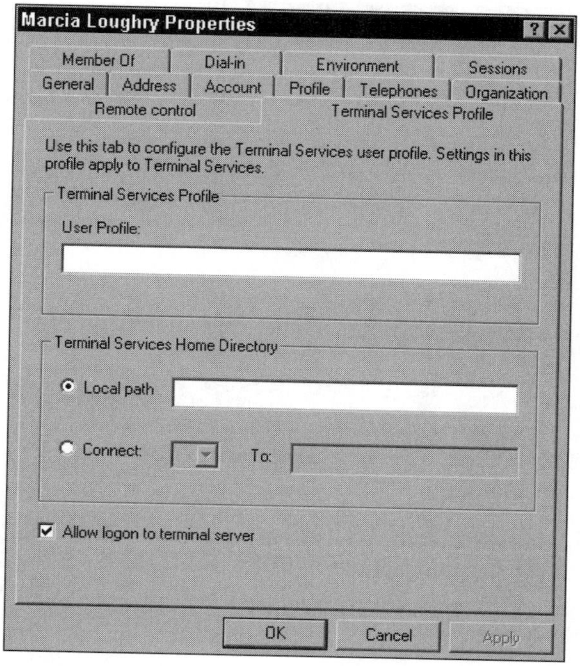

Figure 11-14: The Terminal Services Profile tab.

The Member Of tab lists which groups the user is a member of (see Figure 11-15). Use the Add and Remove buttons to quickly edit group memberships. Near the bottom of this screen is a Set Primary Group button. Every user has a primary group membership. If you specify no group memberships, the Primary Group, by default, is the user's group.

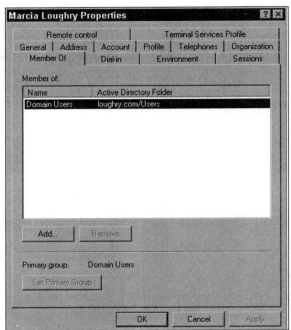

Figure 11-15:
The
Member Of
tab.

You see the Dial-in tab (see Figure 11-16) only if you installed RAS (Remote Access Service) in the domain. All the fields on this tab relate to RAS security settings. RAS is the service that allows users to dial in and access the network.

Rather than spend a lot of time explaining RAS security, which I'd need to do to explain each of the fields on the Dial-in tab, check out the Windows 2000 Resource Kit for more information. RAS security can be quite complex, and I prefer to focus on Active Directory concepts in this book.

The Environment tab (see Figure 11-17) is another tab that relates to Terminal Services. On this tab, you specify whether a program launches at startup and whether client-side drives and printers connect at logon.

Be careful! All the settings you enable on this tab override user-specified settings on the client.

Figure 11-18 shows the Sessions tab, which also refers to Terminal Services. Use this tab to configure timeout limits and connection actions on the user's Terminal Services session.

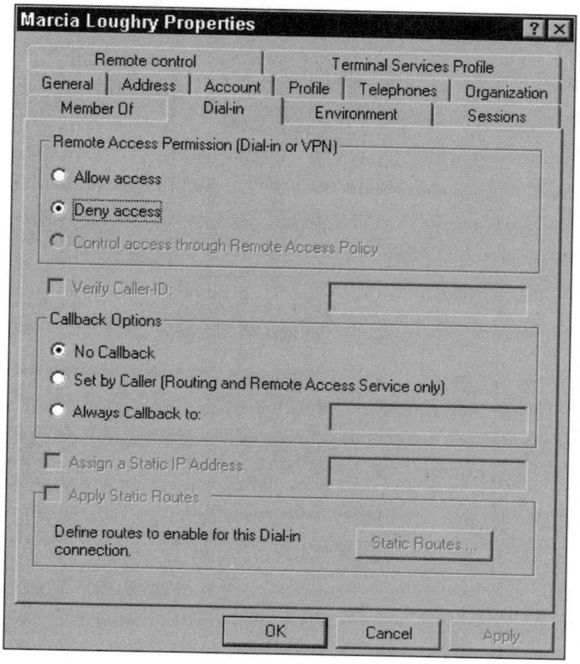

Figure 11-16:
Configure
RAS secu-
rity on the
Dial-in tab.

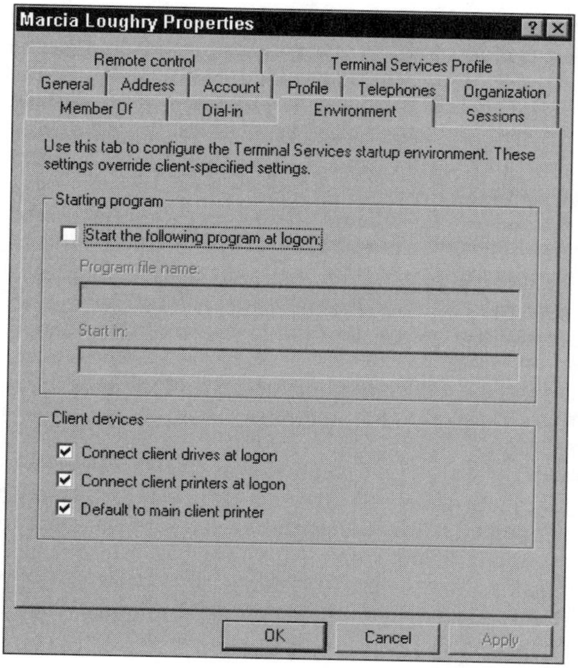

Figure 11-17:
The
Environment
tab.

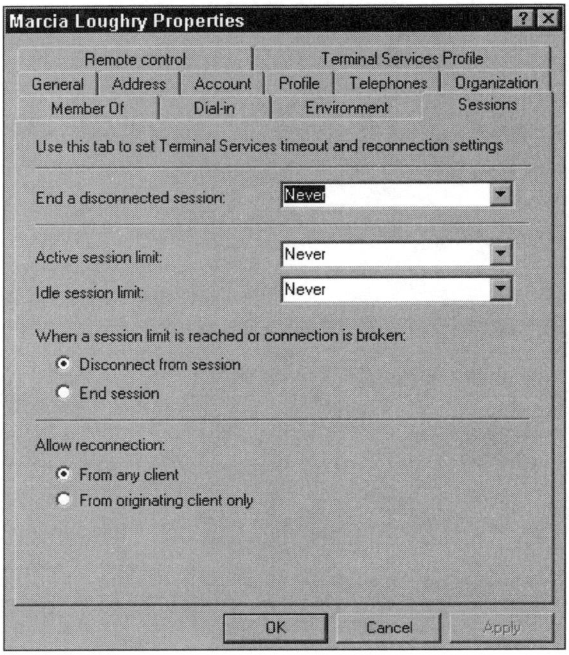

Figure 11-18:
The
Sessions
tab controls
Terminal
Services
timeouts.

As I reviewed the user Properties tabs, I hope you noticed that the more services you run in the domain, the more attributes are available for each user object.

Managing groups

Managing groups is much more efficient than managing individual users. By creating groups and assigning users to these groups, administrators can manage large numbers of users simultaneously. Windows 2000 uses the following two types of groups:

- ✓ **Security groups:** These groups offer a means of gathering multiple users together and granting access to resources. System administrators can create a shared folder, for example, and then create a group that accesses the folder. Users who need access to the folder become members of the new group. You can also associate additional groups with varying access permissions with the shared folder. To one group, you may grant only Read permission to the folder. To another, you may offer Change permission. In large environments, particularly, designating security groups is a much more efficient way to control user permissions than trying to manage individual users.

✔ **Distribution groups:** Distribution groups are new in Windows 2000, and you use them to group users together for non-security-related purposes, such as sending e-mails. System administrators can, for example, create a distribution group for each division or department in an organization. By using these groups, you can target e-mail messages to specific subsets of users.

In the Windows NT world, groups were either local groups or global groups. But in Windows 2000, the scope of a group's influence is more specific, as the following list explains:

✔ **Domain local groups:** Domain local groups are effective only within their local domain. You use them to grant permissions to resources within the domain, and administrators can view them only from within the specified domain.

✔ **Global groups:** Global groups grant permissions to a scope of trusted domains. You can view them anywhere within the tree. You can *nest* global groups — meaning that global groups can contain other global groups. (This process is similar to the Windows NT practice of assigning global groups to local groups.)

✔ **Universal groups:** Universal groups are new in Windows 2000. They are effective and viewable across all domains in a forest. System administrators use universal groups to contain global groups. An administrator can, for example, create separate global distribution groups to contain user accounts of employees at two different branch offices in California. Then the administrator creates a universal distribution group for all employees in California. The two global groups become members of the universal group. Now the administrator can direct e-mails to employees at either of the branch offices or to all the employees in California.

Look at the New Object - Group screen shown in Figure 11-19. (See Chapter 6 for the details on creating a new object.) In the bottom-left portion of the screen, you specify the group scope (Domain local, Global, or Universal). To the right, you specify the group type: Security or Distribution.

Editing groups

After you create a group, you can edit it by accessing the Properties page for that group. From the Active Directory Users and Computers snap-in, right-click the user account and choose Properties from the pop-up menu. The Properties dialog box appears and offers you access to numerous attributes through the tabs at the top of the dialog box.

In Figure 11-20, you see the properties of a group I created that I call NY Users. The General tab of the Properties dialog box shows the information I selected as I created the group.

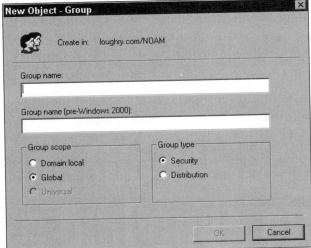

Figure 11-19:
Specify the group scope and type on the New Object - Group screen.

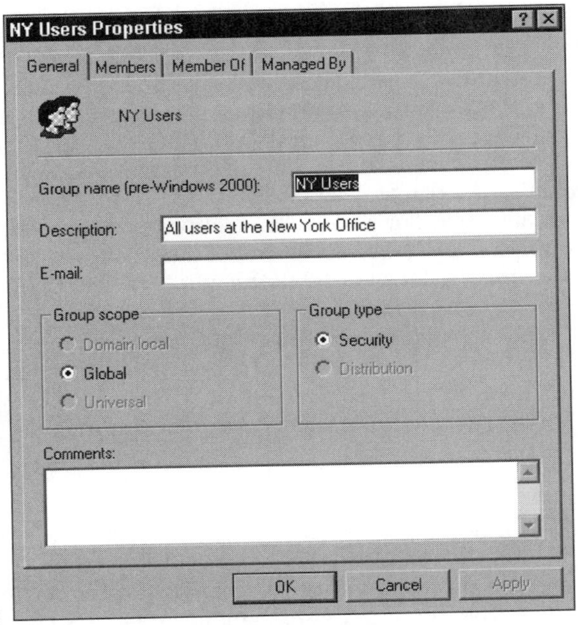

Figure 11-20:
Viewing the General properties of the NY Users group.

The Members tab, shown in Figure 11-21, lists users who belong to the NY Users group. You can use the Add and Remove buttons at the bottom of the screen to add or remove members of the group.

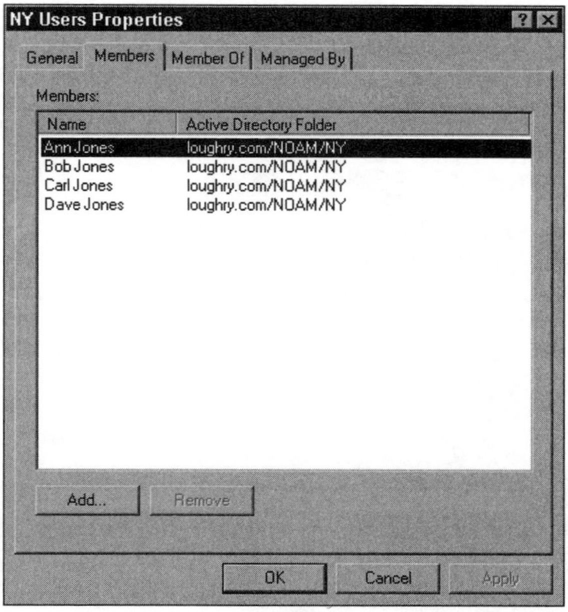

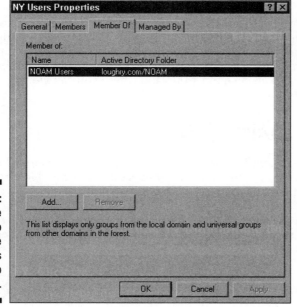

Figure 11-21:
Viewing
members of
the NY
Users group
on the
Members
tab.

On the Member Of tab, shown in Figure 11-22, the Name column shows which groups the NY Users group is a member of. Again, you can edit directly from this screen by using the Add and Remove buttons.

Figure 11-22:
Viewing the
groups to
which the
NY Users
group
belongs.

The Managed By tab, shown in Figure 11-23, shows who has the assignment of managing this group. Someone must hold the final authority on who can gain access to a specific resource. The Managed By screen contains the contact information for the user who's the decision maker for this group.

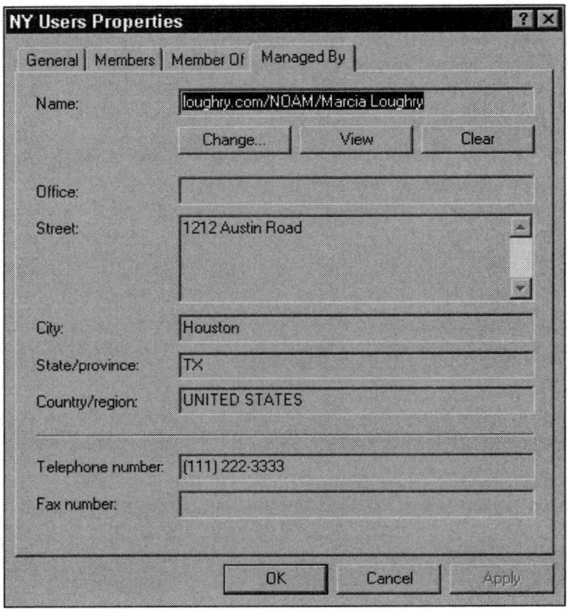

Figure 11-23:
The
Managed
By tab.

As you can see from the Properties tabs for the NY Users group, managing and editing groups isn't a complicated process. You manage both distribution groups and security groups in exactly the same way. Make sure that you specify the appropriate scope as you create the group, because the scope determines how you can use the group and where you can view it.

Creating shared folders

Creating a shared folder is a two-step process. First, you create the shared folder on the server or computer; then you create the shared folder within the Active Directory tree. Just follow these steps:

1. **To create a shared folder on the server, right-click the folder in Windows Explorer and choose Sharing from the menu that appears (see Figure 11-24).**

   Next, you must create the shared folder in the tree.

2. **From the AD Users and Computers snap-in, create a new Shared Folder in the appropriate container of the tree by right-clicking the container and choosing New⇨Shared Folder.**

   The New Object - Shared Folder dialog box opens, as shown in Figure 11-25. As you see in the figure, all you need to supply is a name for the new shared folder and the network path to the folder.

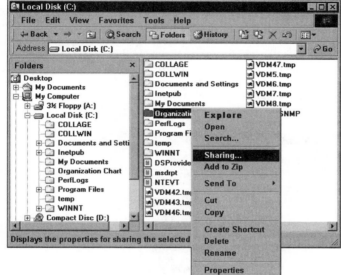

Figure 11-24:
Right-click the folder in Explorer and choose Sharing.

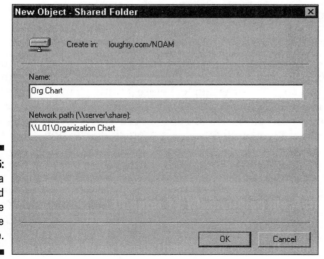

Figure 11-25:
Creating a new shared folder in the appropriate tree.

Managing shared folders

Managing shared folders and files differs somewhat from managing users and groups. After you create the shared folder, you can edit the folder's Properties as appropriate. From the AD Users and Computers snap-in, right-click the folder object and choose Properties from the pop-up menu. The Properties dialog box appears and offers you two tabs at the top.

On the General tab, you can describe the shared folder and view or edit the network path. Click the Keywords button if you want to create keywords that users can use to search the Active Directory when they're trying to locate this folder (see Figure 11-26). In my example, I named the shared folder North America Org Chart, so I added the words *organization* and *org* as keywords. If users want to locate this folder, they can search for either of these words and this folder appears in their search results list.

Figure 11-26:
In the Keywords dialog box, you can designate keywords that can help users in searching the database.

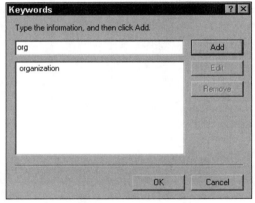

Shared folders also have a Managed By tab. On this tab, you can store the name and contact information for the person responsible for authorizing access to this resource. For example, before granting a user access to a payroll department shared folder, you would probably want to contact a manager in payroll to authorize the user's access. The Managed By tab is where you record the payroll manager's contact information. (Refer to Figure 11-23 to see a Managed By tab.)

You can adjust additional sharing properties from within Explorer, but those are beyond the scope of this book. Here, I deal only with managing the Active Directory. For more information on creating shares in Windows 2000, consult *Windows 2000 Server For Dummies* by Ed Tittel (with Mary Madden and James Michael Stewart), published by IDG Books Worldwide, Inc.

Viewing default users and groups

As you install Active Directory on the Windows 2000 Server, you create certain users and groups by default. I used the Export List feature of Active Directory to create comma-delimited text files showing these users and groups. I then turned those files into Tables 11-1 and 11-2.

Table 11-1	Default Users	
Name	*Type*	*Description*
Administrator	User	Built-in account for administering the computer/domain.
Cert Publishers	Security Group - Global	Enterprise certification and renewal agents.
DnsAdmins	Security Group - Domain Local	DNS Administrators Group.
DnsUpdateProxy	Security Group - Global	DNS clients with permission to perform dynamic updates on behalf of some other clients (such as DHCP servers).
Domain Admins	Security Group - Global	Designated administrators of the domain.
Domain Computers	Security Group - Global	All workstations and servers that join to the domain.
Domain Controllers	Security Group - Global	All domain controllers in the domain.
Domain Guests	Security Group - Global	All domain guests.
Domain Users	Security Group - Global	All domain users.
Enterprise Admins	Security Group - Global	Designated administrators of the enterprise.
Group Policy Creator Owners	Security Group - Global	Members in this group can modify group policy for the domain.
Guest	User	Built-in account for guest access to the computer/domain.

(continued)

Table 11-1 *(continued)*

Name	Type	Description
IUSR_L01	User	Built-in account for anony-mous access to Internet Information Services.
IWAM_L01	User	Built-in account for anony-mous access to Internet Information Services out of process applications.
krbtgt	User	Key Distribution Center Service Account.
RAS and IAS Servers	Security Group - Domain Local	Servers in this group can access remote access prop-erties of users.
Schema Admins	Security Group - Global	Designated administrators of the schema.

Table 11-2   **Default Groups**

Name	Type	Description
Account Operators	Security Group - Built-in Local	Members can administer domain user and group accounts.
Administrators	Security Group - Built-in Local	Administrators have full access to the computer/domain.
Backup Operators	Security Group - Built-in Local	Backup Operators can only use a backup program to back up files and folders onto the computer.
Guests	Security Group - Built-in Local	Guests can operate the computer and save docu-ments but can't install programs or make poten-tially damaging changes to the system files and settings.

Name	Type	Description
Print Operators	Security Group - Built-in Local	Members can administer domain printers.
Replicator	Security Group - Built-in Local	Members support file replication in a domain.
Server Operators	Security Group - Built-in Local	Members can administer domain servers.
Users	Security Group - Built-in Local	Users can operate the computer and save documents but can't install programs or make potentially damaging changes to the system files and settings.

You can use the Export List feature to dump lists of users, groups, and other Active Directory resources. I've already found this feature invaluable! For example, use Export List to dump lists of object attributes, lists of users in a group, or lists of objects in a container.

Chapter 12

Controlling Replication

*I*n a large environment or an environment with slow WAN links, replication traffic can make or break a network. *Replication* is the periodic exchange of database information between the domain controllers within a domain, which ensures that all domain controllers contain updated, consistent data. Your job as a system or network administrator is to plan and control replication traffic. Excessive replication traffic can saturate a network, resulting in slow response times and application time-outs. Fortunately, Microsoft provides tools for the job!

Aside from controlling replication traffic, sites group computers for fast and efficient authentication. As a user logs on to a workstation, for example, a domain controller (DC) authenticates his ID and password. Rather than send the authentication request across a WAN link for processing, the DC compares the IP address of the workstation to the subnets associated with each site. It then sends the authentication request to a domain controller in the local site.

In this chapter, I explain about implementing a site topology, using sites and site links to control replication, and the difference between intrasite and intersite replication. (For more information on planning a site topology to control authentication and replication traffic, see Chapter 5.)

Understanding Replication

Before I show you the tools for managing replication, I should probably tell you a bit more about it. As I mentioned in the preceding section, replication is an exchange of Active Directory information among domain controllers. Active Directory uses *multimaster replication,* which means that any domain controller can respond to service requests and record updates to the directory. Windows NT uses *single-master replication,* which limits database updates to the primary domain controller (PDC).

Active Directory uses site information to make replication and authentication more efficient. By grouping computers into sites, local domain controllers respond to logon requests. Sites also make replication traffic on the network more efficient. Replication can occur in two forms: intrasite and intersite.

Intrasite replication

Directory updates between domain controllers in the same site is known as *intrasite replication* (see Figure 12-1). Domain controllers within a site exchange information more often and more efficiently than do domain controllers in different sites. These frequent updates keep information within a site fresh. Domain controllers within a site are more likely to need fresh information about resources within the site. Updates are less frequent to domain controllers outside the site because those domain controllers are less likely to need up-to-the-minute directory updates.

These frequent intrasite updates are why sites play such an important role in network traffic flow. Sites let you physically group together computers that need to share resource information. Because these DCs are going to exchange information frequently, a site should be limited to computers connected by fast links (such as LAN segments), instead of by slower WAN links. If you create your sites correctly, you optimize network traffic flow.

Active Directory automatically configures the replication topology between domain controllers in the same site, and AD also automatically configures intrasite connections and optimizes replication patterns across these sites.

This automatic replication topology provides multiple routes to each domain controller and is known as *fault tolerance.* Fault tolerance is important because it means that if one domain controller is unavailable, the unavailable DC doesn't block replication to other domain controllers. The directory updates simply follow another path to reach all domain controllers within the site. If you add a new domain controller to the site, Active Directory automatically adjusts the intrasite replication topology to include the new DC.

The DCs don't compress directory updates before sending them within a site as they do in intersite replication. The CPU cycles on the local domain controllers, therefore, remain free to service requests instead of compressing data.

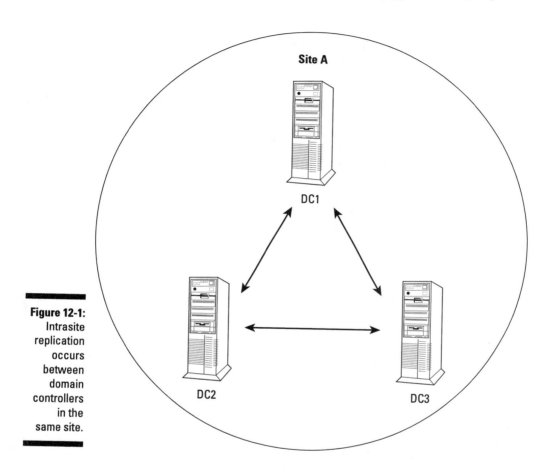

Figure 12-1:
Intrasite
replication
occurs
between
domain
controllers
in the
same site.

Intersite replication

Intersite replication — replication between domain controllers in different
sites — works differently than intrasite replication (see Figure 12-2). In the
figure, the intersite links are represented by the arrows between sites.
(Intrasite links are the arrows within the sites.) Here is where physical-
structure diagrams of your network become invaluable. (See Chapter 5 to
find out how to create these diagrams if you haven't already created them.)
First, Active Directory doesn't create the links between sites automatically.
You create the site links based on the actual network links in your environment. I discuss how to create and configure site links in the section "Creating
site links," a bit later in this chapter. For now, I just want you to understand
how replication works across the links. Without site links, directory updates
don't replicate to other sites.

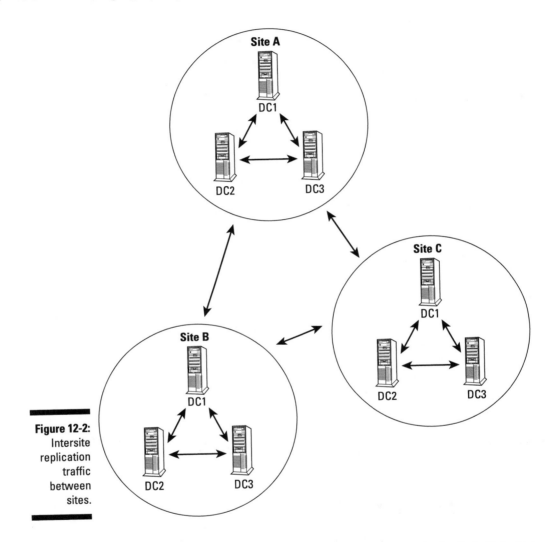

Figure 12-2:
Intersite
replication
traffic
between
sites.

After your site links are in place, you assign a *cost* to each site link. Doing so helps Active Directory determine which site link to make a *primary route* between sites (to which you assign a low cost, such as 1) and which to make a *secondary route* between sites (to which you assign a higher cost, such as 100). (Again, see the section "Creating site links," later in this chapter.) Use the available bandwidth measurements from your diagram to determine which site links are best suited to carry primary replication traffic.

To avoid saturating a network link with replication traffic during busy times of the day, you can associate schedules with the site link that determine when you can use the link for traffic. Remember that replication between sites can occur less frequently than intrasite replication.

Domain controllers automatically compress intersite replication data before transmitting it. This process enables the data to transmit more rapidly.

To optimize server resources, you can establish one server within a site as a *bridgehead server*. The bridgehead server handles all intersite directory replication. This server compresses all directory updates and replicates them to other sites. In turn, the bridgehead server receives directory updates from all other sites. After the bridgehead server receives the updates, it replicates those updates to the other DCs in the site.

Directory partitions and replication

The Active Directory stores the following three different categories of information:

- Schema (see Chapter 13 for more information on the schema)
- Configuration
- Domain

Each of these three categories is known as a *partition,* and the type of partition determines what type of directory information replicates. The following list describes these partitions in more detail:

- **Schema information:** Contains details about the objects and attributes that you can store in the directory tree or forest. Schema information replicates to all domain controllers.

- **Configuration information:** Contains details about the configuration of your Active Directory implementation, such as the structure of the tree or forest. Configuration information replicates to all domain controllers.

- **Domain information:** Contains details about the objects within a domain. Domain information doesn't replicate to all domain controllers — only to domain controllers within the domain. A listing of all domain objects becomes part of the global catalog, which works like an index to help users locate resources. The global catalog information about the domain replicates to all domain controllers.

Propagating updates

Propagating updates is just a fancy way of saying "replicating." I only mention it because you'll probably hear the phrase used in discussions about replication. The updates are the changes you make to Active Directory objects. Propagating the changes refers to copying the changes to all the other domain controllers in the tree. (I guess you sound more impressive saying "the domain controllers are propagating updates throughout the domain" than saying "the domain controllers are replicating." You don't want to make your job sound too easy, do you?)

Implementing a Site Topology

As part of Active Directory planning, you should create a physical structure design to accompany your design for a logical Active Directory structure. (See Chapter 5 if you need help in creating the physical design. Chapter 4 helps you with the logical design.) The physical structure associates the underlying network with the logical structure so that Active Directory functions efficiently on the network.

Sites are the major component of the physical structure. Sites are groupings of subnets that connect to one another via fast links — usually LAN links. All the sites in the physical structure connect together via *site links* and *site link bridges*. (Site link bridges connect specific site links. For more information, see the section "Creating a site link bridge" near the end of this chapter.) Sites, subnets, site links, and site link bridges make up the site topology.

In Figure 12-3, you can see that my network requires four sites. To connect these sites, I must create site links and possibly create site link bridges. Then, by using available bandwidth data, I can assign a cost to each site link and schedule replication traffic across the site links.

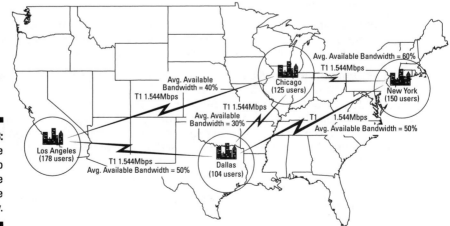

Figure 12-3:
Using a site
map to
create
the site
topology.

Creating sites

Creating sites is easy. *Configuring* the site links is what can getcha! Follow these steps to create a new site:

1. **Start the AD Sites and Services Manager by choosing Start⇨Programs⇨ Administrative Tools⇨Active Directory Sites and Services Manager.**

   The AD Sites and Services screen opens.

   As you install Active Directory, it automatically creates the first site for you and names it Default-First-Site-Name. Not a very original name, but at least it tells you how the site got there. Fortunately, you can rename this site quickly and easily in AD Sites and Services by right-clicking Default-First-Site-Name and choosing Rename from the pop-up menu that appears (see Figure 12-4). I'm working from the site map shown in Figure 12-3, so I'm renaming this site Chicago.

2. **Select the Sites container from the left pane of the AD Sites and Services screen.**

3. **Right-click and choose New Site from the pop-up menu that appears (see Figure 12-5).**

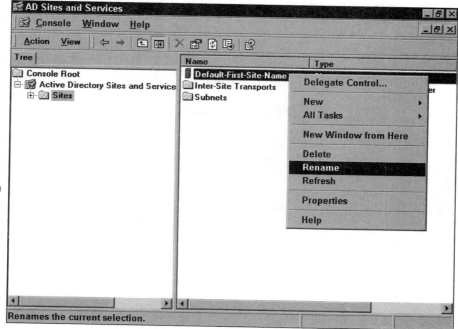

Figure 12-4:
Use the Rename command to change the default name for the site.

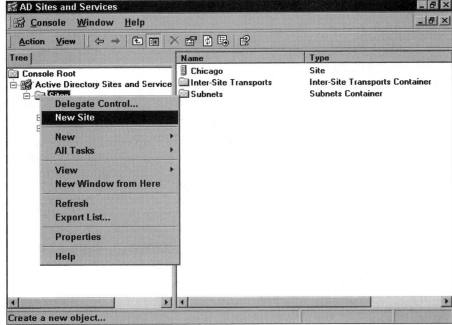

Figure 12-5:
Choose the New Site command to create a new site.

4. **In the New Object - Site dialog box that appears, type a name for the site in the Name text box (see Figure 12-6).**

I'm still following my site map, so I'm naming this site NewYork.

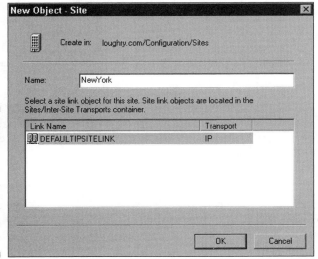

Figure 12-6:
Name the site and associate a site link object in the New Object - Site dialog box.

5. **Choose DEFAULTIPSITELINK as the site link object (no other site links exist yet).**

6. **Click OK.**

   This part of the process is the part that I really like. A set of Active Directory instructions appears that explains what you need to do to complete your site configuration (see Figure 12-7). Could things be any easier?

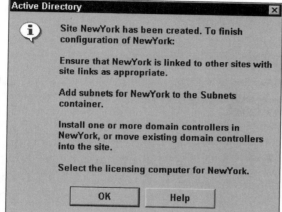

Figure 12-7:
Active
Directory
tells you
how to
complete
your site
configuration.

7. **After you have read the instructions in the message box, click OK to close the box.**

The following sections explain how to do the tasks suggested in the dialog box.

Creating subnets

To identify the subnets that you associate with the site, follow these steps:

1. **On the AD Sites and Services screen, select the Subnets folder that appears beneath the Sites folder.**

2. **Right-click the Subnets folder and choose New Subnet from the pop-up menu that appears (see Figure 12-8).**

3. **In the New Object - Subnet dialog box that appears, type the network address and the subnet mask in the appropriate text boxes (see Figure 12-9).**

   If you don't know the subnet mask for your network, ask your network administrator.

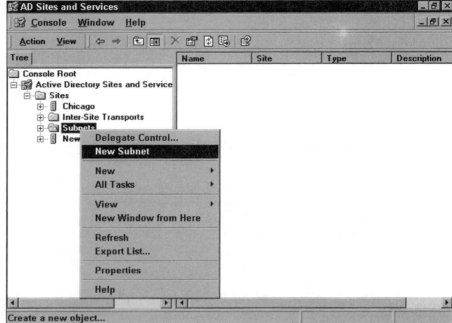

Figure 12-8:
Choose the
New Subnet
command to
create a
new subnet.

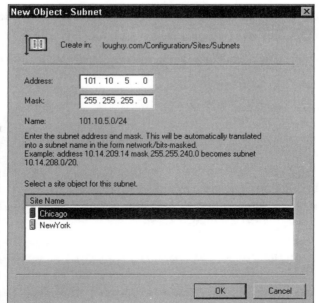

Figure 12-9:
Associate
the subnet
with the
correct site
by choosing
the appro-
priate name
from the
Site Name
text box.

4. **Associate the subnet with the correct site by choosing the appropriate name from the Site Name list box.**

   In my example, I associate the 101.10.5.0 network address with the Chicago site.

5. **Click OK to close the New Object - Subnet dialog box.**

I created all my subnets so that I can show you how the subnets appear in the AD Sites and Services Manager. In Figure 12-10, notice that each subnet lists the network address with /24 following the address. The 24 indicates the number of bits masked by the subnet mask. If the subnet mask were 255.255.0.0, the network address would appear with /16 after it instead.

The subnet mask distinguishes the network address from the host address. The portion of the IP address masked by the subnet mask is the network address. The unmasked portion of the IP address is the host address.

Notice, too, that in the right-hand pane in Figure 12-10, each subnet lists the site with which it associates. In this example, you can see that each subnet corresponds to one of the four sites on my site map back in Figure 12-3.

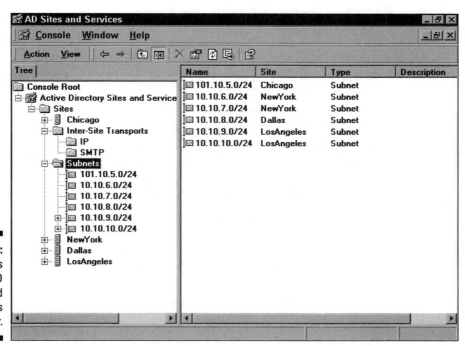

Figure 12-10:
The subnets list in the AD Sites and Services Manager.

Subnetting and subnet masks are beyond the scope of this Active Directory book. For more information, refer to *MCSE TCP/IP For Dummies* by Cameron Brandon (published by IDG Books Worldwide, Inc.).

Creating site links

Creating site links is only a bit more complicated than creating sites. After you create the site links, you schedule traffic and associate a cost with each site link. (Keep reading — I explain schedules and cost a bit later in this section!)

To create and configure a site link you must specify the following items:

- ✔ The sites to be connected
- ✔ A transport protocol
- ✔ A schedule
- ✔ A cost

To create a site link, follow these steps:

1. **On the AD Sites and Services screen, click (or double-click, if necessary) to expand the Inter-Site Transports folder.**

2. **Right-click the IP folder and choose New Site Link from the pop-up menu that appears (see Figure 12-11).**

   You can also choose to create an SMTP site link. But in this example, I use IP because I have T1 connectivity and ample available bandwidth.

3. **In the New Object - Site Link dialog box that appears (see Figure 12-12), type a name for the Site Link in the Name text box.**

4. **From the Sites Not in This Site Link box on the left, select each site that you want to connect with the new link and click the Add button.**

   As you click Add, the site is moved to the Sites in This Site Link box on the right.

   Continue selecting sites and clicking the Add button after each one until all the sites you want included in this link have been added to the box on the right.

5. **When you have added all the sites for the link, click OK to close the New Object - Site Link dialog box.**

   You're finished! You just created your first site link.

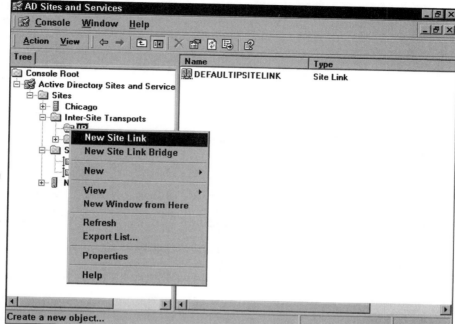

Figure 12-11:
Right-click
the IP folder
and choose
New Site
Link
to create
a new
site link.

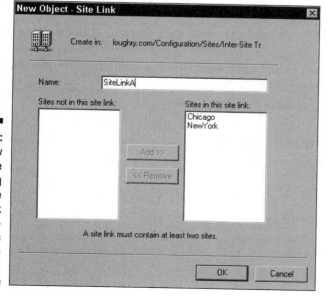

Figure 12-12:
In the New
Object - Site
Link dialog
box, name
the site link
and associate sites
with the
site link.

TIP

Beginning with the Beta 3 version of Windows 2000 Server, site links are transitive, which means that if you have a site link between Site A and Site B and another site link between Site B and Site C, the link between Site A and Site C also is a transitive link. Figure 12-13 illustrates this relationship.

Figure 12-13:
Site links are established between Sites A and B and between B and C, so a transitive link exists between Site A and Site C.

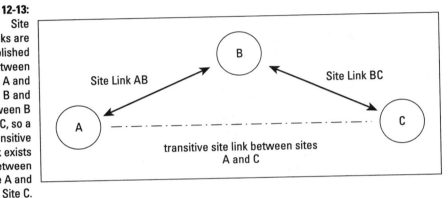

Enabling transitive site links

To enable transitive site links, you need to enable the Bridge All Site Links option on the IP Inter-Site Transport, as I describe in the following steps:

1. **On the AD Sites and Services screen, click (or double-click, if necessary) to expand the Inter-Site Transports folder.**

2. **Right-click the IP folder and choose Properties from the pop-up menu that appears.**

   The IP Properties dialog box opens.

3. **On the General tab, enable the Bridge All Site Links option by clicking the box to place a check mark in it (see Figure 12-14).**

4. **Click OK to close the Properties dialog box.**

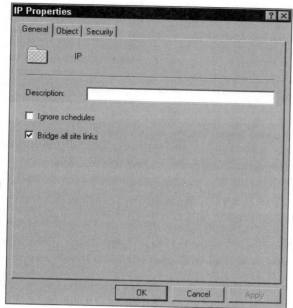

Choosing a transport protocol

Intersite links (links between two sites) transmit directory updates by using either the Internet Protocol (IP) or Simple Mail Transport Protocol (SMTP). Here are the primary differences between the two:

✔ **SMTP:** Traffic is sent via e-mail messages.

   IP: Traffic uses remote procedure call (RPC) communication. A remote procedure call is a message-passing method that enables the system to call procedures from other computers.

✔ **SMTP:** Requires that you install a certificate authority to verify that e-mail messages between domain controllers are authentic.

   IP: Doesn't require a certificate authority because it doesn't send replication traffic as e-mail messages.

Fortunately, Microsoft provides a digital certificate service in Windows 2000. The service runs on a domain controller, which is then known as the *certificate authority* (CA). The CA provides encrypted digital certificates to verify the authenticity of messages.

On slower, less reliable WAN links, choose SMTP Inter-Site Transports so that replication traffic is minimized. You may also choose SMTP on links that have little available bandwidth remaining. On fast links, choose the IP transport for speed.

Creating a schedule

You can further optimize replication traffic on your network by scheduling the traffic to use a site link only at certain times of the day. For example, if more bandwidth is available during evening hours, you can schedule replication between the hours of 7 p.m. and 10 p.m. Or perhaps you want replication traffic to use one site link between 6 a.m. and 6 p.m., but another site link during the remaining hours.

Be aware that when you restrict replication traffic to specific hours of the day, you're making a trade-off. You're sacrificing fresh directory content for efficient network traffic. If you can afford to have slightly stale directory data between sites until the scheduled replication occurs, you may choose to schedule intersite replication to occur infrequently.

To schedule replication traffic on a site link, follow these steps:

1. **On the AD Sites and Services screen, right-click the site link in the right-hand pane and choose Properties from the pop-up menu.**

   The Properties dialog box opens.

2. **Click the Schedule tab.**

   This tab contains a weekly calendar. Use this calendar to block out times during which you want replication to be either available or unavailable on this site link.

3. **After making your selections, click OK to close the Properties dialog box.**

Assigning a cost

You may prefer to have replication traffic use one site link over another whenever possible. Perhaps you have a link that's heavily used, with little available bandwidth. You want to limit replication traffic on this link because of the bandwidth saturation. You have a second link that has plenty of bandwidth available, so you prefer replication traffic to use this second link. But you'd like the first link to act as an alternate replication link if the preferred second link is unavailable. To enable this scenario, you assign a cost to each of the links.

A cost is simply a way of indicating a preference between two links, without restricting use of either link. To indicate your preference, assign a lower cost value to the preferred link, and a higher cost value to the second link. You can use any value between 1 and 100 for the cost value. The values you choose are relative only to the other values you specify. For example, you can enter a cost value of 1 on your preferred link, and 10, 20, or even 100 on the secondary link. As long as the value is higher than 1, the link will be used as a secondary link to the link with a value of 1. If you later add another site link, you'll want to assign a cost value relative to the values of the two existing links. If you assigned a cost value of 10 to the secondary link and now want the new link to be used before the secondary link, assign a cost value between 1 and 10 to the new link.

To assign a cost to a site link, follow these steps:

1. **On the AD Sites and Services screen, right-click the site link and choose Properties from the pop-up menu.**

   The Properties dialog box opens.

2. **On the Cost tab, enter a cost value between 1 and 100.**

   A low value means that traffic frequently uses the site link. So the higher the value, the less frequently traffic uses the site link.

3. **Click OK to close the Properties dialog box.**

Creating a site link bridge

Site link bridges are connectors between two site links. If you enable the Bridge All Site Links option (as I show you how to do in the section "Enabling transitive site links," earlier in this chapter), site link bridges are redundant. They provide the same function as transitive site links.

But if you want total control over replication traffic patterns, you don't want to enable the Bridge All Site Links option; instead you need to create site link bridges between the site links. I don't recommend that you try this process unless you have slow links saturated with traffic and you want to closely control replication traffic. In most cases, this technique creates unnecessary work for the administrator and leaves a large margin for error. A better way to control replication traffic is to assign appropriate cost values to the site links.

A site link bridge essentially creates a replication path among available site links. The bridge groups the site links together so that you can administer them as one object. For example, if you create a site link bridge between a Chicago-NewYork site link and a NewYork-Philadelphia site link, you essentially create a replication path between Chicago and Philadelphia. You can then assign costs and schedules to control use of this site link bridge.

To create a site link bridge, follow these steps:

1. **On the AD Sites and Services screen, click (or double-click, if necessary) to expand the Inter-Site Transports folder.**

2. **Right-click the IP folder and choose New Site Link Bridge from the pop-up menu.**

   The New Object - Site Link Bridge dialog box opens, as shown in Figure 12-15.

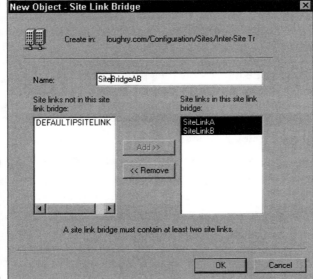

Figure 12-15:
Create a
new
site link
bridge
in this
dialog box.

3. **Type a name for the Site Link Bridge in the Name text box.**

4. **In the Site Links Not in This Site Link Bridge box on the left, select the site links connected by this site link bridge; then click the Add button to move these site links to the Site Links in This Site Link Bridge box on the right.**

5. **After making your selections, click OK to finish creating the site link bridge.**

Again, I don't recommend that you create site link bridges. Because site links are transitive, replication paths are already in place. If you configure the site link bridge in a manner that conflicts with the configured cost values and schedules for its site links, you could cause replication between sites to fail.

Chapter 13

Schema-ing!

In This Chapter

- Understanding the Active Directory schema
- Identifying schema objects
- Accessing schema objects
- Extending the schema
- Exploring the schema master

As you may already know, the Active Directory schema contains definitions of all object classes (or object categories) and attributes that you can store in the directory. Make no mistake about it — understanding the schema is vital to understanding and managing Active Directory!

My goal for this chapter is to help you have a good schema learning experience — unlike my own. When I began learning Active Directory basics, few resources were available: I attended a couple of presentations and found one white paper to read. I sat down with that white paper on several different evenings. Snore! This stuff can be pretty dry. So, in this chapter, I intersperse my "talking" with screen shots from Windows 2000 Server. For best results, follow along on your own server!

Schema 101

The Active Directory schema is part of the NTDS.dit file. Active Directory is a database, and databases store information in tables. The schema is stored in the *schema table,* which is one of three tables in the Active Directory database. (See Chapter 14 for more information on the Active Directory database.)

The schema is all about Active Directory objects. It's a set of definitions that describe Active Directory objects and the objects' descriptive attributes.

These definitions serve as rules, or templates, that dictate how you must describe an object. You have the following two categories of schema definitions:

- ✔ Classes
- ✔ Attributes

Object classes and object attributes are known as *schema objects* and sometimes as *metadata*.

Introducing object classes

An *object class* is a set of mandatory attributes and optional attributes that combine to define a particular class of Active Directory objects (see Figure 13-1). A user is one object class and a printer is another. Obviously, you can't describe these vastly different objects by using the same set of attributes. So the user object class consists of different mandatory and optional attributes than does the printer object class.

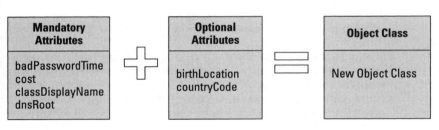

Figure 13-1: Mandatory and optional attributes combine to create object classes.

Mandatory Attributes		Optional Attributes		Object Class
badPasswordTime cost classDisplayName dnsRoot	+	birthLocation countryCode	=	New Object Class

An *attribute* provides information about an object. Each attribute provides information about a different aspect of an object and uses a certain structure and syntax. Attributes combine in various groupings to form object classes.

The object classes and attributes that the schema defines take effect across the entire Active Directory tree or forest. This way, all similar objects in a forest conform to the same conventions. For example, all user objects have the same attributes, although the values of the attributes differ. Similarly, all shared folders are defined by the same attributes, but the values of those attributes differ. The schema itself resides within the Active Directory. As you initially install Active Directory, it automatically installs a base set of schema objects and attributes. (The objects and attributes are read into the Active Directory database from the schema.ini file in the %systemroot%\system32 folder.) The schema is actually part of the NTDS.dit file.

You can view the base schema by using the Active Directory Schema snap-in of the Microsoft Management Console. The Active Directory Schema snap-in is available on the Windows 2000 Resource Kit. You must be a member of the Schema Administrators group to make changes to the schema. (For more information on the Schema Administrators group, see Chapter 1.)

You have to register the schmmgmt.dll before you can use the Active Directory Schema snap-in. The regsvr32 utility, found in the WINNT\System32 folder, adds registry entries that enable you to use the schmmgmt.dll.

To register the DLL file, choose Start⇨Run and type **cmd** in the text box to get to a command prompt. Then at the command prompt, type the following line:

```
regsvr32 schmmgmt.dll
```

Then follow these steps to view the base schema:

1. **Open the Microsoft Management Console (MMC) by choosing Start⇨Run and typing** mmc **in the text box.**

2. **If the Active Directory Schema snap-in isn't already in place, choose Console⇨Add/Remove Snap-in from the menu bar.**

Only members of the Schema Administrators group can modify the schema. Limit membership in this group to a handful of select administrators. Any changes that you make to the schema by using the snap-in are irreversible, so make sure that you don't alter the schema unintentionally.

Figure 13-2 shows the Active Directory Schema in the left-hand pane of the console window. Notice that the schema contains two types of components, classes and attributes, which appear in the right-hand pane.

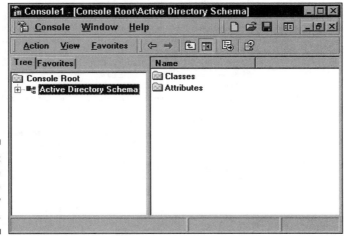

Figure 13-2:
Viewing the Active Directory schema.

Explore a little bit further (just click on any of the folders), and you see the default classes and attributes that make up the base schema of Active Directory. Clicking the Classes folder accesses a list of object classes in the right-hand pane of the console window (see Figure 13-3).

Table B-1 in Appendix B provides a list of object classes that I dumped from the Active Directory schema in my lab by using the Export List feature. The information provided in Table B-1 is the same that you see in abbreviated form in Figure 13-3 but in an easier-to-read format.

Notice that each class that appears in Figure 13-3 includes a name, a type, and a description. Active Directory uses the Type category to create a structure within the directory. A class's type can be either *Structural, Abstract,* or *Auxiliary,* but you can only create new objects in the Structural type category.

The Abstract type serves as a template for creating new Structural classes. The Auxiliary type contains a list of attributes that can be associated with Structural class objects. For more detailed information on these types refer to the Windows 2000 Resource Kit document titled "The Active Directory Schema."

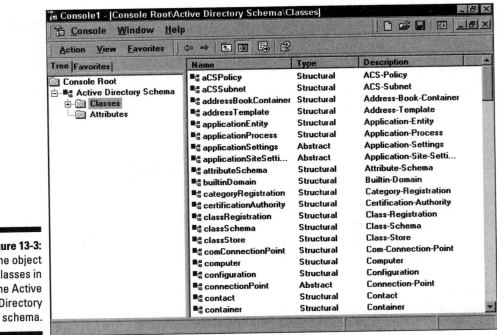

Figure 13-3:
The object classes in the Active Directory schema.

A class with a Structural type follows an inheritance hierarchy that begins with an object class known as top. As is true of any other class, both mandatory and optional attributes define top. Every structural object class descends from top and takes on (inherits) the attributes of top.

Figure 13-4 illustrates a structural-class hierarchy. Top is the parent class to Object Class 1, which inherits attributes from top. In turn, Object Class 1 is the parent class to Object Class 2, which inherits its attributes and becomes parent to Object Class 3. The attributes that pass down from top extend through all the object classes in this branch. You can have several lines of inheritance descending from top — not all object classes descend in a single branch.

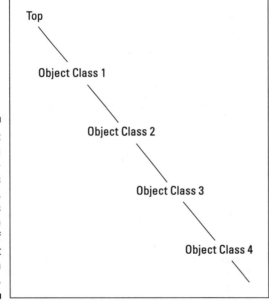

Figure 13-4:
In a structural-class hierarchy, classes inherit the attributes of the object class known as top.

Top

Object Class 1

Object Class 2

Object Class 3

Object Class 4

Examining object attributes

Now take a look at the second component of the Active Directory schema: object attributes. If you still have the console window open, click the Attributes folder to access a list of object attributes, as shown in Figure 13-5. (Refer to Step 2 under "Introducing object classes" for instructions on opening the schema in a Microsoft Management Console window.)

Again, I include a list in Table B-2 in Appendix B that I generated by using the Export List feature so that you can look at these attributes in detail.

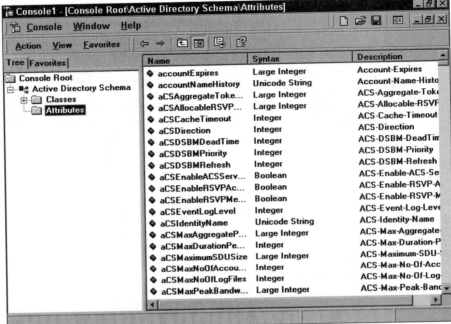

Figure 13-5:
The object
attributes in
the Active
Directory
schema.

Each of these attributes can become part of the definition of an object class. The attribute OID, for example, is a mandatory attribute in every object class. The value of the attribute, however, is different for each object class.

To successfully create an object, the object must match all the criteria that the schema defines. The classSchema object defines the criteria for each class of object. These criteria consist of mandatory attributes and optional attributes. Table B-3 in Appendix B shows the attributes of the classSchema object. The mandatory and optional attributes listed there define the rules for creating objects in the schema.

Similarly, the attributeSchema object defines attributes. The attributeSchema object defines how you create attributes in the schema. Table B-4 in Appendix B lists the mandatory and optional attributes of the attributeSchema object. The table also shows the required syntax for the value of each attribute. If you want to create a new attribute in the schema, the attributeSchema object tells you which attributes are required and which are optional.

I dumped both Tables B-3 and B-4 from one of the DCs in my lab by using the Export List feature. You're likely to find that this feature is very useful for creating lists!

Every user object that you create in the tree must contain all the mandatory attributes that the `classSchema` object specifies. In addition, each user object can contain the optional attributes that you specify for the `User` object class. (You find out how to add classes and attributes in the following section.) Figure 13-6 shows the attributes of the `User` object class.

Figure 13-6:
The
Attributes
tab of the
Properties
dialog box
for the
`User` object
class.

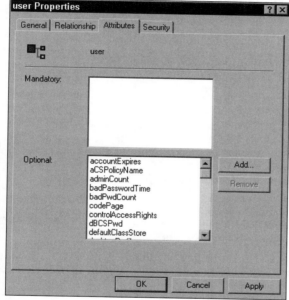

Now look at Figure 13-7, which shows the attributes of the `Server` object class. Notice that the attributes that make up the `Server` object class differ from those that make up the `User` object class.

Figure 13-7:
The
Attributes
tab of the
Properties
dialog box
for the
Server
object class.

Now take a look at all the properties of the User object class, as the following list describes:

✔ **General tab:** Each item that you see on this tab is a mandatory attribute of the User object class (see Figure 13-8).

✔ **Relationship tab:** The parent class of the User object, along with Auxiliary Classes and Possible Superior appear on this tab (see Figure 13-9).

The Relationship tab contains information about inheritance. The parent class is an object from which the User object class inherits attributes. In this example, the User object inherits attributes from a parent object known as organizationalPerson. The User object class can also inherit attributes from any additional classes that appear under Auxiliary Classes or Possible Superior.

To summarize the Relationship tab, the User object class inherits its attributes from its parent class and from any Auxiliary Classes. (Similarly, the parent class inherits attributes from its parent class, and so on.)

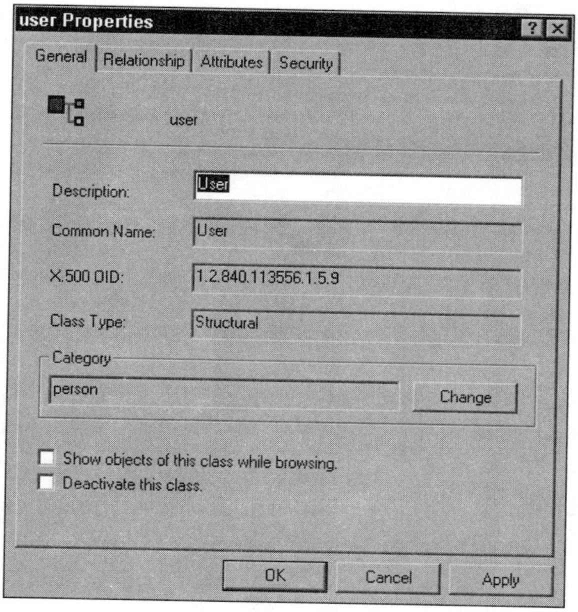

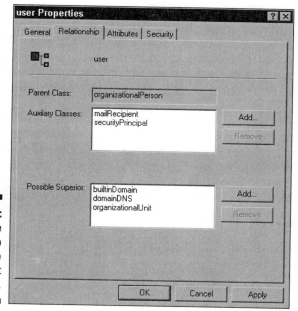

Figure 13-8:
The General
properties
tab of the
User object
class.

Figure 13-9:
The
Relationship
tab of the
User object
class.

✔ **Attributes tab:** This tab lists the mandatory and optional attributes of the User object class (see Figure 13-10). Remember that some attributes are inherited from the parent class.

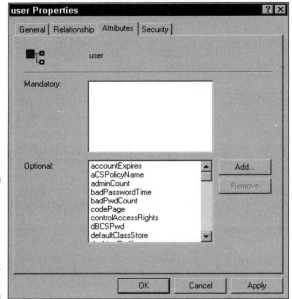

Figure 13-10:
The
Attributes
properties
tab of the
User object
class.

Inherited attributes don't appear on the Attributes tab. You must view the parent object class to see which attributes it passes on to the child object class.

✔ **Security tab:** This tab displays the permissions of each group or user in relationship to User objects (see Figure 13-11). You can see, for example, that the Account Operators group has full control of this object class.

To summarize, the Active Directory schema contains a list of object attributes. From this list, attributes combine in groupings of mandatory and optional attributes to form object classes. (For more detailed information, see Table B-2 in Appendix B.)

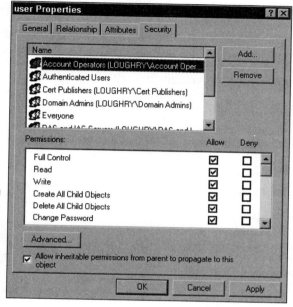

Figure 13-11:
The Security
properties
tab of the
User object
class.

Extending the Schema

Whenever you're not working on production servers, I urge you to explore the classes and attributes of the schema and to become familiar with their syntax. That's the best way to pick up information about the schema!

But keep in mind that changes to the schema are irreversible. If you add an attribute or class, you can't delete it. You can, however, disable it. Be even more cautious if you're modifying an existing class or attribute. Changes to the schema affect every object in the Active Directory (thus every object in the forest), and you certainly don't want to introduce changes without testing them in a lab first.

Adding to or modifying the Active Directory schema is known as *extending* the schema. The schema is the core of the Active Directory database, and you need to treat it with extreme care. Yes, I said it earlier, but it bears repeating: Extending the schema is highly complex. You need to limit membership in the Schema Administrators group to a handful of skilled administrators.

Incorrect modifications to the schema can corrupt your Active Directory database. Whenever possible, use objects and attributes that are already defined by the base schema. Use the tables in Appendix B as a resource to determine which objects and attributes support your needs.

Modifications to the schema can include the following:

- Creating a class
- Extending a class
- Deactivating a class
- Creating an attribute
- Modifying an attribute
- Deactivating an attribute

Notice that deleting a class or attribute isn't an option. After you make changes to the schema, you can't remove them. You can disable (or deactivate) them, but you can't delete them.

Adding classes and attributes

Adding a class or attribute is simple. First, open the Active Directory Schema Manager from the MMC, by choosing Console⇨Add/Remove Snap-in and selecting the Active Directory Schema Manager from the list of available snap-ins.

To add a class, select the Classes folder, right-click, and choose New⇨ Object Class from the pop-up menu. The Create New Class dialog box appears.

To add an attribute, select the Attributes folder, right-click, and choose New⇨Object Attribute from the pop-up menu. The Create New Attribute dialog box appears, as shown in Figure 13-12.

After you add a class or attribute, modifying it is much like modifying any other Active Directory object. Select the class or attribute that you want to modify, right-click, and choose Properties from the pop-up menu.

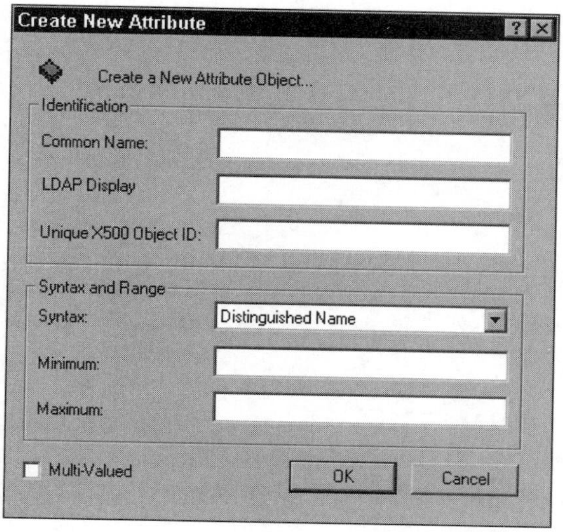

Figure 13-12:
Add an attribute by using the Create New Attribute dialog box.

Deactivating objects

Finally, you can deactivate classes and attributes by using the Active Directory Schema snap-in. If you right-click a particular class or attribute, the Properties dialog box for that object appears, as shown in Figure 13-13. Place a check mark in the box next to the Deactivate This Class option. You can't, however, deactivate the base objects that install automatically with Active Directory. You can only deactivate objects that you add to your schema. But be careful in deactivating objects! Most objects are part of a parent-child inheritance structure, so you may inadvertently alter all the objects in an inheritance branch by deactivating a parent object. Objects that you deactivate, you can also resurrect. Simply remove the check mark that you entered in the box next to Deactivate This Class.

You need to prepare sufficiently if you're going to extend the schema. Consider that adding an object or attribute requires a unique OID (object identifier) that a regulatory authority must issue. In addition, you must specify (among other items) syntax and indexing. You face a lot of restrictions on what you can or can't change within the schema, and these restrictions vary depending on whether the object is a base schema object or an extended object.

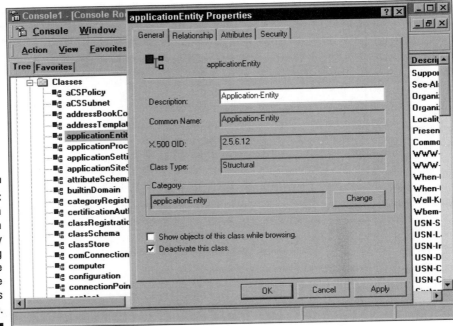

Figure 13-13:
Deactivate a
schema
object by
checking
the
Deactivate
This Class
option.

Because of the serious nature of schema changes, Microsoft has written consistency checks and safety checks into Active Directory. For example, you cannot change the schema unless you are a member of the Schema Administrators group. In addition, the schema — by default — is set for read-only access. You must first make the schema modifiable on one of the domain controllers before you can make changes.

To enable schema modification on a domain controller, open the Active Directory Schema Manager from the MMC, by choosing Console⇨ Add/Remove Snap-in and selecting the Active Directory Schema Manager from the list of available snap-ins. Right-click the Active Directory Schema and choose Change Schema Master from the resulting pop-up menu. At the bottom of the Change Schema Master dialog box (see Figure 13-14), click to place a check in the box next to The Schema May Be Modified on This Server option. (In this example, checking the box lets me modify the schema on my L01.loughry.com server.) Click OK to close the dialog box.

If I seem to be discouraging you from extending the schema — I am. The base schema is pretty complete. I think that you're much more likely to have numerous base schema objects that you don't use in your environment. As directory-enabled devices and networks become more common, equipment vendors are sure to provide utilities to modify the schema to include necessary objects for their products. Similarly, software vendors write directory-enabled applications that modify the schema as necessary for their applications. (For more information on directory-enabled devices and applications, see Chapter 16.)

If you do identify a need to extend the schema, extensive instructions are available in the Windows 2000 Resource Kit and on Microsoft TechNet. The Resource Kit also includes additional utilities for modifying the schema.

Transferring the Schema Master

Changes to the schema can take place on only one domain controller at a time. This DC is known as the *schema master,* and this arrangement is known as *Flexible Single Master Operation* (FSMO). The first domain controller on-line becomes, by default, the schema master. You can easily change the schema master role (also known as the FSMO role) to another server by using the Active Directory Schema snap-in. Open the snap-in using the MMC. When you are in the MMC, choose Console⇨Add/Remove Snap-in and select the Active Directory Schema Manager from the list of available snap-ins.

To change the schema master, right-click the Active Directory Schema in the left-hand pane of the MMC. On the resulting pop-up menu, choose Change Schema Master, and the dialog box that you saw earlier in Figure 13-14 appears. The server that is currently the schema master is displayed near the center of this dialog box. Click the Change button and type a different server name to change the schema master to a different server.

You can also transfer the schema master role by using the NTDSutil tool, but this command-line tool is harder to use. Primarily, you want to use the NTDSutil tool if the schema master crashes and you need to forcefully transfer the role to another server. (This process is known as *seizing* the schema master role.)

To use NTDSutil, choose Start⇨Run and type **cmd** in the text box to get to a command prompt. Then at the command prompt, type **ntdsutil roles ?**

This starts NTDSutil and displays the menu shown in Figure 13-15. At the fsmo maintenance prompt, type **seize schema master**.

Seizing the schema master role is a last-resort action. If the previous schema master comes back on-line after you seize the role, inconsistencies may exist between the two servers. If the new schema master contains newer schema updates, when the old schema master comes back on-line you may lose the new updates.

```
C:\WINNT\System32\cmd.exe - ntdsutil roles ?

C:\>ntdsutil roles ?
ntdsutil: roles
fsmo maintenance: ?

 ?                                    - Print this help information
 Connections                         - Connect to a specific domain controller
 Help                                - Print this help information
 Quit                                - Return to the prior menu
 Seize domain naming master          - Overwrite domain role on connected server
 Seize infrastructure master         - Overwrite infrastructure role on connected se
er
 Seize PDC                           - Overwrite PDC role on connected server
 Seize RID master                    - Overwrite RID role on connected server
 Seize schema master                 - Overwrite schema role on connected server
 Select operation target            - Select sites, servers, domains, roles and Nam
g Contexts
 Transfer domain naming master       - Make connected server the domain naming maste
r
 Transfer infrastructure master      - Make connected server the infrastructure mas
r
 Transfer PDC                        - Make connected server the PDC
 Transfer RID master                 - Make connected server the RID master
 Transfer schema master              - Make connected server the schema master

fsmo maintenance: _
```

Figure 13-15:
Using NTDSutil to seize the schema master role.

Reloading the Schema Cache

Each time that a computer running Active Directory boots up, a copy of the Active Directory schema loads into memory. The memory-resident copy is known as the *schema cache,* and it serves as a performance enhancement because the system can access memory-resident data more quickly than it can access data from disk.

When you make changes to the schema, the changes take place on the disk-based version of the schema before they update in the schema cache. The update begins five minutes after a schema modification. If you make a second change, the five-minute timer starts over again.

Obviously, during the five-minute interval before your schema changes are updated in the schema cache, the two versions (disk and cache) are out of synch. You can shorten the time interval by selecting the Reload the Schema option from the Action menu in the Active Directory Schema Manager, as shown in Figure 13-16.

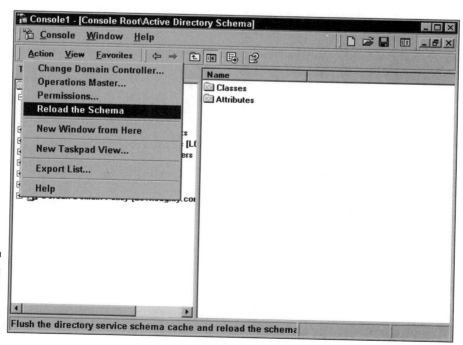

Figure 13-16:
Reloading the schema cache.

Don't use the Reload the Schema option more than once in making a series of changes to the schema. After the schema cache updates, Active Directory creates a new cache from the disk-based database. Thus, two cached copies of the schema can exist during the update process. By triggering Reload the Schema multiple times, you can end up with numerous copies of the schema cached in memory, which can significantly slow the performance of the system. Use the Reload the Schema option only once after completing all your modifications.

Because the schema is part of the Active Directory database, updates to the schema replicate to all domain controllers in the tree or forest. In a large enterprise, *replication latency* (the time frame between the start and finish of replication to all domain controllers) can temporarily result in out-of-synch schemas between domain controllers. Replication latency is unavoidable, but temporary. After all domain controllers have replicated, the updates are available across the domain.

Chapter 14

Maintaining the Active Directory Database

*I*f you're at all familiar with the inner workings of Exchange Server or the Windows Internet Naming Service (WINS) database, maintaining the Active Directory database should come easily to you. But don't despair if this terminology is all new to you! In this chapter, I explain the components of the database and how they interact.

Maintaining the Active Directory database isn't difficult, and Microsoft provides some great tools to help you. Don't let the lingo — terms such as *tombstone* and *fragmentation* — intimidate you, because the database is largely self-sufficient. With a bit of simple maintenance, you can be certain of having a healthy, happy database!

Database Files

Active Directory's database engine is the *Extensible Storage Engine (ESE),* which is based on the Jet database engine that Exchange 5.5 and WINS use. The following key files make up the Active Directory database:

✔ NTDS.dit (the database file)

✔ Log files (sequential records of each change to the database)

Because Active Directory is a distributed database, the ESE enables the database to grow to 16 terabytes. Theoretically, a 16-terabyte database can hold more than 10 million objects, but Microsoft had tested it with only 1.5 million objects at the time this book went to press.

Specifying the location of the datastore

The Active Directory database's NTDS.dit file is also known as the datastore. Only the Jet database can manipulate information within the datastore, but you can administer NTDS.dit off-line by using a utility known as NTDSutil. NTDSutil enables you to take the database off-line so that you can replace the entire NTDS.dit file in case the file becomes corrupt. By default, the location for all database files is the directory C:\WINNT\NTDS.

You specify the location of the database files by using the Active Directory Installation Wizard. To start the wizard, choose Start⇨Run and type **dcpromo** in the text box. Several screens into the wizard, you're prompted to specify a location for the database file and the log files. Figure 14-1 shows the Database and Log Locations screen of the wizard.

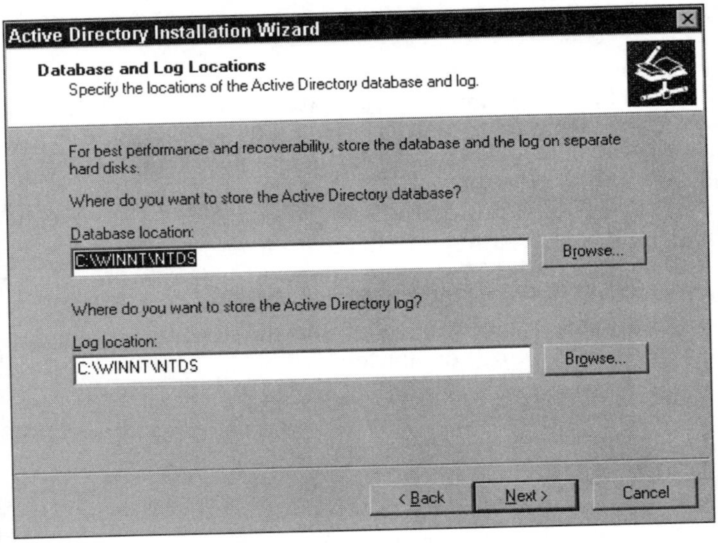

Figure 14-1: Use the Database and Log Locations screen to specify a location for your database files.

Two NTDS.dit files reside on your machine. The first resides at C:\WINNT\SYSTEM32. This file serves as a default template for the Active Directory database. Then, during Active Directory installation, this file copies to the C:\WINNT\NTDS directory. The directory service uses this copied file to start Active Directory. Updates from other domain controllers in the domain also write to this second file.

Optimizing Active Directory disk performance

For best performance, Microsoft recommends that you place the log files on a physical disk separate from where you keep the datastore (NTDS.dit). Doing so provides optimum disk performance because the read and write functions of the log files and datastore aren't vying for the resources of a single disk. For the same reasons, Microsoft further recommends that you place the datastore and log files on separate physical disks from the operating system files and the *page file* (pages of memory that Active Directory writes to disk instead of to RAM). This practice increases the amount of data that you can store in system memory.

Assuming that you have adequate physical disks, the following list describes the ideal disk-management configuration:

✔ Two mirrored physical disks to hold the operating system files

✔ Two mirrored physical disks to hold the database log files

✔ A RAID5 array to hold the datastore

Mirroring and RAID5 are both fault-tolerance mechanisms designed to prevent data loss. *Mirroring* two disks means that the second disk stores an exact copy of the first disk. RAID5 is a bit more complex. A *RAID5 array* is a set of at least three disks that function together. The system stripes data across the disks so that you can recover it in case of a disk failure.

Working with the log files

The log files record transactions to the Active Directory database. In case of a system crash or database corruption, ESE uses the transactions that the log files enumerate to recreate the database. It also uses log files to restore a database to a consistent state after you restore the database from a backup.

Active Directory can record either *sequential* or *circular* logs, although sequential is the default and the preferred type of log. Circular logs overwrite transactions at specific intervals, whereas sequential logs never overwrite transactions. (During garbage-collection intervals, however, Active Directory deletes sequential log files that have committed their transactions to the database.) Sequential logging provides an extra measure of protection in case your database becomes corrupt. By restoring the database from sequential log files, you have a continuous record of transactions. If you restore the database from circular log files, however, you may overwrite some data, leaving you with an incomplete record of transactions.

New data never overwrites sequential log files. They grow until they reach a specified size. After Active Directory commits all the transactions in a log file to the database, it no longer needs that log file. Active Directory's garbage-collection process deletes unnecessary log files every 12 hours (the default garbage-collection interval). If your server never stays up longer than 12 hours between reboots, it never cleans up the old log files and they take up more and more space on the disk. But then again, if your server doesn't stay up for more than 12 hours at a time, you have bigger problems than the garbage-collection interval!

Some administrators prefer circular logging because it helps minimize the amount of logged data that the physical disk stores. You must edit the registry to enable circular logging.

I seldom recommend editing the registry. This action is extremely risky because a wrong change can irreparably corrupt your registry. Please be *very* careful if you decide to try this process.

To edit the registry, follow these steps:

1. **Choose Start⇨Run.**

2. **In the Open text box of the Run dialog box, type** regedt32.

   The Registry Editor appears.

3. **Within the Registry Editor, click to select the HKEY_LOCAL_MACHINE window.**

4. **Double-click through the following sequence of lines to navigate to the circular logging parameter:**

   HKEY_LOCAL_MACHINE
       SYSTEM
           CurrentControlSet
              Services
                 NTDS
                   Parameters

5. **Choose Edit⇨Add Value.**

   The Add Value dialog box opens.

6. **Type** CircularLogging **in the Value Name box; leave the Data Type as REG_SZ (see Figure 14-2).**

Figure 14-2:
Adding the
CircularLog-
ging para-
meter to the
registry.

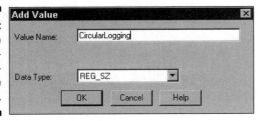

7. **Click OK.**

   The String dialog box appears.

8. **In the Value box, type** 1.

9. **Click OK.**

   Circular logging is now enabled. You should see the CircularLogging parameter, with a value of 1, in the right-hand pane of the Registry Editor.

10. **Close the Registry Editor by clicking the Close button in the upper-right corner of the window.**

Garbage Collection

Garbage collection refers to Active Directory's automated database cleanup that occurs every 12 hours. Garbage collection takes care of the following tasks:

- Deletes old log files
- Deletes tombstones
- Defragments the database file (which I discuss in the following section)

A *tombstone* is an object that you mark for removal from the database. Say, for example, that you remove several computers from the domain. You then *tombstone* each of the computer objects to show that it's obsolete. Each tombstoned object remains in the database for 60 days from the time that you mark it.

You can change the default garbage collection interval by modifying the `garbageCollPeriod` attribute. You can change the default tombstone lifetime by modifying the `tombstoneLifetime` attribute. To modify an attribute, select the attribute in the Active Directory schema, right-click, and choose Properties from the menu that appears. For more information on accessing and modifying the Active Directory schema, see Chapter 13.

Defragmenting the Database

Defragmenting (or *defragging*) the database file rearranges the pages of the file into a more compact format. This process is very similar to what you go through when you defragment the hard drive of your PC.

You can defragment the database either on-line or off-line. On-line defragmenting rearranges the data but doesn't release any freed space back to the file system. Off-line defragmenting rearranges the data and then releases the freed up space back to the file system. To defragment off-line, you must be in Directory Service Repair mode.

To enter Directory Service Repair mode, follow these steps:

1. **Press F8 during the server's boot sequence.**

2. **To enter Directory Service Repair mode, choose Directory Service Repair Mode from the list of options that appears.**

Off-line defragmenting creates a new, compacted copy of the database in a different directory. You can archive the old database file (C:\WINNT\NTDS\NTDS.dit) to a separate directory and replace it with the compacted version, which also carries the name NTDS.dit.

Keep the original database file until you're certain that the compacted file loads correctly.

If you have a very large enterprise, keep an eye on the size of the database. Remember that the database engine is the same Jet engine that WINS uses. Microsoft maintains that a WINS database file can grow to considerably more than 30 or 40MB before it's in danger of becoming corrupt. In practice, I often find that I need to defrag at approximately half that size. On a very large WINS database, I often end up defragging once a week, but the defrag process takes only a minute or two. Active Directory is so new that predicting whether the same database growth issues may arise with the NTDS.dit file is difficult. But I suggest that you monitor the size of the file to watch for this situation.

Backing Up the Active Directory Database

You can take several approaches to backing up the Active Directory database, as the following list describes:

- ✔ Use the off-line defrag process and keep a copy of the new database and log files.
- ✔ Use a third-party backup application that enables you to perform on-line database backups.
- ✔ Use the backup utility that comes with Windows 2000 Server.

The preceding section in this chapter covers the off-line defragmenting process. To save a full copy of the database, make sure that you save all the log files as well.

Numerous third-party backup applications are available for Windows 2000. If you decide to use one of these applications, make sure that you choose one that specifically states that it can perform on-line database backups (or *open-file* backups). These applications are usually sold as product add-ons, or *agents,* that you must purchase in addition to the backup application software.

Finally, you can always opt to use the backup utility that comes with Windows 2000 Server. This utility is a scaled-down version of Seagate's Backup Exec, but it's a perfectly good tool for backing up the Active Directory database. The following sections describe how to use this utility.

Using the backup utility

To start the backup utility, choose Start⇨Programs⇨Accessories⇨ System Tools⇨Backup. This brings you to the Windows 2000 Backup and Recovery Tools screen (see Figure 14-3).

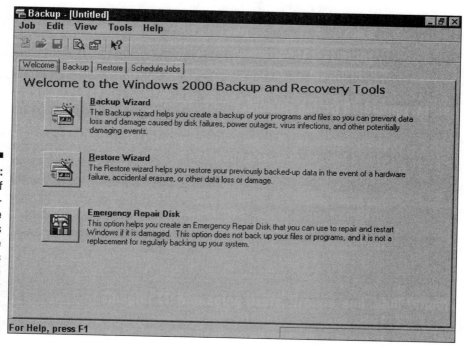

Figure 14-3: Use one of these wizards or use the options on the various tabs to create backups and to restore jobs.

The backup utility is easy to use! As you see on the Welcome screen shown in Figure 14-3, you can choose one of the following three options:

- ✔ Backup Wizard
- ✔ Restore Wizard
- ✔ Emergency Repair Disk

If you prefer to bypass the wizards, you can specify your preferences by using the options on the other three tabs shown on the Welcome screen: Backup, Restore, and Schedule Jobs.

Creating the backup job

To back up the Active Directory database, you must back up the System State files. Click the Backup tab of the backup utility and look at the left-hand pane of the selection window that appears. Find the System State entry and click the adjacent check box to mark it, as shown in Figure 14-4.

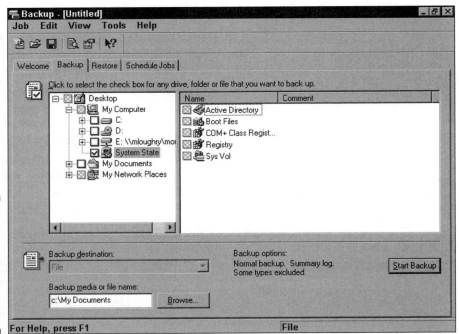

Figure 14-4:
Clicking the System State check box includes Active Directory in the backup.

The right-hand pane of the window shows the files that are backed up after you choose the System State backup option. As you can see, Active Directory is the first option in the list. Selecting this option includes the Active Directory files in the backup job.

I urge you to back up and archive the Active Directory database files regularly. The Active Directory database contains the structure of your entire Windows 2000 network. If the database becomes corrupt, repairing it can take days — if you can repair it at all! This is the type of mishap that system administrators lose their jobs over — don't be caught without a recent backup of the database!

If you do off-line defrags on a regular schedule, make archiving a copy of the database at that time a regular practice.

Database Tables

If you're at all familiar with databases — Microsoft SQL 7 databases, for example — you're aware that they consist of tables that store information in rows and columns. The following three distinct tables compose the Active Directory database file (NTDS.dit):

- ✔ Schema
- ✔ Link
- ✔ Data

Schema table

The Active Directory schema is part of the NTDS.dit file, and the schema exists in the *schema table*. (See Chapter 13 for more information about the Active Directory schema.) The schema table is small and relatively static because you seldom extend the Active Directory schema. You don't need to manage or manipulate the schema table. You can make changes to the schema table by using the Active Directory Schema snap-in.

Link table

The *link table* stores — surprise, surprise! — links between objects and attributes in the Active Directory. User JoeB, for example, is a member of a group known as Acct. The data table stores the user object JoeB, which has a value of Acct in the MemberOf attribute. The data table also stores the group object known as Acct. The link table, however, stores data that represents the link, or relationship, between the two objects.

You don't need to manipulate or manage the link table — simply know that it's one of the tables in NTDS.dit.

Data table

The *data table* contains all the specific data in the Active Directory: users, groups, printers, and so on. Depending on the size of your environment, the data table can be quite large. It's the most dynamic of the three database tables and is, by far, the largest.

The data table stores information about objects in *rows*. It stores the attributes of each object in *columns* (see Figure 14-5).

Object	Attribute	Attribute	Attribute
User1			
User2			
User3			
User4			
User5			

Figure 14-5: How the data table stores objects and attributes.

With hundreds of possible attributes available (see Table B-2 in Appendix B), the data table can be quite large. To store data more efficiently, therefore, the data table allocates space only for attributes that contain a value. The more attributes that you assign to an object, the more space that object requires in the data table.

Look at the example shown in Figure 14-6. User3 has assigned values for each of its three possible attributes. Storing User3, therefore, takes more space in the database than storing User1. Similarly, User5 requires more space to store than User3 because the values of its attributes are longer than those of User3.

You don't directly manipulate or manage the data table. As you add or modify objects in the Active Directory tree, the data table captures those changes automatically.

Figure 14-6:
Only attributes with assigned values require storage space in the database.

Object	Attribute1	Attribute2	Attribute3
User1	xyz		
User2	xyz		
User3	xyz	1234	x1y2
User4	xyz		
User5	xyz	12345678	x1y2z3

Sizing the Database

Except in extremely large enterprises, the Active Directory database is normally less than 1 gigabyte (GB) in size. To enable future growth, however, I recommend setting aside at least 4GB for the database.

The size of the database depends on the number of objects and object attributes that it stores. A database with few user attributes takes up less space than one that sets many user attributes. Before extending the Active Directory database, consider that additional objects and attributes significantly increase the size of the database.

If you integrate DNS with the Active Directory database, the database becomes larger to accommodate the DNS information. Similarly, if you implement digital certificates for security, the database stores the certificates as user attributes, and the database grows exponentially. (A *digital certificate* is an electronic ID card that verifies a user's credentials so that the user can communicate with network resources.)

How you administer users and groups also affects the size of the database. Applying access control settings to a group is more efficient than applying them to each user. Applying settings to a group object also requires less database space than storing them as attributes on each individual user object.

Microsoft has conducted extensive testing on the size of various database objects and attributes. Repeating that data in this book would require too many pages. For more information on the size of various database objects, see the Microsoft white paper "Active Directory Database Sizing." You can find this white paper on Microsoft TechNet (a monthly CD subscription from Microsoft) or at www.microsoft.com.

Part V

Active Directory and Changing Technology

In this part . . .

In these two chapters, you look at some of the exciting
new technologies that Active Directory enables.
Obviously, familiar products such as SQL and Exchange
must change to integrate with Active Directory. But Active
Directory is also a giant step toward distributed computing, directory-enabled applications, and directory-enabled
networks. The possibilities are exciting! I'm sure that
you're going to apply this information to your own Active
Directory environment.

Chapter 15

Active Directory and BackOffice

*T*oday's directory-service environment is a hodgepodge of various directories servicing specific applications. The popularity of distributed-computing environments (in which applications can run on multiple computers throughout the network) is expanding. So the issue of disparate directory services reaches new proportions as administrators manage duplicate user accounts and complex (or nonexistent) interfaces between products. Multiple logon IDs, high support costs, and confusing interfaces are fueling IT's push toward integrating directory services.

Obviously, Microsoft plans to integrate its BackOffice applications with Active Directory. But many enterprises aren't complete Microsoft shops! What about directory-based applications from other vendors? If Microsoft ignores the rest of the development community, it risks losing market share. Microsoft's answer to this call is Active Directory Services Interface, or ADSI.

In this chapter, I explain how Microsoft plans to use ADSI to integrate multiple directory services in an enterprise. I also offer you a look at the possible changes to Microsoft BackOffice products to enable them to take full advantage of Active Directory.

ADSI in a Thimble

ADSI is a very complex topic. But you need to understand its function and its promise because you're likely to have one or more applications with its own dedicated directory. ADSI is likely to loom in your future, one way or another!

Figure 15-1 shows the present directory-service environment. Notice that each directory service relies on a specific application program interface (API) for communication with clients and servers.

What Microsoft provides in ADSI is a set of interfaces that enables independent software vendors (ISVs) to write their applications to interact with a directory by using only this single set of interfaces (see Figure 15-2). ADSI is an open interface, just as ODBC (open database connectivity) is. If you're not familiar with ODBC, it's an interface for relational databases that enables applications to work with any ODBC-compliant database. Similarly, ADSI enables applications to interact with any directory service that's ADSI-compliant.

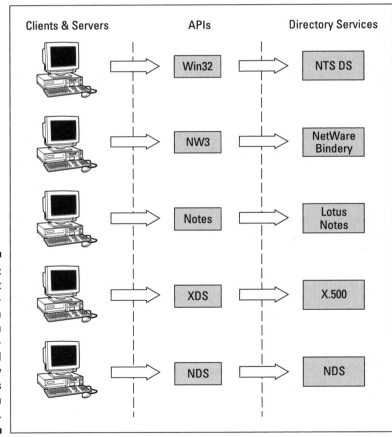

Figure 15-1:
The current communication path between clients/servers and directory services is through the API.

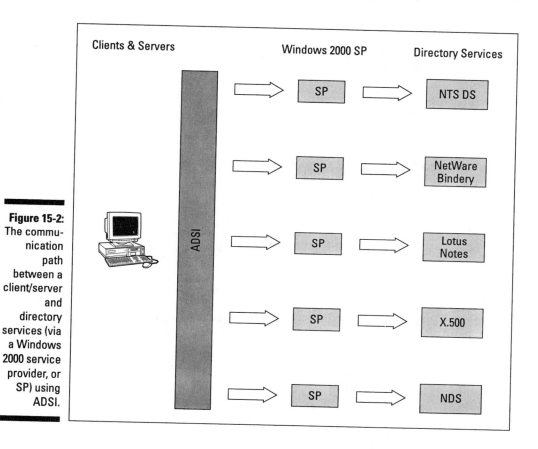

Figure 15-2: The communication path between a client/server and directory services (via a Windows 2000 service provider, or SP) using ADSI.

ADSI objects are actually Component Object Model (COM) objects and are either container objects or leaf objects. These predefined COM objects (which Table 15-1 lists by type) represent objects that you commonly find in a directory service namespace. ADSI is also extensible, which means that developers can add new objects to meet the needs of their applications.

A container object can hold other objects. An OU is an example of a container object. A leaf object can't contain other objects. A user is an example of a leaf object.

Table 15-1	ADSI Objects
Container Objects	*Leaf Objects*
Namespaces	User
Country	Alias
Locality	Service
Organization	Print queue
Organizational unit	Print device
Domain	File share
Computer	Session
Group	Resource

In summary, here are the primary purposes of ADSI:

✔ To ease the administrative burden of a distributed computing environment by using a single interface to interact with independent directory services

✔ To enable software vendors and developers to create applications that work with multiple directory services

Evolving BackOffice Products

Microsoft designed its own group of server applications — the BackOffice products — to take full advantage of Active Directory. The current set of BackOffice products includes the following components:

✔ Exchange Server

✔ Proxy Server

✔ Site Server

✔ Systems Management Server (SMS)

✔ SNA Server

✔ SQL Server

At the time this book went to press, Microsoft hadn't released much specific information regarding Active Directory–related changes to BackOffice applications. The exception, however, is the next version of Exchange, code-named *Platinum*.

The following sections describe the changes known at press time to some of these applications.

Exchange

The next release of Microsoft Exchange, called Platinum, uses Active Directory in place of the Exchange Directory Service, eliminating the need for a separate Exchange directory. Platinum integrates completely with Active Directory, providing enhanced scalability and security for Exchange. By unifying administration of the two directories, Microsoft provides a valuable opportunity to lower administrative support costs.

Although Platinum takes full advantage of Active Directory, it is backward-compatible with previous versions of Exchange that utilize a separate Exchange Directory Service. The current version of Exchange, Exchange 5.5, offers an Active Directory Connector for integration with Active Directory. Microsoft also plans a directory migration tool that enables you to transparently migrate the contents of the Microsoft Exchange directory to Active Directory.

In addition, Microsoft Exchange supports the Active Directory Services Interface, which enables customers to build Microsoft Exchange–based applications today that can be integrated with Active Directory in Microsoft Windows 2000.

Clearly, Exchange is adapting to Active Directory at a very fast pace due to the nature of its directory-based architecture. Microsoft SQL Server and Systems Management Server are additional products that lend themselves to rapid integration with Active Directory. Other BackOffice products will likely integrate with Active Directory at a much slower rate.

Proxy Server

Although I don't have any inside information on the future of BackOffice products, it stands to reason that Microsoft's Internet technology products will benefit most from several new features in Windows 2000:

- ✔ Internet protocol and standards compliance
- ✔ Enhanced IP security
- ✔ Enhanced security services
- ✔ Tight integration with DNS
- ✔ Increased scalability
- ✔ Capacity for directory-enabled networking and directory-enabled applications

Proxy Server should show significant security enhancements and improvements upon integration with Active Directory.

Systems Management Server (SMS)

Expect to see major Active Directory integration in future releases of SMS. Although Microsoft hasn't released development details at the time of this writing, it's clear to me that SMS will benefit greatly from integration with Active Directory, particularly in the area of storing inventory information. Active Directory is the logical storage location for hardware and software inventory data. I can also see it playing an important role in software metering and software distribution. Already, Windows 2000 provides remote OS installation and application installation through group policies.

SQL Server

Clearly, SQL Server and Active Directory will integrate tightly. Microsoft has already revealed that SQL Server security will integrate completely with Active Directory. Access to databases, SQL objects, views, and so on will be configured and managed through Active Directory. SQL Server will also benefit from the enhanced replication features available through Active Directory.

Chapter 16

Transforming the Industry

· ·

In This Chapter

▶ Discovering directory-enabled hardware

▶ Planning for a directory-enabled network (DEN)

▶ Developing applications for Active Directory

· ·

*B*ecause it promises to be widely implemented, Active Directory is having a profound effect on the industry. But as Web-based applications proliferate, Active Directory — by providing a single directory for managing applications, users, and devices — also vigorously addresses the rising cost of ownership that's inherent in supporting distributed applications.

Primarily because of efforts begun by Microsoft and Cisco, Active Directory also presents a new affinity among the operating system, network devices, and distributed applications. Together, these components create a *directory-enabled network* (DEN).

This chapter introduces you to directory-enabled applications, directory-enabled hardware, and directory-enabled networks. Although some of these products are relatively immature, you can't afford not to consider them in the future of your Active Directory implementation.

Independent Software Vendors and Active Directory

Obviously, Microsoft's own BackOffice products are leading the way in Active Directory integration. (BackOffice is a suite of Microsoft products that runs on Windows NT and Windows 2000. In Chapter 15, I talk about what the future holds for Active Directory and BackOffice.) But other software vendors are quickly joining the directory services frenzy. What's all the fuss about? Why are directory-enabled applications so important? The following sections answer these questions.

Understanding the value

Ask any IT manager or CIO to describe his primary mission. His response is likely to include the following:

- ✔ To increase network services to the user community
- ✔ To lower the cost of networked services

Although these aims may sound contradictory, they're not! By using Active Directory–enabled applications, organizations can simultaneously enhance service levels while lowering the total cost of ownership (TCO).

Directory-enabled applications are important because they perform the following functions:

- ✔ **They reduce the administrative burden of system administrators.** Because directory-enabled applications use the Active Directory database instead of a proprietary directory, there is no longer additional work in maintaining multiple user directories.

- ✔ **They enable a single sign-on to access networked resources.** Users are authenticated through Active Directory to use all network resources, including applications.

- ✔ **They enhance application functionality.** Active Directory provides a single, centralized directory database, as well as providing efficient replication across the network.

- ✔ **They improve service to the end user.** Users are no longer required to know the network location of a specific resource. They can access resources through Active Directory.

One of the major problems that directory-enabled applications address is that of consolidating the various directories that different applications use. Nowadays, an enterprise network is apt to have many types of directories: security directories, DHCP (Dynamic Host Configuration Protocol) directories, WINS (Windows Internet Naming Service) directories, DNS (Domain Name Service) directories, messaging directories, and so on (see Figure 16-1).

These various directories seldom have compatible formats, they duplicate user information, and they require lots of administrative time and effort. Sometimes they even require specialized support teams. The elusive dream of many IT managers is for standardized applications that work in a single enterprise-directory structure that can manage all directory resources through a common interface. When this standardization finally comes to pass, it promises to be incredibly cost-effective.

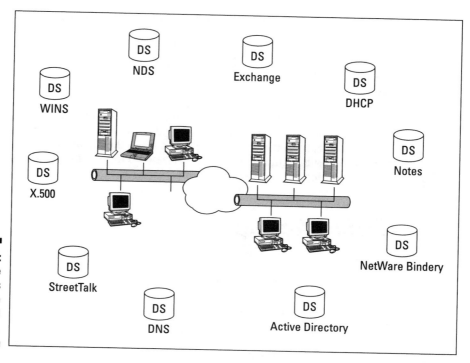

Figure 16-1:
Disparate
directories
proliferate
in a typical
enterprise.

Working powerful magic!

Directory-enabled applications work their magic by integrating access to applications with Active Directory group policies. (Because of their affiliation with policies, you sometimes hear people refer to directory-enabled applications as *policy-powered applications*.) System administrators can automate installation and configuration of a user's applications by applying specially tailored group and security policies. You can think of this automation as a kind of plug-and-play application support.

Policy-based configuration provides access control and prioritization privileges to an application based on a user's Active Directory group membership. Here's an example: Tom is a member of the Sales department and has access to the company's marketing database. Not surprisingly, Tom's assignment is to a group with access privileges that are more limited than those of the corporate marketing director and the CFO. In addition, the company restricts Tom's access during peak usage times so that the database is always available to members of the marketing director's group.

As the preceding example shows, what information Tom can access from the database and when he can access it are determined by the policies attached to the group to which Tom is assigned. The marketing director, on the other hand, has access to a broader base of information and greater availability to that information because she is assigned to a group with different policies attached.

Unfortunately, the full power of directory-enabled application technology isn't available yet. Active Directory is still new technology. Developers are working quickly to develop applications that take advantage of its features. Who knows what enhancements creative developers may come up with before the technology matures?

Early adopting

Microsoft has very ambitious plans for its directory-service product. Following are some of the types of applications that Microsoft expects will incorporate Active Directory in the very near future:

- ✔ Enterprise-resource planning (ERP) applications
- ✔ Client/server database applications
- ✔ Quota-management applications
- ✔ Backup-and-restore applications
- ✔ Systems-management tools
- ✔ Message-queuing applications
- ✔ Transaction-processing applications
- ✔ Groupware applications
- ✔ Document-management applications
- ✔ Directory-synchronization tools

As you can see from the list, Microsoft expects to attract a wide array of application vendors and plans to be particularly well suited for client/server Web applications, which often are distributed applications. Indeed, Microsoft is actively partnering with strategic independent software vendors to encourage Active Directory–enabled application development. But for the moment, the full promise of directory-enabled applications is still in the future.

Directory-Enabled Devices

Leading hardware vendors such as Cisco, Lucent, 3Com, Fore, and others are already producing *directory-enabled devices.* A directory-enabled device is integrated into a global directory services database, where it is represented as a directory object that can be managed using policies and permissions.

Because the Active Directory schema is extensible, specific directory-enabled devices can be added as objects in the directory. Associated attributes define each device's configuration. (For example, a router's attributes might include port1, with a value of 10.10.5.1.) You can automatically manage a directory-enabled device's configuration by making the device a member of a specified group and then associating a policy with that group. Figure 16-2 illustrates this concept. Kinda gives a whole new meaning to the term *smart device,* doesn't it?

Directory-enabled devices include routers, switches, manageable hubs, and servers. Information on current directory-enabled products is widely available on the Internet.

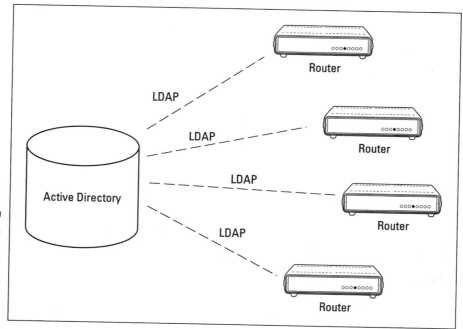

Figure 16-2: Device configuration using directory services.

The Ultimate Goal: Directory-Enabled Networks

The idea of true directory-enabled networking is exciting! If you can imagine applying the power of plug-and-play to an enterprise network, you grasp the concept.

A DEN stores information about network devices, users, and applications by using a global directory service. By associating profiles and policies with users and applications, you can configure guaranteed priority and access to applications, bandwidth, and network devices.

Microsoft and Cisco jointly created the Directory-Enabled Network Initiative in 1997. Oversight of this initiative has since transferred to the Desktop Management Task Force (DMTF), which is a vendor-independent standards organization. Virtually all the major hardware vendors support the DEN initiative. The ultimate goal of the work that DMTF guides is creation of a standardized schema for a global directory service. The broader goal of directory-enabled networks is to establish policy-powered networks that use policies to configure devices that you define in a global directory service.

For detailed information on DEN-related standards and initiatives, consult the following Web sites:

- **DMTF:** www.dmtf.org
- **IETF:** www.ietf.org
- **DEN:** www.universe.digex.net/~murchiso/den/

One important feature of a DEN is the capability to allocate bandwidth based on group policies. For an accounting application, for example, the DEN may guarantee a higher bandwidth than what it provides for Internet browsing. This prioritization of bandwidth ensures that valuable (and limited) network resources are optimally supporting the business needs of the organization.

For vendor-specific information about the DEN initiative, check the Web site of your favorite hardware vendor. Most offer technical briefs or white papers that describe their product offerings and outline their approach to directory-enabled networking.

Again, many aspects of these technologies are still in development. But as you design and manage your network, keep in mind that these new technologies can provide better ways for you to manage, configure, and optimize your network.

Part VI
The Part of Tens

The 5th Wave — By Rich Tennant

"One of the first things you want to do before installing Windows 2000 Server is fog the users to keep them calm during the procedure."

In this part . . .

The Part of Tens is a tradition in *For Dummies* books. It gives you and me an opportunity to add a little fun to the technical topics. Here you discover ten great Internet resources for additional information on Active Directory. You also find — concisely summarized — the ten most important points about Active Directory and, finally, ten troubleshooting tips to help you work through problems related to Active Directory and Windows 2000.

Chapter 17

Ten Most Important Points about Active Directory

*A*ctive Directory is new technology and contains lots of new terms and concepts. I thought, therefore, that condensing a few of the most important things that I've picked up about Active Directory and putting them into a short list might prove helpful to you — sorta like a cheat sheet! So — drum roll, please — following are my ten most important points about Active Directory!

Active Directory Is Based on DNS

Saying that Active Directory is DNS-based means that DNS is an integral part of the directory service. Bottom line: Active Directory simply can't function without DNS! You certainly aren't required to use the Microsoft DNS, but here are some advantages to doing so:

✔ Microsoft DNS supports SRV records, which Active Directory requires.

✔ Microsoft DNS supports Dynamic DNS (DDNS), which Active Directory doesn't require — but that I *strongly recommend* for it.

✔ Although you can use some other DNS service that supports SRV records and DDNS, Microsoft DNS can store DNS data in Active Directory. By storing DNS data in the directory, you remove DNS replication from the network because Active Directory replication includes the DNS data. Other DNS services can't store DNS data in the directory.

Your Active Directory Structure Isn't Based on Your Network Topology

Active Directory is based on the logical hierarchy of your organization. It organizes and manages resources in a user-friendly way. Network topology has no bearing on how you structure domains, trees, forests, and OUs. These items are all based on the logical business processes of the organization and not on the location of resources on the network. (For additional information on the logical Active Directory structure, see Chapter 4.) Sites and site connectors adapt the logical Active Directory structure to the physical realities of the network topology. (Chapter 12 provides additional information on sites and site connectors.)

Native Mode Refers to Domain Controllers in a Single Domain

Many people have the misconception that a Windows 2000 network running in native mode can't include any Windows 95/98 or Windows NT 3.51 and 4.0 computers. Not true!

Native mode affects the domain controllers only. Your network can still include Windows 95/98 and Windows NT clients running the Active Directory client software. You can even have Windows NT member servers.

The important functions that only native mode offers affect domain controllers. After you implement native mode, you lose backward compatibility with Windows NT PDCs and BDCs, which use a Security Access Manager (SAM) database instead of the Active Directory.

Furthermore, all the domains in a tree or forest don't need to be in native mode. One domain can be in mixed mode while others are in native mode. You can even manually establish trusts between native mode domains and Windows NT 3.51 and 4.0 domains. (See Chapter 3 for more information about native mode and mixed mode.)

Trees and Forests Use Transitive Trusts

In Windows 2000, two-way, transitive trust relationships connect all domains in a tree and in a forest. The domain administrators don't need to add these trusts — Active Directory automatically creates the trusts after you add a domain to a tree or a forest. One-way, nontransitive trusts, however, didn't just vanish! Domain administrators can still create one-way, nontransitive trusts whenever necessary. (Chapter 7 provides additional information on trusts.)

No More Browser Elections!

Yes! Finally! At last! After you implement Active Directory, users can search the Active Directory database for the resources they need. They don't need to know server and domain names to find printers and shares, and they don't need to browse the network to find resources. This capability means no more master browser elections in your domains because browsing becomes obsolete; no more annoying browser election messages in your event logs; and no more Windows 95 clients becoming browse masters — in short, one less headache for the system administrator!

For a DC, 128MB of RAM Isn't Enough

Windows 2000 Server requires 64MB of RAM, but Microsoft recommends 128MB. In my opinion, that's wishful thinking! Having only 128MB is fine for a member server, but for domain controllers, 128MB isn't at all sufficient. I recommend that you install a minimum of 256MB of memory in your domain controllers.

A Tree Can Consist of One Domain . . . and Often Should!

Because you now can delegate control of Active Directory objects, multiple domains aren't always necessary. A tree can consist of a single domain with objects grouped and organized by OUs. This configuration suffices for a surprisingly large number of companies. Just because you need multiple domains in Windows NT doesn't mean that you need multiple domains in an Active Directory environment. (See Chapter 4 for additional information on designing a logical directory structure.)

An Active Directory domain can contain millions of objects, so you seldom need multiple domains to accommodate large enterprises. You can nest OUs within other OUs for organizational purposes, so you don't need multiple domains to organize resources. You can search for resources rather than browse for them, so long lists of computer names don't dictate additional domains.

The only really good reason to add additional domains is to accommodate various security policies. IT officers with total cost of ownership (TCO) concerns should clearly identify valid reasons for additional domains. In short, people too often create multiple domains for political, rather than technical, purposes.

Not All Active Directory Domain Controllers Are Created Equal

You've probably read the Microsoft literature that says all domain controllers are the same in Windows 2000. Active Directory uses a multiple-master domain model, and, supposedly, no domain controller has a special role over any of the other domain controllers. This statement, however, isn't strictly true.

Some services can't function in a multiple-master environment, meaning that changes can't take place on more than one domain controller at a time. Some domain controllers, therefore, do assume a single-master operations role and are known as *operations masters*.

Here are the five categories of operations masters:

- ✓ **Schema master:** Maintains the master copy of the schema. (One per forest)
- ✓ **PDC emulator:** Emulates a primary domain controller for backward compatibility with Windows NT. (One per domain)
- ✓ **Domain naming master:** Tracks object names throughout a forest to ensure that they are unique. Also tracks cross-references to objects in other directories. (One per forest)
- ✓ **Infrastructure master:** Tracks object references among domains and maintains a list of deleted child objects. (One per domain)
- ✓ **Relative identifier (RID) master:** Tracks the assignment of SIDs (security identifiers) throughout the domain. (One per domain)

Usually, the first domain controller that you create in the first domain assumes the operations master roles. You can assign these roles to other domain controllers in the domain or forest, but only one domain controller at a time can hold each operations master role.

KCC Knows Best

In configuring replication connections between domain controllers, the Knowledge Consistency Checker (KCC) — a service that runs on the domain controllers — knows more than you do. The KCC automatically creates and configures connections for optimum replication. You rarely run across a case in which you need to change the connections. Changing them is tempting (simply because, as system administrator, you *can* change them), but for intrasite replication, the KCC usually does a better job.

Plan, Plan, Plan

The single most important thing to know about Active Directory is that you can't just turn it on and expect to operate in an efficient manner. To function effectively, an Active Directory implementation requires lots of planning. I do believe that Active Directory can lower total cost of ownership by reducing hardware costs and enabling centralized administration. But if the implementation isn't planned correctly, it ends up costing you money.

Before implementing Active Directory you should plan the following:

- The logical Active Directory structure (Chapter 4)
- The namespace (Chapter 3)
- The administrative model (Chapter 4)
- The security model (Chapter 4)
- The site topology (Chapter 5)

Active Directory has a lot to offer. With the potential for directory-enabled applications and directory-enabled networks, the possibilities are awesome. But the technology is complex — you can't just throw it into production and expect good results.

Chapter 18

Ten Cool Web Links for Active Directory Info

In This Chapter

▶ Finding technical articles and up-to-date facts

▶ Discussing questions with other system administrators

▶ Reviewing new products and processes

*W*ith all the technical information available on the Web, you can easily reach a state of information overload. So I'm saving you some searching by providing in this chapter some of my favorite Active Directory– and Windows 2000–related Web sites. Enjoy!

Microsoft Web Site

Of course, the Microsoft Web site contains scads of information about Active Directory. Check the Windows 2000 Server area, the TechNet area, and the developer area. Most of the good stuff on Active Directory is at the following URL:

```
www.microsoft.com/windows/SERVER/TECHNICAL/
        DIRECTORY/DEFAULT.ASP
```

Windows NT Magazine

This magazine has always been one of my favorites — I've subscribed since shortly after the magazine first came out. The writers target the feature articles toward system administrators, and they include solid technical facts. The online archive is a valuable resource. You can access *Windows NT Magazine* at the following URL:

```
www.winntmag.com
```

CIFS Central

Everything that you ever wanted to know about LDAP (Lightweight Directory Access Protocol) you can find at this site! Check out the following Web address:

```
www.cifs.com/2ndcifsconf/Microsoft-Leach2/index.html
```

Windows NT FAQ

Just the FAQs, ma'am, just the FAQs. This site contains good technical discussion forums. Look for it at the following URL:

```
www.ntfaq.com/
```

Planet IT — Windows 2000

You find lots of good stuff at this nicely done site — feature articles, product reviews, downloads, roundtable discussions, and more. Navigate to Planet IT at the following address:

```
www.planetit.com/techcenters/windows_2000
```

ENT Online

ENT Online is the Independent Newspaper for Windows NT Enterprise computing. You find lots of good technical articles here. Just go to the following URL:

```
www.entmag.com/
```

NT Systems Journal

The *NT Systems Journal* is a monthly magazine containing features, news, product reviews, and regular columns. The feature articles are usually right on the money, and its View from the Field column is usually relevant as well. Check it out at the following Web address:

```
www.ntsystems.com/
```

Windows TechEdge

Another online magazine site that stays on top of the current issues with Windows 2000 and Microsoft products, *Windows TechEdge* offers some great technical analysis features. You want to check this site often by typing the following URL into your browser:

```
www.windowstechedge.com/
```

MCP Magazine

In addition to publishing timely articles, *MCP Magazine* presents lots of great information on Microsoft certifications. But the best part of the site is its discussion forum. Here you can find postings from other system administrators encountering the same technical issues that you run into. It's definitely worth a bookmark! Point your browser to the following address:

```
www.mcpmag.com/
```

i386 the NT Source

This site has lots of performance tips and articles that cover NT and Windows 2000. Find it at the following URL:

```
www.i386.com
```

Messaging Magazine

Okay, so this is actually number 11! Although *Messaging Magazine* isn't really an Active Directory–related site, you can find good articles and information here regarding global directory services, directory security, and similar topics. As Active Directory rolls out, I expect to see a great deal of information here on integrating AD with Exchange and other messaging systems. In the meantime, it's an excellent site that I threw in as a bonus! Check it out at the following address:

```
www.ema.org/html/pubs/messmag.htm
```

Chapter 19

Ten Troubleshooting Tips for Active Directory

In This Chapter

▶ Problems installing Active Directory

▶ Trouble with modifying the schema

▶ Difficulties in restoring the Active Directory database

I would love to tell you that all my Active Directory efforts have been flawless. Alas, that's not true. I spent hours resolving some issues and needed help on others. So in the true spirit of cooperation with my fellow administrators — and because my editor tells me I should — I would like to share some troubleshooting tips for Active Directory.

Domain Controller Fails to Promote

Sometimes, as you're running the Active Directory Installation Wizard to promote a domain controller into an existing domain, the wizard fails, giving an error message that tells you that the domain isn't a valid Active Directory domain. This error is usually a DNS problem. Make certain that you installed DNS correctly and that it's functioning correctly; then run the wizard again.

Twice while I was attempting to promote a server to a domain controller, the wizard failed because of a DNS error. After fixing the error, I needed to run the wizard to demote the domain controller, even though the installation hadn't completed successfully, before I could successfully promote the server.

AD Installation Wizard Hangs

Your servers must be time-synchronized before you attempt to run the Active Directory Installation Wizard. If the time on the servers is off by five minutes in either direction, the installation wizard can hang endlessly. I mean literally that it can hang up for *hours,* and the server never promotes. To resolve the problem, cancel the wizard, synchronize the date and time on the servers, and then restart the installation wizard.

Synchronizing the date and time is easy. Just choose Start➪Settings➪ Control Panel; then double-click the Date/Time icon. I'm sure that you can figure out the calendar and clock adjustments on your own!

New Domain User Can't Log On

Occasionally, a new user can't log on to the domain with a newly created ID. This error is usually a replication latency problem, meaning that the nearest domain controllers haven't yet received the updated account information. After the domain controllers are in synch, the user can log on.

The same situation often occurs if you reset a password. After the local domain controllers receive the updated account information, the user can log on.

If the problem persists, check the event logs to make sure that the domain controllers are replicating successfully.

Can't Log On to a Domain

Any number of things can prevent a user from logging on to a domain. If you know that the user account and password are valid and the account isn't so new that replication may not have finished, consider these questions:

✔ Is TCP/IP configured correctly on the client computer?

✔ Is a domain controller available?

✔ Is a global catalog server available? (User authentication also requires global catalog servers.)

Directory Services Client Setup Doesn't Run

The Directory Services Client upgrades client computers running Windows 95 and Windows 98. If you can't get the client setup to run, make sure that the client computer is running Internet Explorer 4.01 or higher and that the Active Desktop is enabled.

Monitoring Active Directory Resources

In troubleshooting server and network problems, many administrators turn to performance analysis software to gather statistical data. To monitor Active Directory by using the Microsoft Performance Monitor, open the software and choose NTDS from the list of performance monitor objects. You can use dozens of counters to track Active Directory statistics. You may find some of the following useful:

- DRA Pending Replication Synchronizations (to check replication status)
- LDAP Client Sessions (to determine the current number of client sessions)
- Kerberos Authentications (to see how many Kerberos authentications have taken place)

Active Directory Data Didn't Restore with System State Data

If you use the Windows 2000 Restore Wizard to restore System State data from a backup, you can restore the Active Directory database only to its original location. If you specify an alternative location for the System State files, or if you try to restore files to a remote computer, the Active Directory database doesn't restore.

Can't Modify the Schema

Make sure that you're a member of the Schema Administrators group. If you're not, open the Schema Administrators group in AD Users and Computers and add your ID to the group. If you still can't modify the Active Directory schema, the schema master server is probably unavailable. Test network connections to the schema master. If the server has crashed, you may need to seize the schema master role, as I describe in Chapter 13.

Can't Detect Hardware During Setup

Okay, so this isn't actually an Active Directory problem, but it still could happen to you. Developers ran into this problem frequently during the early beta days of Windows 2000. If setup doesn't recognize your hardware, check the HCL (Hardware Compatibility List) on the Microsoft Web site to make sure that it lists your hardware. If the hardware appears on the list, but setup still can't detect the hardware, fixing the problem is usually just a matter of downloading an updated driver from the hardware vendor's Web site. If you continue to have problems installing or configuring the device, contact the hardware vendor for assistance.

Can't Upgrade from Windows NT 4.0

I've seen this happen only twice — so far. In the first case, the computer didn't meet the minimum hardware requirements for Windows NT Server. After upgrading the hardware, the upgrade ran successfully.

The second failed upgrade was simple to resolve but could have been very costly to the organization. Not knowing that the Enterprise Edition of Windows NT 4.0 was loaded on the server (because I didn't look!), I attempted to upgrade by using Windows 2000 Server — and it's not an upgrade that Microsoft supports. You can upgrade only to Windows 2000 Advanced Server or Datacenter Server from the Enterprise Edition of Windows NT 4.0. Be sure that you know which version of Windows NT was loaded on your server before buying a new version of Windows 2000 Server!

Part VII

Appendixes

The 5th Wave   By Rich Tennant

What helps the Windows 2000 operating system communicate with hardware?

That's easy — a massive, worldwide advertising campaign.

In this part . . .

I've included the following appendixes in this book for you to use as references:

- ✔ Appendix A is a list of the helpful utilities available in the Windows 2000 Resource Kit.

- ✔ Appendix B lists the classes and attributes defined in the Active Directory schema, as well as the mandatory and optional attributes that define the classSchema and attributeSchema objects.

- ✔ Appendix C is a listing of country codes and state codes that you can use when you are developing a standard naming convention for your Active Directory implementation.

- ✔ Appendix D is a glossary of terms to help you get familiar with the lingo.

- ✔ Appendix E tells you how to use the programs and utilities on the CD that accompanies this book.

Appendix A

Windows 2000 Tools and Utilities

· ·

*T*he tools and utilities in this appendix are available in the Windows 2000 Resource Kit. Many of them may be familiar if you use the Windows NT Resource Kit utilities. Others are new with Windows 2000 and Active Directory. A few utilities are missing descriptions because that information was not yet available from Microsoft at the time this book went to press.

Table A-1	Windows 2000 Tools and Utilities
Tool or Utility	*Description*
32-Bit UUDecode and UUEncode Utility	Encodes and decodes files according to the UUEncoding standard.
Active Directory Administration Tool	An LDAP administration tool.
Active Directory Replication Monitor	Enables you to monitor replication.
Active Directory Schema Manager	Enables you to manage the schema.
Addusers	Adds multiple users from a comma-delimited text file.
ADSI Edit	Enables you to view the Active Directory namespace and to manage ACLs.
API Monitor	Monitors the API calls that a process makes.
AppleTalk Device Analyzer	Analyzes AppleTalk Network Devices.
Applications as Services Utility	Enables applications to run as services.
Associate	Adds file extension executable program associations to the Registry.
Atmarp	ATM ARP Service Information Tool (Atmarp).
Atmlane	ATM LAN Emulation Client Information.

(continued)

Table A-1 *(continued)*

Tool or Utility	Description
Auditpol	Enables user to modify the audit policy of local or remote computers.
Auto-Boot Batch File	Enables you to start a custom batch file at bootup without needing to log on to that computer.
Automated Installation Tool	Pre-installs applications as part of an automated setup.
Browser Monitor	Monitors the status of browsers on selected domains.
Browstats	General-purpose network-browser diagnostic tool.
Certmgr	Certificate Manager enables you to manage digital security certificates.
Chgprint	Change Printer Utility enables you to change printer configurations.
Choice	Prompts user to make a choice in a batch program.
Clip	Dumps STDIN to Clipboard.
Clipboard Buffer Manager	Manages multiple text buffers, enabling user to store and retrieve them from the Clipboard.
Command Scheduler	Schedules commands on a local or remote computer to occur once or regularly.
Compound File Layout User Tool	Optimizes layout of compound document files for the Internet.
Compreg	Compares local and remote Registry keys and outputs differences.
Compress	Compresses files.
CPU Usage by Processes	Shows the percentage of total CPU usage per process.
Custcon	Console Key Customizer enables you to customize the keys on the console.
Custom Interface Manager	Adjusts and customizes user interface.

Tool or Utility	Description
Default Printer	Shows a list of available printers and enables user to easily select a default printer.
Delrp	Delete File and Reparse Points.
Delsrv	Unregisters a service with the service control manager.
Dependency Walker	Displays a hierarchical diagram of the dependent modules of an executable file or DLL.
Deployment Planning Guide	A text file containing information on planning a Windows 2000 deployment. It's primarily geared toward Windows 2000 Professional, but you'll find value for server deployments as well.
Dh	A utility to display the system heap.
Dhcmp	
DHCP Objects	Locates DHCP objects on a network.
Dhcpcmd	Manages DHCP servers.
Dhcploc	Locates DHCP servers on a network.
Diruse	Determines the amount of disk space that a directory occupies.
Disk Probe	Enables users with Administrator privileges to directly edit, save, and copy data on the physical hard drive that's not accessible in any other way.
Diskmap	Displays information about a disk and the contents of its Partition Table.
Diskuse	Scans a directory tree and reports the amount of space that each user uses.
Distributed Systems Guide	A text file containing information on distributed systems.
Dnscmd	A DNS administrative tool that enables an administrator to administer and obtain statistics from local and remote DNS servers.

(continued)

Table A-1 *(continued)*

Tool or Utility	Description
Domain Monitor	Monitors the status of servers and domain controllers for a domain and its trusted domains.
Driver	Displays information on installed device drivers, their files, and their code.
Dsacls	Command line tool for ACL management.
Dsastat	Enables you to compare information in directory trees.
Dumpel	Dumps an Event Log to a tab-separated text file.
Dxdiag	A DirectX diagnostics tool.
Exetype	Identifies the operating-system environment and processor necessary to run a particular executable file.
Expand	Expands files.
Extensible Performance Counter List	Displays information on extensible performance counter DLLs installed on a computer.
Extract	Tool for extracting CAB (cabinet) files.
File and Directory Comparison	Compares two text files or folders and displays differences.
Filever	Displays version information on executable files.
Findgrp	Lists a user's direct and indirect group memberships.
Forfiles	
Freedisk	Checks for free disk space, returning a 0 if you have enough space for an operation and a 1 if you don't.
FT Registry Information Editor	Edits the Registry for fault tolerance settings.
Getmac	A link layer address viewer that displays a computer's MAC (Ethernet) layer address and binding order.

Tool or Utility	Description
Getsid	Compares the security IDs of two user accounts.
Gettype	Detects the system install type.
Gflags	Enables a user to edit NtGlobalFlag settings for the Windows NT operating system.
Global	Lists contents of global groups across domains and workstations.
Group Copy	Copies the user names in an existing group to another group in the same or a different domain.
Heapmon	Enables a user to view system heap information.
Ifmember	Checks whether a user is a member of a specified group.
Instsrv	Installs and uninstalls executable services and assigns names to them.
Intbind	Interrupt Affinity Tool.
Internetworking Guide	A text file that provides information on internetworking Windows 2000 products.
Ipsecpol	Utility that assists in managing Internet protocol security policy.
Kernprof	Kernel profiler that provides counters for and profiles of various functions of the operating system Kernel.
Kill	Enables a user to terminate selected tasks or processes.
Kixstart32	Processes logon scripts and provides an enhanced batch language.
Ksetup	Kerberos setup that configures a Windows 2000 Professional computer for MIT Kerberos interoperability.
Ktpass	Kerberos Keytab Setup configures a computer running UNIX or a UNIX- based service as a security principal in Active Directory.

(continued)

Table A-1 *(continued)*

Tool or Utility	Description
Link Check Wizard	Scans all the shortcut (link) files on a computer and enables user to remove dead ones.
Linkd	
List	Displays and searches a text file.
Local	Lists contents of local groups across domains and workstations.
Lock Floppy Disk Drives	Enables batch processing of files in a directory or tree.
Logevent	Logs events to a local or remote computer.
Logoff	Logs off a user.
Logtime	Logs start or finish times of programs running in a batch file.
Memory Leak Tester	Appropriates system memory to test performance in low-memory situations.
Memsnap	Takes a snapshot of memory resources that running processes consume.
Mibcc	Compiles Management Information Bases for Simple Network Management Protocol.
Microsoft Printer Migrator	Backs up or migrates a print server.
Movetree	Enables you to move objects within the Active Directory tree.
Munge	Searches for and replaces strings in a file.
Netafx	Network configuration tool.
Netcmd	Network command prompt utility.
Netdiag	Enables you to test to connectivity between devices on the network.
Netdom	Enables administrators to manage domains.
Netsvc	Remotely starts and stops the status of services on a network.

Tool or Utility	Description
Network Connections	Displays current network connections.
Network Share Monitor	Monitors and manages shared folders on multiple computers.
Nlmon	Lists and tests domains and trust relationships.
Nltest	Tests domain trust relationships.
Now	Echoes the current date and time plus any arguments that you pass to it.
Nss2doc	
Ntdsutil	Command-line tool for database management and FSMO management.
Ntrights	Grants or revokes Windows NT rights to or from users or groups.
Oh	Shows the handles of open windows, processes, or objects.
OLE/COM Object Viewer	Browses, configures, and tests Microsoft COM (Component Object Model) classes installed on a computer.
OS/2 API Information	Describes which APIs for the OS/2 operating system Windows NT supports and which it doesn't.
Page Fault Monitor	Lists the source and number of page faults that an application's function calls generate.
Passprop	Sets domain policy flags for password complexity and for whether you can lock out the administrator account.
Pathman	Adds or removes components of the system or user path.
Perfmtr	Performance analysis tool.
Perl	C-like scripting language ported from UNIX to Windows NT.
Perm	Displays a user's access permissions for a file or directory.

(continued)

Table A-1 *(continued)*

Tool or Utility	Description
Permcopy	Copies file- and share-level permissions from one share to another.
Pmon	Shows per-process usage of CPU and memory.
Point-to-Point Tunneling Protocol Ping Utility	Verifies that the required protocol and port for Point-to-Point Tunneling Protocol are routing from a PPTP client to a PPTP server.
Posix Tools	
Process Viewer	Displays information about a running process and enables you to stop it.
Professional and Server Fundamentals Guide	Document that details the fundamentals of Windows 2000 Server and Windows 2000.
Professional.Pstat	Shows the status of all running processes and threads.
Ptree	Queries the process inheritance tree and kill processes on local or remote computers.
Pulist	Lists processes running on local or remote computers.
Raslist	Displays Remote Access Service server announcements from a network.
RASmon	Monitors RAS (Remote Access Service) connections.
Rasusers	Lists Remote Access Service users on a domain or computer.
Rcmd	Provides secure client and server for remotely running command-line programs.
Reg	Command-line utility for editing the Registry.
Regback	Backs up all or part of the Registry.
Regdump	Dumps all or part of the Registry to standard output.

Tool or Utility	Description
Regfind	Searches and optionally replaces Registry data.
Regina Scripting Language	Scripting language useful for batch processing and OLE automation.
Regini	Modifies Registry entries with a batch file.
Regrest	Restores all or part of the Registry.
Remailer	Manipulates Registry entries on local or remote computers from the command prompt.
Remapkey	Tool for remapping the keyboard layout.
Remote	Runs command-line programs on remote computers.
Remote Clipboard Viewer	Shows contents of a remote computer's Clipboard and enables users to cut and paste data to and from it.
Remote Shutdown GUI	Shuts down or reboots a local or remote computer.
Repadmin	Command-line utility for managing replication.
Resource Kit Tools Help	Help utility that assists you in accessing information and using tools from the Resource Kit.
Rkill	Enumerates and kills processes on a remote computer.
Rmtshare	Sets up and deletes shares remotely.
Robocopy	Maintains multiple mirror images of large folder trees on network servers.
RPC Connectivity Verification Tool	Checks whether Windows 2000 Server services are responding to remote procedure-call requests from network clients.
RSDIAG	Remote storage diagnostic utility.
RSDIR	Remote Storage File Information Utility.
Sc	Shows services and their status.

(continued)

Table A-1 *(continued)*

Tool or Utility	Description
Scanreg	Searches for a string in Registry key-names, value names, and value data.
Sclist	Shows services and their statuses.
Secadd	Adds user permissions to a Registry key.
Security Administration Tools	Manages access-control policies.
Security Migrator	Enables a user to run a process in the security context of a different user.
Service Monitoring Tool	Monitors services on local or remote computers and notifies the administrator if their status changes.
Setup Manager	Generates answer files for unattended installations or upgrades on multiple computers.
Setx	Sets environmental variables in the user or computer environment.
Showacls	Lists the access rights for files and folders.
Showdisk	Displays configuration and fault-tolerance information for primary partitions and logical drives.
Showgrps	Shows the groups to which a user belongs.
Showmbrs	Shows the usernames of members of a group.
Shutdown	Shuts down or reboots a local or remote computer.
Sleep	Causes a computer to wait for a specified amount of time.
SNMP Monitor	Monitors Simple Network Management Protocol variables for multiple nodes and logs them to a database.
SNMP Troubleshooting Tool	Works with Simple Mail Transport Protocol to reroute mail from mail server to mail server for a generic user.

Tool or Utility	Description
Snmputil	Queries a Simple Network Management Protocol host or community for Management Information Base values.
Soon	Schedules commands to run within the next 24 hours.
Srvcheck	Enumerates shares and their user permissions.
Srvinfo	Displays network, disk drive, and services installed on a local or remote server.
Srvinstw	Installs and deletes services and device drivers on a local or remote computer.
Su	Migrates security information between users, groups, and domains.
Sysprep	Prepares a system before creating an image to use for multiple installations.
Takeown	Utility for taking ownership.
TCP/IP Core Networking Guide	Document that provides information about networking with TCP/IP.
TCP/IP Remote Shell Service	Provides a command-line shell or single command execution service for remote users.
Telephony Location Manager	Configures telephony locations and properties for portable computers.
TextViewer	Displays contents of multiple text files on local or shared drives.
Time Zone Editor	Creates and edits time zone entries for the Date/Time option in Control Panel.
Timeout	Pauses execution of a command for a period that you specify.
Timethis	Times how long a given command takes to execute.
Timezone	Updates daylight-savings information for a time zone in the Registry.

(continued)

Table A-1 *(continued)*

Tool or Utility	Description
Tlist	Lists IDs and names of processes running on the local computer.
Translate	Translates error codes into explanations.
Trustdom	Displays, creates, and deletes trust relationships between domains.
Typeperf	Displays real-time data from Performance Monitor counters in a command window.
User Profile Deletion Utility	Deletes Windows NT user profiles.
Userdump	Displays the processes running in user mode on the system.
Usrstat	Lists usernames, full names, and last logon date and time for all user accounts in a domain.
Usrtogrp	Adds users to a group from a text file.
Visual File Information	Checks for corruption and changes in files; saves information in tab-delimited text files.
Waitfor	Synchronizes a task across multiple computers.
Whoami	Returns the username and computer of the user who's currently logged on.
Windows 2000 Event Log Database	Lists Event Log messages and related information.
Windows 2000 Messages	Provides explanations of Windows NT error messages.
Windows 2000 Online Books	On-line documentation about Windows 2000.
Windows 2000 Resource Kit Release Notes	Microsoft release notes about the Resource Kit.
Windows Scripting Host	Enables VBScript and JavaScript to run natively within Windows 95 and 98 and Windows NT.
Winmsdp	Provides information about system configuration and status.

Tool or Utility	Description
Winschk	Manages Windows Internet Name Service activities and databases.
Winscl	An administrative tool for managing WINS.
Wsremote	A Winsock remote console.

Appendix B

Schema Classes and Attributes

• •

*T*he tables in this appendix list the classes and attributes available within the Active Directory schema. (See Chapter 13 for a refresher on the schema, classes, or attributes.) Table B-1 lists all the classes in the Active Directory schema. Table B-2 lists all the attributes in the Active Directory schema.

Table B-3 shows the attributes of the classSchema object, which defines the criteria for each class of object. These criteria consist of mandatory attributes and optional attributes. The mandatory and optional attributes listed here define the rules for creating objects in the schema. Similarly, Table B-4 lists the mandatory and optional attributes of the attributeSchema object, as well as the required syntax for the value of each attribute. The attributeSchema object defines how you create attributes in the schema. If you want to create a new attribute in the schema, the attributeSchema object tells you which attributes are required and which are optional.

I created these tables by using the Export List feature in the Active Directory Schema utility. To access the Export List feature, open the Active Directory Schema snap-in and then click the Classes object. (See Chapter 13 if you need additional help in opening the snap-in.) When the listing of classes appears in the right-hand pane, right-click the Classes object and choose Export List from the pop-up menu. The list is exported to a comma-delimited text file, which means that the spaces between columns are replaced with commas. I then imported the text file into Microsoft Word.

Table B-1	Active Directory Schema Classes	
Name	*Type*	*Description*
aCSPolicy	Structural	ACS-Policy
aCSSubnet	Structural	ACS-Subnet
addressBookContainer	Structural	Address-Book-Container
addressTemplate	Structural	Address-Template
applicationEntity	Structural	Application-Entity

(continued)

Table B-1 *(continued)*

Name	Type	Description
applicationProcess	Structural	Application-Process
applicationSettings	Abstract	Application-Settings
applicationSiteSettings	Abstract	Application-Site-Settings
attributeSchema	Structural	Attribute-Schema
builtinDomain	Structural	Builtin-Domain
categoryRegistration	Structural	Category-Registration
certificationAuthority	Structural	Certification-Authority
classRegistration	Structural	Class-Registration
classSchema	Structural	Class-Schema
classStore	Structural	Class-Store
comConnectionPoint	Structural	Com-Connection-Point
computer	Structural	Computer
configuration	Structural	Configuration
connectionPoint	Abstract	Connection-Point
contact	Structural	Contact
container	Structural	Container
controlAccessRight	Structural	Control-Access-Right
country	Abstract	Country
cRLDistributionPoint	Structural	CRL-Distribution-Point
crossRef	Structural	Cross-Ref
crossRefContainer	Structural	Cross-Ref-Container
device	Abstract	Device
dfsConfiguration	Structural	Dfs-Configuration
dHCPClass	Structural	DHCP-Class
displaySpecifier	Structural	Display-Specifier
displayTemplate	Structural	Display-Template
dMD	Structural	DMD
dnsNode	Structural	Dns-Node

Name	Type	Description
dnsZone	Structural	Dns-Zone
domain	Abstract	Domain
domainDNS	Structural	Domain-DNS
domainPolicy	Structural	Domain-Policy
dSA	Structural	DSA
dSUISettings	Structural	DS-UI-Settings
fileLinkTracking	Structural	File-Link-Tracking
fileLinkTrackingEntry	Structural	File-Link-Tracking-Entry
foreignSecurityPrincipal	Structural	Foreign-Security-Principal
fTDfs	Structural	FT-Dfs
group	Structural	Group
groupOfNames	Abstract	Group-Of-Names
groupPolicyContainer	Structural	Group-Policy-Container
indexServerCatalog	Structural	Index-Server-Catalog
infrastructureUpdate	Structural	Infrastructure-Update
intellimirrorGroup	Structural	Intellimirror-Group
intellimirrorSCP	Structural	Intellimirror-SCP
interSiteTransport	Structural	Inter-Site-Transport
interSiteTransportContainer	Structural	Inter-Site-Transport-Container
ipsecBase	Abstract	Ipsec-Base
ipsecFilter	Structural	Ipsec-Filter
ipsecISAKMPPolicy	Structural	Ipsec-ISAKMP-Policy
ipsecNegotiationPolicy	Structural	Ipsec-Negotiation-Policy
ipsecNFA	Structural	Ipsec-NFA
ipsecPolicy	Structural	Ipsec-Policy
leaf	Abstract	Leaf
licensingSiteSettings	Structural	Licensing-Site-Settings

(continued0

Table B-1 *(continued)*

Name	Type	Description
linkTrackObjectMoveTable	Structural	Link-Track-Object-Move-Table
linkTrackOMTEntry	Structural	Link-Track-OMT-Entry
linkTrackVolEntry	Structural	Link-Track-Vol-Entry
linkTrackVolumeTable	Structural	Link-Track-Volume-Table
locality	Structural	Locality
lostAndFound	Structural	Lost-And-Found
mailRecipient	Auxiliary	Mail-Recipient
meeting	Structural	Meeting
msExchConfigurationContainer	Structural	MS-Exch-Configuration-Container
mSMQConfiguration	Structural	MSMQ-Configuration
mSMQEnterpriseSettings	Structural	MSMQ-Enterprise-Settings
mSMQMigratedUser	Structural	MSMQ-Migrated-User
mSMQQueue	Structural	MSMQ-Queue
mSMQSettings	Structural	MSMQ-Settings
mSMQSiteLink	Structural	MSMQ-Site-Link
mS-SQL-OLAPCube	Structural	MS-SQL-OLAPCube
mS-SQL-OLAPDatabase	Structural	MS-SQL-OLAPDatabase
mS-SQL-OLAPServer	Structural	MS-SQL-OLAPServer
mS-SQL-SQLDatabase	Structural	MS-SQL-SQLDatabase
mS-SQL-SQLPublication	Structural	MS-SQL-SQLPublication
mS-SQL-SQLRepository	Structural	MS-SQL-SQLRepository
mS-SQL-SQLServer	Structural	MS-SQL-SQLServer
nTDSConnection	Structural	NTDS-Connection
nTDSDSA	Structural	NTDS-DSA
nTDSService	Structural	NTDS-Service
nTDSSiteSettings	Structural	NTDS-Site-Settings
nTFRSMember	Structural	NTFRS-Member

Name	Type	Description
nTFRSReplicaSet	Structural	NTFRS-Replica-Set
nTFRSSettings	Structural	NTFRS-Settings
nTFRSSubscriber	Structural	NTFRS-Subscriber
nTFRSSubscriptions	Structural	NTFRS-Subscriptions
organization	Structural	Organization
organizationalPerson	Abstract	Organizational-Person
organizationalRole	Structural	Organizational-Role
organizationalUnit	Structural	Organizational-Unit
packageRegistration	Structural	Package-Registration
person	Abstract	Person
physicalLocation	Structural	Physical-Location
pKICertificateTemplate	Structural	PKI-Certificate-Template
pKIEnrollmentService	Structural	PKI-Enrollment-Service
printQueue	Structural	Print-Queue
queryPolicy	Structural	Query-Policy
remoteMailRecipient	Structural	Remote-Mail-Recipient
remoteStorageServicePoint	Structural	Remote-Storage-Service-Point
residentialPerson	Structural	Residential-Person
rIDManager	Structural	RID-Manager
rIDSet	Structural	RID-Set
rpcContainer	Structural	Rpc-Container
rpcEntry	Abstract	rpc-Entry
rpcGroup	Structural	rpc-Group
rpcProfile	Structural	rpc-Profile
rpcProfileElement	Structural	rpc-Profile-Element
rpcServer	Structural	rpc-Server
rpcServerElement	Structural	rpc-Server-Element

(continued)

Table B-1 *(continued)*

Name	Type	Description
rRASAdministration ConnectionPoint	Structural	RRAS-Administration-Connection-Point
rRASAdministrationDictionary	Structural	RRAS-Administration-Dictionary
samDomain	Auxiliary	Sam-Domain
samDomainBase	Auxiliary	Sam-Domain-Base
samServer	Structural	Sam-Server
secret	Structural	Secret
securityObject	Abstract	Security-Object
securityPrincipal	Auxiliary	Security-Principal
server	Structural	Server
serversContainer	Structural	Servers-Container
serviceAdministrationPoint	Structural	Service-Administration-Point
serviceClass	Structural	Service-Class
serviceConnectionPoint	Structural	Service-Connection-Point
serviceInstance	Structural	Service-Instance
site	Structural	Site
siteLink	Structural	Site-Link
siteLinkBridge	Structural	Site-Link-Bridge
sitesContainer	Structural	Sites-Container
storage	Structural	Storage
subnet	Structural	Subnet
subnetContainer	Structural	Subnet-Container
subSchema	Structural	SubSchema
top	Abstract	Top
trustedDomain	Structural	Trusted-Domain
typeLibrary	Structural	Type-Library
user	Structural	User
volume	Structural	Volume

Table B-2	**Active Directory Schema Attributes**	
Name	**Syntax**	**Description**
accountExpires	Large Integer	Account-Expires
accountNameHistory	Unicode String	Account-Name-History
aCSAggregateToken RatePerUser	Large Integer	ACS-Aggregate-Token-Rate-Per-User
aCSAllocableRSVP Bandwidth	Large Integer	ACS-Allocable-RSVP Bandwidth
aCSCacheTimeout	Integer	ACS-Cache-Timeout
aCSDirection	Integer	ACS-Direction
aCSDSBMDeadTime	Integer	ACS-DSBM-DeadTime
aCSDSBMPriority	Integer	ACS-DSBM-Priority
aCSDSBMRefresh	Integer	ACS-DSBM-Refresh
aCSEnableACSService	Boolean	ACS-Enable-ACS-Service
aCSEnableRSVP Accounting	Boolean	ACS-Enable-RSVP-Accounting
aCSEnableRSVP MessageLogging	Boolean	ACS-Enable-RSVP-Message-Logging
aCSEventLogLevel	Integer	ACS-Event-Log-Level
aCSIdentityName	Unicode String	ACS-Identity-Name
aCSMaxAggregate PeakRatePerUser	Large Integer	ACS-Max-Aggregate-Peak-Rate-Per-User
aCSMaxDurationPerFlow	Integer	ACS-Max-Duration-Per-Flow
aCSMaximumSDUSize	Large Integer	ACS-Maximum-SDU-Size
aCSMaxNoOfAccountFiles	Integer	ACS-Max-No-Of-Account-Files
aCSMaxNoOfLogFiles	Integer	ACS-Max-No-Of-Log-Files
aCSMaxPeakBandwidth	Large Integer	ACS-Max-Peak-Bandwidth
aCSMaxPeakBandwidth PerFlow	Large Integer	ACS-Max-Peak-Bandwidth-Per-Flow
aCSMaxSizeOfRSVP AccountFile	Integer	ACS-Max-Size-Of-RSVP-Account-File

(continued)

Table B-2 *(continued)*

Name	Syntax	Description
aCSMaxSizeOfRSVPLogFile	Integer	ACS-Max-Size-Of-RSVP-Log-File
aCSMaxTokenBucketPerFlow	Large Integer	ACS-Max-Token-Bucket-Per-Flow
aCSMaxTokenRatePerFlow	Large Integer	ACS-Max-Token-Rate-Per-Flow
aCSMinimumDelayVariation	Large Integer	ACS-Minimum-Delay-Variation
aCSMinimumLatency	Large Integer	ACS-Minimum-Latency
aCSMinimumPolicedSize	Large Integer	ACS-Minimum-Policed-Size
aCSNonReservedMaxSDUSize	Large Integer	ACS-Non-Reserved-Max-SDU-Size
aCSNonReservedMinPolicedSize	Large Integer	ACS-Non-Reserved-Min-Policed-Size
aCSNonReservedPeakRate	Large Integer	ACS-Non-Reserved-Peak-Rate
aCSNonReservedTokenSize	Large Integer	ACS-Non-Reserved-Token-Size
aCSNonReservedTxLimit	Large Integer	ACS-Non-Reserved-Tx-Limit
aCSNonReservedTxSize	Large Integer	ACS-Non-Reserved-Tx-Size
aCSPermissionBits	Large Integer	ACS-Permission-Bits
aCSPolicyName	Unicode String	ACS-Policy-Name
aCSPriority	Integer	ACS-Priority
aCSRSVPAccountFilesLocation	Unicode String	ACS-RSVP-Account-Files-Location
aCSRSVPLogFilesLocation	Unicode String	ACS-RSVP-Log-Files-Location
aCSServerList	Unicode String	ACS-Server-List
aCSServiceType	Integer	ACS-Service-Type
aCSTimeOfDay	Unicode String	ACS-Time-Of-Day
aCSTotalNoOfFlows	Integer	ACS-Total-No-Of-Flows
additionalTrustedServiceNames	Unicode String	Additional-Trusted-Service-Names

Name	Syntax	Description
addressBookRoots	Distinguished Name	Address-Book-Roots
addressEntryDisplayTable	Octet String	Address-Entry-Display-Table
addressEntryDisplay TableMSDOS	Octet String	Address-Entry-Display-Table-MSDOS
addressSyntax	Octet String	Address-Syntax
addressType	Case Insensitive String	Address-Type
adminContextMenu	Unicode String	Admin-Context-Menu
adminCount	Integer	Admin-Count
adminDescription	Unicode String	Admin-Description
adminDisplayName	Unicode String	Admin-Display-Name
adminPropertyPages	Unicode String	Admin-Property-Pages
allowedAttributes	Object Identifier	Allowed-Attributes
allowedAttributesEffective	Object Identifier	Allowed-Attributes-Effective
allowedChildClasses	Object Identifier	Allowed-Child-Classes
allowedChild ClassesEffective	Object Identifier	Allowed-Child-Classes-Effective
altSecurityIdentities	Unicode String	Alt-Security-Identities
aNR	Unicode String	ANR
applicationName	Unicode String	Application-Name
appliesTo	Unicode String	Applies-To
appSchemaVersion	Integer	App-Schema-Version
assetNumber	Unicode String	Asset-Number
assistant	Distinguished Name	Assistant
assocNTAccount	Octet String	Assoc-NT-Account
attributeDisplayNames	Unicode String	Attribute-Display-Names
attributeID	Object Identifier	Attribute-ID
attributeSecurityGUID	Octet String	Attribute-Security-GUID

(continued)

Table B-2 *(continued)*

Name	Syntax	Description
attributeSyntax	Object Identifier	Attribute-Syntax
attributeTypes	Unicode String	Attribute-Types
auditingPolicy	Octet String	Auditing-Policy
authenticationOptions	Integer	Authentication-Options
authorityRevocationList	Octet String	Authority-Revocation-List
auxiliaryClass	Object Identifier	Auxiliary-Class
badPasswordTime	Large Integer	Bad-Password-Time
badPwdCount	Integer	Bad-Pwd-Count
birthLocation	Octet String	Birth-Location
bridgeheadServerListBL	Distinguished Name	Bridgehead-Server-List-BL
bridgeheadTransportList	Distinguished Name	Bridgehead-Transport-List
builtinCreationTime	Large Integer	Builtin-Creation-Time
builtinModifiedCount	Large Integer	Builtin-Modified-Count
businessCategory	Unicode String	Business-Category
bytesPerMinute	Integer	Bytes-Per-Minute
c	Unicode String	Country-Name
cACertificate	Octet String	CA-Certificate
cACertificateDN	Unicode String	CA-Certificate-DN
cAConnect	Unicode String	CA-Connect
canonicalName	Unicode String	Canonical-Name
canUpgradeScript	Unicode String	Can-Upgrade-Script
catalogs	Unicode String	Catalogs
categories	Unicode String	Categories
categoryId	Octet String	Category-Id
cAUsages	Unicode String	CA-Usages
cAWEBURL	Unicode String	CA-WEB-URL

Name	Syntax	Description
certificateAuthorityObject	Distinguished Name	Certificate-Authority-Object
certificateRevocationList	Octet String	Certificate-Revocation-List
certificateTemplates	Unicode String	Certificate-Templates
classDisplayName	Unicode String	Class-Display-Name
cn	Unicode String	Common-Name
co	Unicode String	Text-Country
codePage	Integer	Code-Page
cOMClassID	Unicode String	COM-ClassID
cOMCLSID	Unicode String	COM-CLSID
cOMInterfaceID	Unicode String	COM-InterfaceID
comment	Unicode String	User-Comment
cOMOtherProgId	Unicode String	COM-Other-Prog-Id
company	Unicode String	Company
cOMProgID	Unicode String	COM-ProgID
cOMTreatAsClassId	Unicode String	COM-Treat-As-Class-Id
cOMTypelibId	Unicode String	COM-Typelib-Id
cOMUniqueLIBID	Unicode String	COM-Unique-LIBID
contentIndexingAllowed	Boolean	Content-Indexing-Allowed
contextMenu	Unicode String	Context-Menu
controlAccessRights	Octet String	Control-Access-Rights
cost	Integer	Cost
countryCode	Integer	Country-Code
createDialog	Unicode String	Create-Dialog
createTimeStamp	Generalized Time	Create-Time-Stamp
createWizardExt	Unicode String	Create-Wizard-Ext
creationTime	Large Integer	Creation-Time
creationWizard	Unicode String	Creation-Wizard

(continued)

Table B-2 (continued)

Name	Syntax	Description
creator	Unicode String	Creator
cRLObject	Distinguished Name	CRL-Object
cRLPartitioned RevocationList	Octet String	CRL-Partitioned-Revocation-List
crossCertificatePair	Octet String	Cross-Certificate-Pair
currentLocation	Octet String	Current-Location
currentParentCA	Distinguished Name	Current-Parent-CA
currentValue	Octet String	Current-Value
currMachineId	Octet String	Curr-Machine-Id
dBCSPwd	Octet String	DBCS-Pwd
dc	Unicode String	Domain-Component
defaultClassStore	Distinguished Name	Default-Class-Store
defaultGroup	Distinguished Name	Default-Group
defaultHidingValue	Boolean	Default-Hiding-Value
defaultLocalPolicyObject	Distinguished Name	Default-Local-Policy-Object
defaultObjectCategory	Distinguished Name	Default-Object-Category
defaultPriority	Integer	Default-Priority
defaultSecurityDescriptor	Unicode String	Default-Security-Descriptor
deltaRevocationList	Octet String	Delta-Revocation-List
department	Unicode String	Department
description	Unicode String	Description
desktopProfile	Unicode String	Desktop-Profile
destinationIndicator	Print Case String	Destination-Indicator
dhcpClasses	Octet String	dhcp-Classes
dhcpFlags	Large Integer	dhcp-Flags

Name	*Syntax*	*Description*
dhcpIdentification	Unicode String	dhcp-Identification
dhcpMask	Print Case String	dhcp-Mask
dhcpMaxKey	Large Integer	dhcp-MaxKey
dhcpObjDescription	Unicode String	dhcp-Obj-Description
dhcpObjName	Unicode String	dhcp-Obj-Name
dhcpOptions	Octet String	dhcp-Options
dhcpProperties	Octet String	dhcp-Properties
dhcpRanges	Print Case String	dhcp-Ranges
dhcpReservations	Print Case String	dhcp-Reservations
dhcpServers	Print Case String	dhcp-Servers
dhcpSites	Print Case String	dhcp-Sites
dhcpState	Print Case String	dhcp-State
dhcpSubnets	Print Case String	dhcp-Subnets
dhcpType	Integer	dhcp-Type
dhcpUniqueKey	Large Integer	dhcp-Unique-Key
dhcpUpdateTime	Large Integer	dhcp-Update-Time
directReports	Distinguished Name	Reports
displayName	Unicode String	Display-Name
displayNamePrintable	Print Case String	Display-Name-Printable
distinguishedName	Distinguished Name	Obj-Dist-Name
dITContentRules	Unicode String	DIT-Content-Rules
division	Unicode String	Division
dMDLocation	Distinguished Name	DMD-Location
dmdName	Unicode String	DMD-Name
dNReferenceUpdate	Distinguished Name	DN-Reference-Update

(continued)

Table B-2 *(continued)*

Name	Syntax	Description
dnsAllowDynamic	Boolean	Dns-Allow-Dynamic
dnsAllowXFR	Boolean	Dns-Allow-XFR
dNSHostName	Unicode String	DNS-Host-Name
dnsNotifySecondaries	Integer	Dns-Notify-Secondaries
dNSProperty	Octet String	DNS-Property
dnsRecord	Octet String	Dns-Record
dnsRoot	Unicode String	Dns-Root
dnsSecureSecondaries	Integer	Dns-Secure-Secondaries
domainCAs	Distinguished Name	Domain-Certificate-Authorities
domainCrossRef	Distinguished Name	Domain-Cross-Ref
domainID	Distinguished Name	Domain-ID
domainIdentifier	Integer	Domain-Identifier
domainPolicyObject	Distinguished Name	Domain-Policy-Object
domainPolicyReference	Distinguished Name	Domain-Policy-Reference
domainReplica	Unicode String	Domain-Replica
domainWidePolicy	Octet String	Domain-Wide-Policy
driverName	Unicode String	Driver-Name
driverVersion	Integer	Driver-Version
dSASignature	Octet String	DSA-Signature
dSCorePropagationData	Generalized Time	DS-Core-Propagation-Data
dSHeuristics	Unicode String	DS-Heuristics
dSUIAdminMaximum	Integer	DS-UI-Admin-Maximum
dSUIAdminNotification	Unicode String	DS-UI-Admin-Notification
dSUIShellMaximum	Integer	DS-UI-Shell-Maximum
dynamicLDAPServer	Distinguished Name	Dynamic-LDAP-Server
eFSPolicy	Octet String	EFSPolicy
employeeID	Unicode String	Employee-ID

Name	Syntax	Description
employeeNumber	Unicode String	Employee-Number
employeeType	Unicode String	Employee-Type
enabled	Boolean	Enabled
enabledConnection	Boolean	Enabled-Connection
enrollmentProviders	Unicode String	Enrollment-Providers
extendedAttributeInfo	Unicode String	Extended-Attribute-Info
extendedCharsAllowed	Boolean	Extended-Chars-Allowed
extendedClassInfo	Unicode String	Extended-Class-Info
extensionName	Unicode String	Extension-Name
facsimileTelephoneNumber	Unicode String	Facsimile-Telephone-Number
fileExtPriority	Unicode String	File-Ext-Priority
flags	Integer	Flags
flatName	Unicode String	Flat-Name
forceLogoff	Large Integer	Force-Logoff
foreignIdentifier	Octet String	Foreign-Identifier
friendlyNames	Unicode String	Friendly-Names
fromEntry	Boolean	From-Entry
fromServer	Distinguished Name	From-Server
frsComputerReference	Distinguished Name	Frs-Computer-Reference
frsComputerReferenceBL	Distinguished Name	Frs-Computer-Reference-BL
fRSControlDataCreation	Unicode String	FRS-Control-Data-Creation
fRSControlInboundBacklog	Unicode String	FRS-Control-Inbound-Backlog
fRSControlOutboundBacklog	Unicode String	FRS-Control-Outbound-Backlog
fRSDirectoryFilter	Unicode String	FRS-Directory-Filter
fRSDSPoll	Integer	FRS-DS-Poll
fRSExtensions	Octet String	FRS-Extensions
fRSFaultCondition	Unicode String	FRS-Fault-Condition

(continued)

Table B-2 *(continued)*

Name	Syntax	Description
fRSFileFilter	Unicode String	FRS-File-Filter
fRSFlags	Integer	FRS-Flags
fRSLevelLimit	Integer	FRS-Level-Limit
fRSMemberReference	Distinguished Name	FRS-Member-Reference
fRSMemberReferenceBL	Distinguished Name	FRS-Member-Reference-BL
fRSPartnerAuthLevel	Integer	FRS-Partner-Auth-Level
fRSPrimaryMember	Distinguished Name	FRS-Primary-Member
fRSReplicaSetGUID	Octet String	FRS-Replica-Set-GUID
fRSReplicaSetType	Integer	FRS-Replica-Set-Type
fRSRootPath	Unicode String	FRS-Root-Path
fRSRootSecurity	NT Security Descriptor	FRS-Root-Security
fRSServiceCommand	Unicode String	FRS-Service-Command
fRSServiceCommandStatus	Unicode String	FRS-Service-Command-Status
fRSStagingPath	Unicode String	FRS-Staging-Path
fRSTimeLastCommand	UTC Coded Time	FRS-Time-Last-Command
fRSTimeLastConfigChange	UTC Coded Time	FRS-Time-Last-Config-Change
fRSUpdateTimeout	Integer	FRS-Update-Timeout
fRSVersion	Unicode String	FRS-Version
fRSVersionGUID	Octet String	FRS-Version-GUID
fRSWorkingPath	Unicode String	FRS-Working-Path
fSMORoleOwner	Distinguished Name	FSMO-Role-Owner
garbageCollPeriod	Integer	Garbage-Coll-Period
generatedConnection	Boolean	Generated-Connection
generationQualifier	Unicode String	Generation-Qualifier
givenName	Unicode String	Given-Name
globalAddressList	Distinguished Name	Global-Address-List

Name	Syntax	Description
governsID	Object Identifier	Governs-ID
gPCFileSysPath	Unicode String	GPC-File-Sys-Path
gPCFunctionalityVersion	Integer	GPC-Functionality-Version
gPCMachineExtensionNames	Unicode String	GPC-Machine-Extension-Names
gPCUserExtensionNames	Unicode String	GPC-User-Extension-Names
gPLink	Unicode String	GP-Link
gPOptions	Integer	GP-Options
groupAttributes	Integer	Group-Attributes
groupMembershipSAM	Octet String	Group-Membership-SAM
groupPriority	Unicode String	Group-Priority
groupsToIgnore	Unicode String	Groups-to-Ignore
groupType	Integer	Group-Type
hasMasterNCs	Distinguished Name	Has-Master-NCs
hasPartialReplicaNCs	Distinguished Name	Has-Partial-Replica-NCs
helpData16	Octet String	Help-Data16
helpData32	Octet String	Help-Data32
helpFileName	Unicode String	Help-File-Name
homeDirectory	Unicode String	Home-Directory
homeDrive	Unicode String	Home-Drive
homePhone	Unicode String	Phone-Home-Primary
homePostalAddress	Unicode String	Address-Home
iconPath	Unicode String	Icon-Path
implementedCategories	Octet String	Implemented-Categories
indexedScopes	Unicode String	IndexedScopes
info	Unicode String	Comment
initialAuthIncoming	Unicode String	Initial-Auth-Incoming
initialAuthOutgoing	Unicode String	Initial-Auth-Outgoing

(continued)

Table B-2 *(continued)*

Name	Syntax	Description
initials	Unicode String	Initials
installUiLevel	Integer	Install-Ui-Level
instanceType	Integer	Instance-Type
internationalISDNNumber	Numerical String	International-ISDN-Number
interSiteTopologyFailover	Integer	Inter-Site-Topology-Failover
interSiteTopologyGenerator	Distinguished Name	Inter-Site-Topology-Generator
interSiteTopologyRenew	Integer	Inter-Site-Topology-Renew
invocationId	Octet String	Invocation-Id
ipPhone	Unicode String	Phone-Ip-Primary
ipsecData	Octet String	Ipsec-Data
ipsecDataType	Integer	Ipsec-Data-Type
ipsecFilterReference	Distinguished Name	Ipsec-Filter-Reference
ipsecID	Unicode String	Ipsec-ID
ipsecISAKMPReference	Distinguished Name	Ipsec-ISAKMP-Reference
ipsecName	Unicode String	Ipsec-Name
iPSECNegotiationPolicyAction	Unicode String	IPSEC-Negotiation-Policy-Action
ipsecNegotiation-PolicyReference	Distinguished Name	Ipsec-Negotiation-Policy-Reference
iPSECNegotiationPolicyType	Unicode String	IPSEC-Negotiation-Policy-Type
ipsecNFAReference	Distinguished Name	Ipsec-NFA-Reference
ipsecOwnersReference	Distinguished Name	Ipsec-Owners-Reference
ipsecPolicyReference	Distinguished Name	Ipsec-Policy-Reference
isCriticalSystemObject	Boolean	Is-Critical-System-Object
isDefunct	Boolean	Is-Defunct
isDeleted	Boolean	Is-Deleted
isEphemeral	Boolean	Is-Ephemeral

Name	Syntax	Description
isMemberOfPartial AttributeSet	Boolean	Is-Member-Of-Partial-Attribute-Set
isPrivilegeHolder	Distinguished Name	Is-Privilege-Holder
isSingleValued	Boolean	Is-Single-Valued
keywords	Unicode String	Keywords
knowledgeInformation	Case Insensitive String	Knowledge-Information
l	Unicode String	Locality-Name
lastBackupRestoration Time	Large Integer	Last-Backup-Restoration-Time
lastContentIndexed	Large Integer	Last-Content-Indexed
lastKnownParent	Distinguished Name	Last-Known-Parent
lastLogoff	Large Integer	Last-Logoff
lastLogon	Large Integer	Last-Logon
lastSetTime	Large Integer	Last-Set-Time
lastUpdateSequence	Unicode String	Last-Update-Sequence
lDAPAdminLimits	Unicode String	LDAP-Admin-Limits
lDAPDisplayName	Unicode String	LDAP-Display-Name
lDAPIPDenyList	Octet String	LDAP-IPDeny-List
legacyExchangeDN	Case Insensitive String	Legacy-Exchange-DN
linkID	Integer	Link-ID
linkTrackSecret	Octet String	Link-Track-Secret
lmPwdHistory	Octet String	Lm-Pwd-History
localeID	Integer	Locale-ID
localizationDisplayId	Integer	Localization-Display-Id
localizedDescription	Unicode String	Localized-Description
localPolicyFlags	Integer	Local-Policy-Flags
localPolicyReference	Distinguished Name	Local-Policy-Reference
location	Unicode String	Location
lockoutDuration	Large Integer	Lockout-Duration

(continued)

Table B-2 *(continued)*

Name	Syntax	Description
lockOutObservationWindow	Large Integer	Lock-Out-Observation-Window
lockoutThreshold	Integer	Lockout-Threshold
lockoutTime	Large Integer	Lockout-Time
logonCount	Integer	Logon-Count
logonHours	Octet String	Logon-Hours
logonWorkstation	Octet String	Logon-Workstation
lSACreationTime	Large Integer	LSA-Creation-Time
lSAModifiedCount	Large Integer	LSA-Modified-Count
machineArchitecture	Enumeration	Machine-Architecture
machinePassword ChangeInterval	Large Integer	Machine-Password-Change-Interval
machineRole	Enumeration	Machine-Role
machineWidePolicy	Octet String	Machine-Wide-Policy
mail	Unicode String	E-mail-Addresses
mailAddress	Unicode String	SMTP-Mail-Address
managedBy	Distinguished Name	Managed-By
managedObjects	Distinguished Name	Managed-Objects
manager	Distinguished Name	Manager
mAPIID	Integer	MAPI-ID
marshalledInterface	Octet String	Marshalled-Interface
masteredBy	Distinguished Name	Mastered-By
maxPwdAge	Large Integer	Max-Pwd-Age
maxRenewAge	Large Integer	Max-Renew-Age
maxStorage	Large Integer	Max-Storage
maxTicketAge	Large Integer	Max-Ticket-Age
mayContain	Object Identifier	May-Contain
meetingAdvertiseScope	Unicode String	meetingAdvertiseScope

Name	Syntax	Description
meetingApplication	Unicode String	meetingApplication
meetingBandwidth	Integer	meetingBandwidth
meetingBlob	Octet String	meetingBlob
meetingContactInfo	Unicode String	meetingContactInfo
meetingDescription	Unicode String	meetingDescription
meetingEndTime	UTC Coded Time	meetingEndTime
meetingID	Unicode String	meetingID
meetingIP	Unicode String	meetingIP
meetingIsEncrypted	Unicode String	meetingIsEncrypted
meetingKeyword	Unicode String	meetingKeyword
meetingLanguage	Unicode String	meetingLanguage
meetingLocation	Unicode String	meetingLocation
meetingMaxParticipants	Integer	meetingMaxParticipants
meetingName	Unicode String	meetingName
meetingOriginator	Unicode String	meetingOriginator
meetingOwner	Unicode String	meetingOwner
meetingProtocol	Unicode String	meetingProtocol
meetingRating	Unicode String	meetingRating
meetingRecurrence	Unicode String	meetingRecurrence
meetingScope	Unicode String	meetingScope
meetingStartTime	UTC Coded Time	meetingStartTime
meetingType	Unicode String	meetingType
meetingURL	Unicode String	meetingURL
member	Distinguished Name	Member
memberOf	Distinguished Name	Is-Member-Of-DL
mhsORAddress	Unicode String	MHS-OR-Address
middleName	Unicode String	Other-Name
minPwdAge	Large Integer	Min-Pwd-Age

(continued)

Table B-2 *(continued)*

Name	Syntax	Description
minPwdLength	Integer	Min-Pwd-Length
minTicketAge	Large Integer	Min-Ticket-Age
mobile	Unicode String	Phone-Mobile-Primary
modifiedCount	Large Integer	Modified-Count
modifiedCountAtLastProm	Large Integer	Modified-Count-At-Last-Prom
modifyTimeStamp	Generalized Time	Modify-Time-Stamp
moniker	Octet String	Moniker
monikerDisplayName	Unicode String	Moniker-Display-Name
moveTreeState	Octet String	Move-Tree-State
mscopeId	Print Case String	Mscope-Id
mS-DS-Consistency ChildCount	Integer	MS-DS-Consistency-Child-Count
mS-DS-ConsistencyGuid	Octet String	MS-DS-Consistency-Guid
mS-DS-CreatorSID	SID	MS-DS-Creator-SID
mS-DS-Machine AccountQuota	Integer	MS-DS-Machine-Account-Quota
mS-DS-ReplicatesNCReason	DN Binary	MS-DS-Replicates-NC-Reason
msiFileList	Unicode String	Msi-File-List
msiScript	Octet String	Msi-Script
msiScriptName	Unicode String	Msi-Script-Name
msiScriptPath	Unicode String	Msi-Script-Path
msiScriptSize	Integer	Msi-Script-Size
mSMQAuthenticate	Boolean	MSMQ-Authenticate
mSMQBasePriority	Integer	MSMQ-Base-Priority
mSMQComputerType	Case Insensitive String	MSMQ-Computer-Type
mSMQCost	Integer	MSMQ-Cost
mSMQCSPName	Case Insensitive String	MSMQ-CSP-Name

Name	Syntax	Description
mSMQDependent ClientService	Boolean	MSMQ-Dependent-Client-Service
mSMQDependent ClientServices	Boolean	MSMQ-Dependent-Client-Services
mSMQDigests	Octet String	MSMQ-Digests
mSMQDigestsMig	Octet String	MSMQ-Digests-Mig
mSMQDsService	Boolean	MSMQ-Ds-Service
mSMQDsServices	Boolean	MSMQ-Ds-Services
mSMQEncryptKey	Octet String	MSMQ-Encrypt-Key
mSMQForeign	Boolean	MSMQ-Foreign
mSMQInRoutingServers	Distinguished Name	MSMQ-In-Routing-Servers
mSMQInterval1	Integer	MSMQ-Interval1
mSMQInterval2	Integer	MSMQ-Interval2
mSMQJournal	Boolean	MSMQ-Journal
mSMQJournalQuota	Integer	MSMQ-Journal-Quota
mSMQLabel	Case Insensitive String	MSMQ-Label
mSMQLongLived	Integer	MSMQ-Long-Lived
mSMQMigrated	Boolean	MSMQ-Migrated
mSMQNameStyle	Boolean	MSMQ-Name-Style
mSMQNt4Flags	Integer	MSMQ-Nt4-Flags
mSMQNt4Stub	Integer	MSMQ-Nt4-Stub
mSMQOSType	Integer	MSMQ-OS-Type
mSMQOutRoutingServers	Distinguished Name	MSMQ-Out-Routing-Servers
mSMQOwnerID	Octet String	MSMQ-Owner-ID
mSMQPrevSiteGates	Distinguished Name	MSMQ-Prev-Site-Gates
mSMQPrivacyLevel	Enumeration	MSMQ-Privacy-Level
mSMQQMID	Octet String	MSMQ-QM-ID
mSMQQueueJournalQuota	Integer	MSMQ-Queue-Journal-Quota

(continued)

Table B-2 *(continued)*

Name	Syntax	Description
mSMQQueueNameExt	Unicode String	MSMQ-Queue-Name-Ext
mSMQQueueQuota	Integer	MSMQ-Queue-Quota
mSMQQueueType	Octet String	MSMQ-Queue-Type
mSMQQuota	Integer	MSMQ-Quota
mSMQRoutingService	Boolean	MSMQ-Routing-Service
mSMQRoutingServices	Boolean	MSMQ-Routing-Services
mSMQServices	Integer	MSMQ-Services
mSMQServiceType	Integer	MSMQ-Service-Type
mSMQSignCertificates	Octet String	MSMQ-Sign-Certificates
mSMQSignCertificatesMig	Octet String	MSMQ-Sign-Certificates-Mig
mSMQSignKey	Octet String	MSMQ-Sign-Key
mSMQSite1	Distinguished Name	MSMQ-Site-1
mSMQSite2	Distinguished Name	MSMQ-Site-2
mSMQSiteForeign	Boolean	MSMQ-Site-Foreign
mSMQSiteGates	Distinguished Name	MSMQ-Site-Gates
mSMQSiteGatesMig	Distinguished Name	MSMQ-Site-Gates-Mig
mSMQSiteID	Octet String	MSMQ-Site-ID
mSMQSiteName	Case Insensitive String	MSMQ-Site-Name
mSMQSites	Octet String	MSMQ-Sites
mSMQTransactional	Boolean	MSMQ-Transactional
mSMQUserSid	Octet String	MSMQ-User-Sid
mSMQVersion	Integer	MSMQ-Version
msNPAllowDialin	Boolean	msNPAllowDialin
msNPCalledStationID	IA5-String	msNPCalledStationID
msNPCallingStationID	IA5-String	msNPCallingStationID
msNPSavedCallingStationID	IA5-String	msNPSavedCallingStationID
msRADIUSCallbackNumber	IA5-String	msRADIUSCallbackNumber

Name	*Syntax*	*Description*
msRADIUSFramedIPAddress	Integer	msRADIUSFramedIPAddress
msRADIUSFramedRoute	IA5-String	msRADIUSFramedRoute
msRADIUSServiceType	Integer	msRADIUSServiceType
msRASSavedCallbackNumber	IA5-String	msRASSavedCallback-Number
msRASSavedFramed IPAddress	Integer	msRASSavedFramed-IPAddress
msRASSavedFramedRoute	IA5-String	msRASSavedFramedRoute
msRRASAttribute	Unicode String	ms-RRAS-Attribute
msRRASVendorAttributeEntry	Unicode String	ms-RRAS-Vendor-Attribute-Entry
mS-SQL-Alias	Unicode String	MS-SQL-Alias
mS-SQL-AllowAnonymous Subscription	Boolean	MS-SQL-Allow-AnonymousSubscription
mS-SQL-AllowImmediate UpdatingSubscription	Boolean	MS-SQL-AllowImmediate-UpdatingSubscription
mS-SQL-AllowKnown PullSubscription	Boolean	MS-SQL-AllowKnown-PullSubscription
mS-SQL-AllowQueued UpdatingSubscription	Boolean	MS-SQL-AllowQueued-UpdatingSubscription
mS-SQL-AllowSnapshot FilesFTPDownloading	Boolean	MS-SQL-AllowSnapshotFiles-FTPDownloading
mS-SQL-AppleTalk	Unicode String	MS-SQL-AppleTalk
mS-SQL-Applications	Unicode String	MS-SQL-Applications
mS-SQL-Build	Integer	MS-SQL-Build
mS-SQL-CharacterSet	Integer	MS-SQL-CharacterSet
mS-SQL-Clustered	Boolean	MS-SQL-Clustered
mS-SQL-ConnectionURL	Unicode String	MS-SQL-ConnectionURL
mS-SQL-Contact	Unicode String	MS-SQL-Contact
mS-SQL-CreationDate	Unicode String	MS-SQL-CreationDate
mS-SQL-Database	Unicode String	MS-SQL-Database

(continued)

Table B-2 *(continued)*

Name	Syntax	Description
mS-SQL-Description	Unicode String	MS-SQL-Description
mS-SQL-GPSHeight	Unicode String	MS-SQL-GPSHeight
mS-SQL-GPSLatitude	Unicode String	MS-SQL-GPSLatitude
mS-SQL-GPSLongitude	Unicode String	MS-SQL-GPSLongitude
mS-SQL-InformationDirectory	Boolean	MS-SQL-InformationDirectory
mS-SQL-InformationURL	Unicode String	MS-SQL-InformationURL
mS-SQL-Keywords	Unicode String	MS-SQL-Keywords
mS-SQL-Language	Unicode String	MS-SQL-Language
mS-SQL-LastBackupDate	Unicode String	MS-SQL-LastBackupDate
mS-SQL-LastDiagnosticDate	Unicode String	MS-SQL-LastDiagnosticDate
mS-SQL-LastUpdatedDate	Unicode String	MS-SQL-LastUpdatedDate
mS-SQL-Location	Unicode String	MS-SQL-Location
mS-SQL-Memory	Large Integer	MS-SQL-Memory
mS-SQL-MultiProtocol	Unicode String	MS-SQL-MultiProtocol
mS-SQL-Name	Unicode String	MS-SQL-Name
mS-SQL-NamedPipe	Unicode String	MS-SQL-NamedPipe
mS-SQL-PublicationURL	Unicode String	MS-SQL-PublicationURL
mS-SQL-Publisher	Unicode String	MS-SQL-Publisher
mS-SQL-RegisteredOwner	Unicode String	MS-SQL-RegisteredOwner
mS-SQL-ServiceAccount	Unicode String	MS-SQL-ServiceAccount
mS-SQL-Size	Large Integer	MS-SQL-Size
mS-SQL-SortOrder	Unicode String	MS-SQL-SortOrder
mS-SQL-SPX	Unicode String	MS-SQL-SPX
mS-SQL-Status	Large Integer	MS-SQL-Status
mS-SQL-TCPIP	Unicode String	MS-SQL-TCPIP
mS-SQL-ThirdParty	Boolean	MS-SQL-ThirdParty
mS-SQL-Type	Unicode String	MS-SQL-Type

Name	Syntax	Description
mS-SQL-UnicodeSortOrder	Integer	MS-SQL-UnicodeSortOrder
mS-SQL-Version	Unicode String	MS-SQL-Version
mS-SQL-Vines	Unicode String	MS-SQL-Vines
mustContain	Object Identifier	Must-Contain
name	Unicode String	RDN
nameServiceFlags	Integer	Name-Service-Flags
nCName	Distinguished Name	NC-Name
nETBIOSName	Unicode String	NETBIOS-Name
netbootAllowNewClients	Boolean	Netboot-Allow-New-Clients
netbootAnswerOnly ValidClients	Boolean	Netboot-Answer-Only-Valid-Clients
netbootAnswerRequests	Boolean	Netboot-Answer-Requests
netbootCurrentClientCount	Integer	Netboot-Current-Client-Count
netbootGUID	Octet String	Netboot-GUID
netbootInitialization	Unicode String	Netboot-Initialization
netbootIntelliMirrorOSes	Unicode String	Netboot-IntelliMirror-OSes
netbootLimitClients	Boolean	Netboot-Limit-Clients
netbootLocallyInstalledOSes	Unicode String	Netboot-Locally-Installed-OSes
netbootMachineFilePath	Unicode String	Netboot-Machine-File-Path
netbootMaxClients	Integer	Netboot-Max-Clients
netbootMirrorDataFile	Unicode String	Netboot-Mirror-Data-File
netbootNewMachine NamingPolicy	Unicode String	Netboot-New-Machine-Naming-Policy
netbootNewMachineOU	Distinguished Name	Netboot-New-Machine-OU
netbootSCPBL	Distinguished Name	Netboot-SCP-BL
netbootServer	Distinguished Name	Netboot-Server
netbootSIFFile	Unicode String	Netboot-SIF-File
netbootTools	Unicode String	Netboot-Tools

(continued)

Table B-2 *(continued)*

Name	Syntax	Description
networkAddress	Case Insensitive String	Network-Address
nextLevelStore	Distinguished Name	Next-Level-Store
nextRid	Integer	Next-Rid
nonSecurityMember	Distinguished Name	Non-Security-Member
nonSecurityMemberBL	Distinguished Name	Non-Security-Member-BL
notes	Unicode String	Additional-Information
notificationList	Distinguished Name	Notification-List
nTGroupMembers	Octet String	NT-Group-Members
nTMixedDomain	Integer	NT-Mixed-Domain
ntPwdHistory	Octet String	Nt-Pwd-History
nTSecurityDescriptor	NT Security Descriptor	NT-Security-Descriptor
o	Unicode String	Organization-Name
objectCategory	Distinguished Name	Object-Category
objectClass	Object Identifier	Object-Class
objectClassCategory	Enumeration	Object-Class-Category
objectClasses	Unicode String	Object-Classes
objectCount	Integer	Object-Count
objectGUID	Octet String	Object-Guid
objectSid	SID	Object-Sid
objectVersion	Integer	Object-Version
oEMInformation	Unicode String	OEM-Information
oMObjectClass	Octet String	OM-Object-Class
oMSyntax	Integer	OM-Syntax
oMTGuid	Octet String	OMT-Guid
oMTIndxGuid	Octet String	OMT-Indx-Guid
operatingSystem	Unicode String	Operating-System
operatingSystemHotfix	Unicode String	Operating-System-Hotfix

Name	*Syntax*	*Description*
operatingSystemServicePack	Unicode String	Operating-System-Service-Pack
operatingSystemVersion	Unicode String	Operating-System-Version
operatorCount	Integer	Operator-Count
optionDescription	Unicode String	Option-Description
options	Integer	Options
optionsLocation	Print Case String	Options-Location
originalDisplayTable	Octet String	Original-Display-Table
originalDisplayTableMSDOS	Octet String	Original-Display-Table-MSDOS
otherFacsimileTelephone Number	Unicode String	Phone-Fax-Other
otherHomePhone	Unicode String	Phone-Home-Other
otherIpPhone	Unicode String	Phone-Ip-Other
otherLoginWorkstations	Unicode String	Other-Login-Workstations
otherMailbox	Unicode String	Other-Mailbox
otherMobile	Unicode String	Phone-Mobile-Other
otherPager	Unicode String	Phone-Pager-Other
otherTelephone	Unicode String	Phone-Office-Other
otherWellKnownObjects	DN Binary	Other-Well-Known-Objects
ou	Unicode String	Organizational-Unit-Name
owner	Distinguished Name	Owner
packageFlags	Integer	Package-Flags
packageName	Unicode String	Package-Name
packageType	Integer	Package-Type
pager	Unicode String	Phone-Pager-Primary
parentCA	Distinguished Name	Parent-CA
parentCACertificateChain	Octet String	Parent-CA-Certificate-Chain
parentGUID	Octet String	Parent-GUID
partialAttributeDeletionList	Octet String	Partial-Attribute-Deletion-List

(continued)

Table B-2 *(continued)*

Name	Syntax	Description
partialAttributeSet	Octet String	Partial-Attribute-Set
pekKeyChangeInterval	Large Integer	Pek-Key-Change-Interval
pekList	Octet String	Pek-List
pendingCACertificates	Octet String	Pending-CA-Certificates
pendingParentCA	Distinguished Name	Pending-Parent-CA
perMsgDialogDisplayTable	Octet String	Per-Msg-Dialog-Display-Table
perRecipDialogDisplayTable	Octet String	Per-Recip-Dialog-Display-Table
personalTitle	Unicode String	Personal-Title
physicalDeliveryOfficeName	Unicode String	Physical-Delivery-Office-Name
physicalLocationObject	Distinguished Name	Physical-Location-Object
pKICriticalExtensions	Unicode String	PKI-Critical-Extensions
pKIDefaultCSPs	Unicode String	PKI-Default-CSPs
pKIDefaultKeySpec	Integer	PKI-Default-Key-Spec
pKIEnrollmentAccess	NT Security Descriptor	PKI-Enrollment-Access
pKIExpirationPeriod	Octet String	PKI-Expiration-Period
pKIExtendedKeyUsage	Unicode String	PKI-Extended-Key-Usage
pKIKeyUsage	Octet String	PKI-Key-Usage
pKIMaxIssuingDepth	Integer	PKI-Max-Issuing-Depth
pKIOverlapPeriod	Octet String	PKI-Overlap-Period
pKT	Octet String	PKT
pKTGuid	Octet String	PKT-Guid
policyReplicationFlags	Integer	Policy-Replication-Flags
portName	Unicode String	Port-Name
possibleInferiors	Object Identifier	Possible-Inferiors
possSuperiors	Object Identifier	Poss-Superiors

Name	Syntax	Description
postalAddress	Unicode String	Postal-Address
postalCode	Unicode String	Postal-Code
postOfficeBox	Unicode String	Post-Office-Box
preferredDeliveryMethod	Enumeration	Preferred-Delivery-Method
preferredOU	Distinguished Name	Preferred-OU
prefixMap	Octet String	Prefix-Map
presentationAddress	Address	Presentation-Address
previousCACertificates	Octet String	Previous-CA-Certificates
previousParentCA	Distinguished Name	Previous-Parent-CA
primaryGroupID	Integer	Primary-Group-ID
primaryInternational-ISDNNumber	Unicode String	Phone-ISDN-Primary
primaryTelexNumber	Unicode String	Telex-Primary
printAttributes	Integer	Print-Attributes
printBinNames	Unicode String	Print-Bin-Names
printCollate	Boolean	Print-Collate
printColor	Boolean	Print-Color
printDuplexSupported	Boolean	Print-Duplex-Supported
printEndTime	Integer	Print-End-Time
printerName	Unicode String	Printer-Name
printFormName	Unicode String	Print-Form-Name
printKeepPrintedJobs	Boolean	Print-Keep-Printed-Jobs
printLanguage	Unicode String	Print-Language
printMACAddress	Unicode String	Print-MAC-Address
printMaxCopies	Integer	Print-Max-Copies
printMaxResolutionSupported	Integer	Print-Max-Resolution-Supported
printMaxXExtent	Integer	Print-Max-X-Extent
printMaxYExtent	Integer	Print-Max-Y-Extent

(continued)

Table B-2 *(continued)*

Name	Syntax	Description
printMediaReady	Unicode String	Print-Media-Ready
printMediaSupported	Unicode String	Print-Media-Supported
printMemory	Integer	Print-Memory
printMinXExtent	Integer	Print-Min-X-Extent
printMinYExtent	Integer	Print-Min-Y-Extent
printNetworkAddress	Unicode String	Print-Network-Address
printNotify	Unicode String	Print-Notify
printNumberUp	Integer	Print-Number-Up
printOrientationsSupported	Unicode String	Print-Orientations-Supported
printOwner	Unicode String	Print-Owner
printPagesPerMinute	Integer	Print-Pages-Per-Minute
printRate	Integer	Print-Rate
printRateUnit	Unicode String	Print-Rate-Unit
printSeparatorFile	Unicode String	Print-Separator-File
printShareName	Unicode String	Print-Share-Name
printSpooling	Unicode String	Print-Spooling
printStaplingSupported	Boolean	Print-Stapling-Supported
printStartTime	Integer	Print-Start-Time
printStatus	Unicode String	Print-Status
priority	Integer	Priority
priorSetTime	Large Integer	Prior-Set-Time
priorValue	Octet String	Prior-Value
privateKey	Octet String	Private-Key
privilegeAttributes	Integer	Privilege-Attributes
privilegeDisplayName	Unicode String	Privilege-Display-Name
privilegeHolder	Distinguished Name	Privilege-Holder
privilegeValue	Large Integer	Privilege-Value
productCode	Octet String	Product-Code

Name	Syntax	Description
profilePath	Unicode String	Profile-Path
proxiedObjectName	DN Binary	Proxied-Object-Name
proxyAddresses	Unicode String	Proxy-Addresses
proxyGenerationEnabled	Boolean	Proxy-Generation-Enabled
proxyLifetime	Large Integer	Proxy-Lifetime
publicKeyPolicy	Octet String	Public-Key-Policy
purportedSearch	Unicode String	Purported-Search
pwdHistoryLength	Integer	Pwd-History-Length
pwdLastSet	Large Integer	Pwd-Last-Set
pwdProperties	Integer	Pwd-Properties
qualityOfService	Integer	Quality-Of-Service
queryFilter	Unicode String	Query-Filter
queryPoint	Unicode String	QueryPoint
queryPolicyBL	Distinguished Name	Query-Policy-BL
queryPolicyObject	Distinguished Name	Query-Policy-Object
rangeLower	Integer	Range-Lower
rangeUpper	Integer	Range-Upper
rDNAttID	Object Identifier	RDN-Att-ID
registeredAddress	Octet String	Registered-Address
remoteServerName	Unicode String	Remote-Server-Name
remoteSource	Unicode String	Remote-Source
remoteSourceType	Integer	Remote-Source-Type
remoteStorageGUID	Unicode String	Remote-Storage-GUID
replicaSource	Unicode String	Replica-Source
replInterval	Integer	Repl-Interval
replPropertyMetaData	Octet String	Repl-Property-Meta-Data
replTopologyStayOfExecution	Integer	Repl-Topology-Stay-Of-Execution
replUpToDateVector	Octet String	Repl-UpToDate-Vector

(continued)

Table B-2 *(continued)*

Name	Syntax	Description
repsFrom	Replica Link	Reps-From
repsTo	Replica Link	Reps-To
requiredCategories	Octet String	Required-Categories
retiredReplDSASignatures	Octet String	Retired-Repl-DSA-Signatures
revision	Integer	Revision
rid	Integer	Rid
rIDAllocationPool	Large Integer	RID-Allocation-Pool
rIDAvailablePool	Large Integer	RID-Available-Pool
rIDManagerReference	Distinguished Name	RID-Manager-Reference
rIDNextRID	Integer	RID-Next-RID
rIDPreviousAllocationPool	Large Integer	RID-Previous-Allocation-Pool
rIDSetReferences	Distinguished Name	RID-Set-References
rIDUsedPool	Large Integer	RID-Used-Pool
rightsGuid	Unicode String	Rights-Guid
roleOccupant	Distinguished Name	Role-Occupant
rootTrust	Distinguished Name	Root-Trust
rpcNsAnnotation	Unicode String	Rpc-Ns-Annotation
rpcNsBindings	Unicode String	Rpc-Ns-Bindings
rpcNsCodeset	Unicode String	Rpc-Ns-Codeset
rpcNsEntryFlags	Integer	Rpc-Ns-Entry-Flags
rpcNsGroup	Unicode String	Rpc-Ns-Group
rpcNsInterfaceID	Unicode String	Rpc-Ns-Interface-ID
rpcNsObjectID	Unicode String	Rpc-Ns-Object-ID
rpcNsPriority	Integer	Rpc-Ns-Priority
rpcNsProfileEntry	Unicode String	Rpc-Ns-Profile-Entry
rpcNsTransferSyntax	Unicode String	Rpc-Ns-Transfer-Syntax
sAMAccountName	Unicode String	SAM-Account-Name
sAMAccountType	Integer	SAM-Account-Type

Name	Syntax	Description
schedule	Octet String	Schedule
schemaFlagsEx	Integer	Schema-Flags-Ex
schemaIDGUID	Octet String	Schema-ID-GUID
schemaInfo	Octet String	Schema-Info
schemaUpdate	Generalized Time	Schema-Update
schemaVersion	Integer	Schema-Version
scopeFlags	Integer	Scope-Flags
scriptPath	Unicode String	Script-Path
sDRightsEffective	Integer	SD-Rights-Effective
searchFlags	Enumeration	Search-Flags
searchGuide	Octet String	Search-Guide
securityIdentifier	SID	Security-Identifier
seeAlso	Distinguished Name	See-Also
seqNotification	Integer	Seq-Notification
serialNumber	Print Case String	Serial-Number
serverName	Unicode String	Server-Name
serverReference	Distinguished Name	Server-Reference
serverReferenceBL	Distinguished Name	Server-Reference-BL
serverRole	Integer	Server-Role
serverState	Integer	Server-State
serviceBindingInformation	Unicode String	Service-Binding-Information
serviceClassID	Octet String	Service-Class-ID
serviceClassInfo	Octet String	Service-Class-Info
serviceClassName	Unicode String	Service-Class-Name
serviceDNSName	Unicode String	Service-DNS-Name
serviceDNSNameType	Unicode String	Service-DNS-Name-Type
serviceInstanceVersion	Octet String	Service-Instance-Version
servicePrincipalName	Unicode String	Service-Principal-Name

(continued)

Table B-2 *(continued)*

Name	Syntax	Description
setupCommand	Unicode String	Setup-Command
shellContextMenu	Unicode String	Shell-Context-Menu
shellPropertyPages	Unicode String	Shell-Property-Pages
shortServerName	Unicode String	Short-Server-Name
showInAddressBook	Distinguished Name	Show-In-Address-Book
showInAdvancedViewOnly	Boolean	Show-In-Advanced-View-Only
sIDHistory	SID	SID-History
signatureAlgorithms	Unicode String	Signature-Algorithms
siteGUID	Octet String	Site-GUID
siteLinkList	Distinguished Name	Site-Link-List
siteList	Distinguished Name	Site-List
siteObject	Distinguished Name	Site-Object
siteObjectBL	Distinguished Name	Site-Object-BL
siteServer	Distinguished Name	Site-Server
sn	Unicode String	Surname
sPNMappings	Unicode String	SPN-Mappings
st	Unicode String	State-Or-Province-Name
street	Unicode String	Street-Address
streetAddress	Unicode String	Address
subClassOf	Object Identifier	Sub-Class-Of
subRefs	Distinguished Name	Sub-Refs
subSchemaSubEntry	Distinguished Name	SubSchemaSubEntry
superiorDNSRoot	Unicode String	Superior-DNS-Root
superScopeDescription	Unicode String	Super-Scope-Description
superScopes	Print Case String	Super-Scopes
supplementalCredentials	Octet String	Supplemental-Credentials
supportedApplicationContext	Octet String	Supported-Application-Context

Name	Syntax	Description
syncAttributes	Integer	Sync-Attributes
syncMembership	Distinguished Name	Sync-Membership
syncWithObject	Distinguished Name	Sync-With-Object
syncWithSID	SID	Sync-With-SID
systemAuxiliaryClass	Object Identifier	System-Auxiliary-Class
systemFlags	Integer	System-Flags
systemMayContain	Object Identifier	System-May-Contain
systemMustContain	Object Identifier	System-Must-Contain
systemOnly	Boolean	System-Only
systemPossSuperiors	Object Identifier	System-Poss-Superiors
telephoneNumber	Unicode String	Telephone-Number
teletexTerminalIdentifier	Octet String	Teletex-Terminal-Identifier
telexNumber	Octet String	Telex-Number
templateRoots	Distinguished Name	Template-Roots
terminalServer	Octet String	Terminal-Server
textEncodedORAddress	Unicode String	Text-Encoded-OR-Address
thumbnailLogo	Octet String	Logo
thumbnailPhoto	Octet String	Picture
timeRefresh	Large Integer	Time-Refresh
timeVolChange	Large Integer	Time-Vol-Change
title	Unicode String	Title
tokenGroups	SID	Token-Groups
tokenGroupsNoGCAcceptable	SID	Token-Groups-No-GC-Acceptable
tombstoneLifetime	Integer	Tombstone-Lifetime
transportAddressAttribute	Object Identifier	Transport-Address-Attribute
transportDLLName	Unicode String	Transport-DLL-Name
transportType	Distinguished Name	Transport-Type

(continued)

Table B-2 *(continued)*

Name	Syntax	Description
treatAsLeaf	Boolean	Treat-As-Leaf
treeName	Unicode String	Tree-Name
trustAttributes	Integer	Trust-Attributes
trustAuthIncoming	Octet String	Trust-Auth-Incoming
trustAuthOutgoing	Octet String	Trust-Auth-Outgoing
trustDirection	Integer	Trust-Direction
trustParent	Distinguished Name	Trust-Parent
trustPartner	Unicode String	Trust-Partner
trustPosixOffset	Integer	Trust-Posix-Offset
trustType	Integer	Trust-Type
uASCompat	Integer	UAS-Compat
uNCName	Unicode String	UNC-Name
unicodePwd	Octet String	Unicode-Pwd
upgradeProductCode	Octet String	Upgrade-Product-Code
uPNSuffixes	Unicode String	UPN-Suffixes
url	Unicode String	WWW-Page-Other
userAccountControl	Integer	User-Account-Control
userCert	Octet String	User-Cert
userCertificate	Octet String	X509-Cert
userParameters	Unicode String	User-Parameters
userPassword	Octet String	User-Password
userPrincipalName	Unicode String	User-Principal-Name
userSharedFolder	Unicode String	User-Shared-Folder
userSharedFolderOther	Unicode String	User-Shared-Folder-Other
userSMIMECertificate	Octet String	User-SMIME-Certificate
userWorkstations	Unicode String	User-Workstations
uSNChanged	Large Integer	USN-Changed
uSNCreated	Large Integer	USN-Created

Name	Syntax	Description
uSNDSALastObjRemoved	Large Integer	USN-DSA-Last-Obj-Removed
USNIntersite	Integer	USN-Intersite
uSNLastObjRem	Large Integer	USN-Last-Obj-Rem
uSNSource	Large Integer	USN-Source
validAccesses	Integer	Valid-Accesses
vendor	Unicode String	Vendor
versionNumber	Integer	Version-Number
versionNumberHi	Integer	Version-Number-Hi
versionNumberLo	Integer	Version-Number-Lo
volTableGUID	Octet String	Vol-Table-GUID
volTableIdxGUID	Octet String	Vol-Table-Idx-GUID
volumeCount	Integer	Volume-Count
wbemPath	Unicode String	Wbem-Path
wellKnownObjects	DN Binary	Well-Known-Objects
whenChanged	Generalized Time	When-Changed
whenCreated	Generalized Time	When-Created
winsockAddresses	Octet String	Winsock-Addresses
wWWHomePage	Unicode String	WWW-Home-Page
x121Address	Numerical String	X121-Address

Table B-3	Attributes of the classSchema Object			
Name	**Type**	**System**	**Description**	**Source Class**
systemPossSuperiors	Optional	Yes	System-Poss-Superiors	classSchema
systemOnly	Optional	Yes	System-Only	classSchema
systemMustContain	Optional	Yes	System-Must-Contain	classSchema
systemMayContain	Optional	Yes	System-May-Contain	classSchema

(continued)

Table B-3 *(continued)*

Name	Type	System	Description	Source Class
systemAuxiliaryClass	Optional	Yes	System-Auxiliary-Class	classSchema
schemaFlagsEx	Optional	Yes	Schema-Flags-Ex	classSchema
rDNAttID	Optional	Yes	RDN-Att-ID	classSchema
possSuperiors	Optional	Yes	Poss-Superiors	classSchema
mustContain	Optional	Yes	Must-Contain	classSchema
mayContain	Optional	Yes	May-Contain	classSchema
lDAPDisplayName	Optional	Yes	LDAP-Display-Name	classSchema
isDefunct	Optional	Yes	Is-Defunct	classSchema
defaultSecurityDescriptor	Optional	Yes	Default-Security-Descriptor	classSchema
defaultHidingValue	Optional	Yes	Default-Hiding-Value	classSchema
classDisplayName	Optional	Yes	Class-Display-Name	classSchema
auxiliaryClass	Optional	Yes	Auxiliary-Class	classSchema
subClassOf	Mandatory	Yes	Sub-Class-Of	classSchema
schemaIDGUID	Mandatory	Yes	Schema-ID-GUID	classSchema
objectClassCategory	Mandatory	Yes	Object-Class-Category	classSchema
governsID	Mandatory	Yes	Governs-ID	classSchema
defaultObjectCategory	Mandatory	Yes	Default-Object-Category	classSchema
cn	Mandatory	Yes	Common-Name	classSchema
url	Optional	Yes	WWW-Page-Other	top
wWWHomePage	Optional	Yes	WWW-Home-Page	top

Name	Type	System	Description	Source Class
whenCreated	Optional	Yes	When-Created	top
whenChanged	Optional	Yes	When-Changed	top
wellKnownObjects	Optional	Yes	Well-Known-Objects	top
wbemPath	Optional	Yes	Wbem-Path	top
uSNSource	Optional	Yes	USN-Source	top
uSNLastObjRem	Optional	Yes	USN-Last-Obj-Rem	top
USNIntersite	Optional	Yes	USN-Intersite	top
uSNDSALastObjObjects	Optional	Yes	USN-DSA-Last-Obj-Removed	top
uSNCreated	Optional	Yes	USN-Created	top
uSNChanged	Optional	Yes	USN-Changed	top
systemFlags	Optional	Yes	System-Flags	top
subSchemaSubEntry	Optional	Yes	SubSchema-SubEntry	top
subRefs	Optional	Yes	Sub-Refs	top
siteObjectBL	Optional	Yes	Site-Object-BL	top
serverReferenceBL	Optional	Yes	Server-Reference-BL	top
sDRightsEffective	Optional	Yes	SD-Rights-Effective	top
revision	Optional	Yes	Revision	top
repsTo	Optional	Yes	Reps-To	top
repsFrom	Optional	Yes	Reps-From	top
directReports	Optional	Yes	Reports	top
replUpToDateVector	Optional	Yes	Repl-UpToDate-Vector	top
replPropertyMetaData	Optional	Yes	Repl-Property-Meta-Data	top

(continued)

Table B-3 *(continued)*

Name	Type	System	Description	Source Class
name	Optional	Yes	RDN	top
queryPolicyBL	Optional	Yes	Query-Policy-BL	top
proxyAddresses	Optional	Yes	Proxy-Addresses	top
proxiedObjectName	Optional	Yes	Proxied-Object-Name	top
possibleInferiors	Optional	Yes	Possible-Inferiors	top
partialAttributeSet	Optional	Yes	Partial-Attribute-Set	top
partialAttribute DeletionList	Optional	Yes	Partial-Attribute-Deletion-List	top
otherWell KnownObjects	Optional	Yes	Other-Well-Known-Objects	top
objectVersion	Optional	Yes	Object-Version	top
objectGUID	Optional	Yes	Object-Guid	top
distinguishedName	Optional	Yes	Obj-Dist-Name	top
nonSecurity MemberBL	Optional	Yes	Non-Security-Member-BL	top
netbootSCPBL	Optional	Yes	Netboot-SCP-BL	top
mS-DS-ConsistencyGuid	Optional	Yes	MS-DS-Consistency-Guid	top
mS-DS-ConsistencyChild Count	Optional	Yes	MS-DS-Consistency-Child-Count	top
modifyTimeStamp	Optional	Yes	Modify-Time-Stamp	top
masteredBy	Optional	Yes	Mastered-By	top
managedObjects	Optional	Yes	Managed-Objects	top
lastKnownParent	Optional	Yes	Last-Known-Parent	top

Name	Type	System	Description	Source Class
isPrivilegeHolder	Optional	Yes	Is-Privilege-Holder	top
memberOf	Optional	Yes	Is-Member-Of-DL	top
isDeleted	Optional	Yes	Is-Deleted	top
isCritical SystemObject	Optional	Yes	Is-Critical-System-Object	top
showInAdvanced ViewOnly	Optional	Yes	Show-In-Advanced-View-Only	top
fSMORoleOwner	Optional	Yes	FSMO-Role-Owner	top
fRSMember ReferenceBL	Optional	Yes	FRS-Member-Reference-BL	top
frsComputer ReferenceBL	Optional	Yes	Frs-Computer-Reference-BL	top
fromEntry	Optional	Yes	From-Entry	top
flags	Optional	Yes	Flags	top
extensionName	Optional	Yes	Extension-Name	top
dSASignature	Optional	Yes	DSA-Signature	top
dSCore PropagationData	Optional	Yes	DS-Core-Propagation-Data	top
displayName Printable	Optional	Yes	Display-Name-Printable	top
displayName	Optional	Yes	Display-Name	top
description	Optional	Yes	Description	top
createTimeStamp	Optional	Yes	Create-Time-Stamp	top
cn	Optional	Yes	Common-Name	top
canonicalName	Optional	Yes	Canonical-Name	top

(continued)

Table B-3 *(continued)*

Name	Type	System	Description	Source Class
bridgehead ServerListBL	Optional	Yes	Bridgehead-Server-List-BL	top
allowedChild-ClassesEffective	Optional	Yes	Allowed-Child-Classes-Effective	top
allowedChildClasses	Optional	Yes	Allowed-Child-Classes	top
allowedAttributes Effective	Optional	Yes	Allowed-Attributes-Effective	top
allowedAttributes	Optional	Yes	Allowed-Attributes	top
adminDisplayName	Optional	Yes	Admin-Display-Name	top
adminDescription	Optional	Yes	Admin-Description	top
objectClass	Mandatory	Yes	Object-Class	top
objectCategory	Mandatory	Yes	Object-Category	top
nTSecurityDescriptor	Mandatory	Yes	NT-Security-Descriptor	top
instanceType	Mandatory	Yes	Instance-Type	top

Table B-4 Attributes of the `attributeSchema` Object

Name	Type	System	Description	Source Class
systemOnly	Optional	Yes	System-Only	attributeSchema
searchFlags	Optional	Yes	Search-Flags	attributeSchema
schemaFlagsEx	Optional	Yes	Schema-Flags-Ex	attributeSchema
rangeUpper	Optional	Yes	Range-Upper	attributeSchema
rangeLower	Optional	Yes	Range-Lower	attributeSchema
oMObjectClass	Optional	Yes	OM-Object-Class	attributeSchema

Name	Type	System	Description	Source Class
mAPIID	Optional	Yes	MAPI-ID	attributeSchema
linkID	Optional	Yes	Link-ID	attributeSchema
isMemberOfPartial AttributeSet	Optional	Yes	Is-Member-Of-Partial-Attribute-Set	attributeSchema
isEphemeral	Optional	Yes	Is-Ephemeral	attributeSchema
isDefunct	Optional	Yes	Is-Defunct	attributeSchema
extendedChars Allowed	Optional	Yes	Extended-Chars-Allowed	attributeSchema
classDisplayName	Optional	Yes	Class-Display-Name	attributeSchema
attributeSecurity GUID	Optional	Yes	Attribute-Security-GUID	attributeSchema
schemaIDGUID	Mandatory	Yes	Schema-ID-GUID	attributeSchema
oMSyntax	Mandatory	Yes	OM-Syntax	attributeSchema
lDAPDisplayName	Mandatory	Yes	LDAP-Display-Name	attributeSchema
isSingleValued	Mandatory	Yes	Is-Single-Valued	attributeSchema
cn	Mandatory	Yes	Common-Name	attributeSchema
attributeSyntax	Mandatory	Yes	Attribute-Syntax	attributeSchema
attributeID	Mandatory	Yes	Attribute-ID	attributeSchema
url	Optional	Yes	WWW-Page-Other	top
wWWHomePage	Optional	Yes	WWW-Home-Page	top
whenCreated	Optional	Yes	When-Created	top
whenChanged	Optional	Yes	When-Changed	top
wellKnownObjects	Optional	Yes	Well-Known-Objects	top
wbemPath	Optional	Yes	Wbem-Path	top
uSNSource	Optional	Yes	USN-Source	top
uSNLastObjRem	Optional	Yes	USN-Last-Obj-Rem	top

(continued)

Table B-4 *(continued)*

Name	Type	System	Description	Source Class
USNIntersite	Optional	Yes	USN-Intersite	top
uSNDSALastObjRemoved	Optional	Yes	USN-DSA-Last-Obj-Removed	top
uSNCreated	Optional	Yes	USN-Created	top
uSNChanged	Optional	Yes	USN-Changed	top
systemFlags	Optional	Yes	System-Flags	top
subSchemaSubEntry	Optional	Yes	SubSchema-SubEntry	top
subRefs	Optional	Yes	Sub-Refs	top
siteObjectBL	Optional	Yes	Site-Object-BL	top
serverReferenceBL	Optional	Yes	Server-Reference-BL	top
sDRightsEffective	Optional	Yes	SD-Rights-Effective	top
revision	Optional	Yes	Revision	top
repsTo	Optional	Yes	Reps-To	top
repsFrom	Optional	Yes	Reps-From	top
directReports	Optional	Yes	Reports	top
replUpToDateVector	Optional	Yes	Repl-UpToDate-Vector	top
replPropertyMetaData	Optional	Yes	Repl-Property-Meta-Data	top
name	Optional	Yes	RDN	top
queryPolicyBL	Optional	Yes	Query-Policy-BL	top
proxyAddresses	Optional	Yes	Proxy-Addresses	top
proxiedObjectName	Optional	Yes	Proxied-Object-Name	top
possibleInferiors	Optional	Yes	Possible-Inferiors	top
partialAttributeSet	Optional	Yes	Partial-Attribute-Set	top

Name	Type	System	Description	Source Class
partialAttribute DeletionList	Optional	Yes	Partial-Attribute-Deletion-List	top
otherWellKnown Objects	Optional	Yes	Other-Well-Known-Objects	top
objectVersion	Optional	Yes	Object-Version	top
objectGUID	Optional	Yes	Object-Guid	top
distinguishedName	Optional	Yes	Obj-Dist-Name	top
nonSecurity MemberBL	Optional	Yes	Non-Security-Member-BL	top
netbootSCPBL	Optional	Yes	Netboot-SCP-BL	top
mS-DS-ConsistencyGuid	Optional	Yes	MS-DS-Consistency-Guid	top
mS-DS-Consistency ChildCount	Optional	Yes	MS-DS-Consistency-Child-Count	top
modifyTimeStamp	Optional	Yes	Modify-Time-Stamp	top
masteredBy	Optional	Yes	Mastered-By	top
managedObjects	Optional	Yes	Managed-Objects	top
lastKnownParent	Optional	Yes	Last-Known-Parent	top
isPrivilegeHolder	Optional	Yes	Is-Privilege-Holder	top
memberOf	Optional	Yes	Is-Member-Of-DL	top
isDeleted	Optional	Yes	Is-Deleted	top
isCritical SystemObject	Optional	Yes	Is-Critical-System-Object	top
showInAdvanced ViewOnly	Optional	Yes	Show-In-Advanced-View-Only	top
fSMORoleOwner	Optional	Yes	FSMO-Role-Owner	top
fRSMember ReferenceBL	Optional	Yes	FRS-Member-Reference-BL	top

(continued)

Table B-4 *(continued)*

Name	Type	System	Description	Source Class
frsComputer ReferenceBL	Optional	Yes	Frs-Computer-Reference-BL	top
fromEntry	Optional	Yes	From-Entry	top
flags	Optional	Yes	Flags	top
extensionName	Optional	Yes	Extension-Name	top
dSASignature	Optional	Yes	DSA-Signature	top
dSCore PropagationData	Optional	Yes	DS-Core-Propagation-Data	top
displayName Printable	Optional	Yes	Display-Name-Printable	top
displayName	Optional	Yes	Display-Name	top
description	Optional	Yes	Description	top
createTimeStamp	Optional	Yes	Create-Time-Stamp	top
cn	Optional	Yes	Common-Name	top
canonicalName	Optional	Yes	Canonical-Name	top
bridgehead ServerListBL	Optional	Yes	Bridgehead-Server-List-BL	top
allowedChildClasses Effective	Optional	Yes	Allowed-Child-Classes Effective	top
allowedChild Classes	Optional	Yes	Allowed-Child-Classes	top
allowedAttributes Effective	Optional	Yes	Allowed-Attributes-Effective	top
allowedAttributes	Optional	Yes	Allowed-Attributes	top
adminDisplayName	Optional	Yes	Admin-Display-Name	top

Name	Type	System	Description	Source Class
adminDescription	Optional	Yes	Admin-Description	top
objectClass	Mandatory	Yes	Object-Class	top
objectCategory	Mandatory	Yes	Object-Category	top
nTSecurityDescriptor	Mandatory	Yes	NT-Security-Descriptor	top
instanceType	Mandatory	Yes	Instance-Type	top

Appendix C

Country and State Codes

● ●

*T*he country and state codes listed in this appendix can help you as you devise naming conventions for your namespace. (Refer to Chapters 3 and 4 for additional information on creating a namespace.) These codes are widely accepted standards that are commonly used in DNS and domain naming.

Table C-1		ISO Country Codes	
Country	*Code*	*Country*	*Code*
Afghanistan	AFG	Bangladesh	BGD
Albania	ALB	Barbados	BRB
Algeria	DZA	Belarus	BLR
American Samoa	ASM	Belgium	BEL
Andorra	AND	Belize	BLZ
Angola	AGO	Benin	BEN
Anguilla	AIA	Bermuda	BMU
Antarctica	ATA	Bhutan	BTN
Antigua and Barbuda	ATG	Bolivia	BOL
Argentina	ARG	Bosnia-Herzegovina	BIH
Armenia	ARM	Botswana	BWA
Aruba	ABW	Bouvet Island	BVT
Australia	AUS	Brazil	BRA
Austria	AUT	British Indian Ocean Territory	IOT
Azerbaijan	AZE	Brunei Darussalam	BRN
Bahamas	BHS	Bulgaria	BGR
Bahrain	BHR	Burkina Faso	BFA

(continued)

Table C-1 *(continued)*

Country	Code	Country	Code
Burundi	BDI	East Timor	TMP
Cambodia	KHM	Ecuador	ECU
Cameroon	CMR	Egypt	EGY
Canada	CAN	El Salvador	SLV
Cape Verde	CPV	Equatorial Guinea	GNQ
Cayman Islands	CYM	Eritrea	ETI
Central African Republic	CAF	Estonia	EST
Chad	TCD	Ethiopia	ETH
Chile	CHL	Falkland Islands (Malvinas)	FLK
China	CHN	Faroe Islands	FRO
Christmas Island	CXR	Fiji	FJI
Cocos (Keeling) Islands	CCK	Finland	FIN
Colombia	COL	France	FRA
Comoros	COM	France, Metropolitan	FXX
Congo	COG	French Guiana	GUF
Congo, The Democratic Republic of the	COD	French Polynesia	PYF
Cook Islands	COK	French Southern Territories	ATF
Costa Rica	CRI	Gabon	GAB
Côte d'Ivoire	CIV	Gambia	GMB
Croatia	HRV	Georgia	GEO
Cuba	CUB	Germany	DEU
Cyprus	CYP	Ghana	GHA
Czech Republic	CZE	Gibraltar	GIB
Denmark	DNK	Greece	GRC
Djibouti	DJI	Greenland	GRL
Dominica	DMA	Grenada	GRD
Dominican Republic	DOM	Guadeloupe	GLP

Country	Code	Country	Code
Guam	GUM	Korea, Republic of	KOR
Guatemala	GTM	Kuwait	KWT
Guinea	GIN	Kyrgyzstan	KGZ
Guinea-Bissau	GNB	Lao People's Democratic Republic	LAO
Guyana	GUY	Latvia	LVA
Haiti	HTI	Lebanon	LBN
Heard and McDonald Islands	HMD	Lesotho	LSO
Holy See (Vatican City State)	VAT	Liberia	LBR
Honduras	HND	Libyan Arab Jamahiriya	LBY
Hong Kong	HKG	Liechtenstein	LIE
Hungary	HUN	Lithuania	LTU
Iceland	ISL	Luxembourg	LUX
India	IND	Macau	MAC
Indonesia	IDN	Macedonia, The Former Yugoslav Republic of	MKD
Iran, Islamic Republic of	IRN	Madagascar	MDG
Iraq	IRQ	Malawi	MWI
Ireland	IRL	Malaysia	MYS
Israel	ISR	Maldives	MDV
Italy	ITA	Mali	MLI
Jamaica	JAM	Malta	MLT
Japan	JPN	Marshall Islands	MHL
Jordan	JOR	Martinique	MTQ
Kazakhstan	KAZ	Mauritania	MRT
Kenya	KEN	Mauritius	MUS
Kiribati	KIR	Mayotte	MYT
Korea, Democratic People's Republic of	PRK	Mexico	MEX

(continued)

Table C-1 *(continued)*

Country	Code	Country	Code
Micronesia, Federated States of	FSM	Paraguay	PRY
Moldova, Republic of	MDA	Peru	PER
Monaco	MCO	Philippines	PHL
Mongolia	MNG	Pitcairn	PCN
Montserrat	MSR	Poland	POL
Morocco	MAR	Portugal	PRT
Mozambique	MOZ	Puerto Rico	PRI
Myanmar	MMR	Qatar	QAT
Namibia	NAM	Reunion	REU
Nauru	NRU	Romania	ROM
Nepal	NPL	Russian Federation	RUS
Netherlands	NLD	Rwanda	RWA
Netherlands Antilles	ANT	Saint Kitts and Nevis	KNA
New Caledonia	NCL	Saint Lucia	LCA
New Zealand	NZL	Saint Vincent and the Grenadines	VCT
Nicaragua	NIC	Samoa	WSM
Niger	NER	San Marino	SMR
Nigeria	NGA	São Tomé and Principe	STP
Niue	NIU	Saudi Arabia	SAU
Norfolk Island	NFK	Senegal	SEN
Northern Mariana Islands	MNP	Seychelles	SYC
Norway	NOR	Sierra Leone	SLE
Oman	OMN	Singapore	SGP
Pakistan	PAK	Slovakia (Slovak Republic)	SVK
Palau	PLW	Slovenia	SVN
Panama	PAN	Solomon Islands	SLB
Papua New Guinea	PNG	Somalia	SOM

Country	Code	Country	Code
South Africa	ZAF	Uganda	UGA
South Georgia and the South Sandwich Islands	SGS	Ukraine	UKR
Spain	ESP	United Arab Emirates	ARE
Sri Lanka	LKA	United Kingdom	GBR
St. Helena	SHN	United States	USA
St. Pierre and Miquelon	SPM	U.S. Minor Outlying Islands	UMI
Sudan	SDN	Uruguay	URY
Suriname	SUR	Uzbekistan	UZB
Svalbard and Jan Mayen Islands	SJM	Vanuatu	VUT
Swaziland	SWZ	Venezuela	VEN
Sweden	SWE	Viet Nam	VNM
Switzerland	CHE	Virgin Islands (British)	VGB
Syrian Arab Republic	SYR	Virgin Islands (U.S.)	VIR
Taiwan, Province of China	TWN	Wallis and Futuna Islands	WLF
Tajikistan	TJK	Western Sahara	ESH
Tanzania, United Republic of	TZA	Yemen	YEM
Thailand	THA	Yugoslavia	YUG
Togo	TGO	Zambia	ZMB
Tokelau	TKL	Zimbabwe	ZWE
Tonga	TON		
Trinidad and Tobago	TTO		
Tunisia	TUN		
Turkey	TUR		
Turkmenistan	TKM		
Turks and Caicos Islands	TCA		
Tuvalu	TUV		

Table C-2		U.S. Postal State Abbreviations	
State	*Code*	*State*	*Code*
Alabama	AL	Nevada	NV
Alaska	AK	New Hampshire	NH
Arizona	AZ	New Jersey	NJ
Arkansas	AR	New Mexico	NM
California	CA	New York	NY
Colorado	CO	North Carolina	NC
Connecticut	CT	North Dakota	ND
Delaware	DE	Ohio	OH
District of Columbia	DC	Oklahoma	OK
Florida	FL	Oregon	OR
Georgia	GA	Pennsylvania	PA
Hawaii	HI	Puerto Rico	PR
Idaho	ID	Rhode Island	RI
Illinois	IL	South Carolina	SC
Indiana	IN	South Dakota	SD
Iowa	IA	Tennessee	TN
Kansas	KS	Texas	TX
Kentucky	KY	Utah	UT
Louisiana	LA	Vermont	VT
Maine	ME	Virginia	VA
Maryland	MD	Washington	WA
Massachusetts	MA	West Virginia	WV
Michigan	MI	Wisconsin	WI
Minnesota	MN	Wyoming	WY
Mississippi	MS		
Missouri	MO		
Montana	MT		
Nebraska	NE		

Appendix D

Glossary

Reading along about Active Directory and then suddenly running into a term with which you're not familiar can be quite distracting and frustrating. It can really put a crimp in your learning curve.

I'm providing this glossary as a quick guide to the new terms that you run across in this book. By using this handy reference, you don't have to go digging around in various chapters to find the definition you're seeking.

Words appearing in *italics* within a definition refer to terms that I define elsewhere in this glossary.

Access Control Entry (ACE)

The individual items of an *Access Control List (ACL)*. Each entry in the ACL is known as an Access Control Entry, or ACE. Access Control Entries specify which users can access the resource and what access permissions (read/write, read-only, and so on) the user may exercise.

Access Control List (ACL)

An ACL details which users may access a network resource. (See also *Access Control Entry*.)

Account domain

In a Windows NT *single-master domain model* or *multiple-master domain model*, the master domain contains domain-user accounts and so is known as the account domain.

Active Directory Services Interface (ADSI)

The programming interface that applications use to access the Active Directory.

American National Standards Institute (ANSI)

A nonprofit organization that coordinates voluntary standardization efforts within the United States.

Application programming interface (API)

The programming interface that applications use to send requests to the operating system.

Attribute

A parameter describing an *object*. Objects consist of required attributes and optional attributes.

Authentication

The process of validating a user's ID and password and granting access to network resources.

Bandwidth

The amount of data that you transmit over a communications channel in a particular amount of time, usually one second. Available bandwidth on a network refers to the amount of bandwidth available for use, excluding normal network traffic.

Bindery

A flat-file database in NetWare that contains security information. It was used in earlier versions of NetWare, and many organizations still use bindery mode for backward compatibility with NetWare 3 servers.

Bridgehead server

One server within a *site* that handles all intersite directory *replication*. This server compresses and replicates to other sites all directory updates. In turn, the bridgehead server receives directory updates from all other sites. After the bridgehead server receives the updates, it replicates those updates to the other *domain controllers* in the site.

Canonical name

A *DNS* resource record identifying a nickname or alias given to a network host.

Child domain

Subordinate *domains* that branch downward from the *root,* or *parent,* domain.

Circular log

Log files record system events or transactions. A circular log file overwrites existing entries after the log file reaches a specified size or age. You can set Windows NT event log files, for example, to overwrite information after seven days.

Complete-trust model

One of the four methods in Windows NT that you use to group *domains* for administrative purposes. This model can be an administrator's nightmare. Every domain in the complete-trust model *trusts* every other domain. In a structure consisting of more than three or four domains, administration becomes very time-consuming. The complete-trust model is sometimes known as the full-mesh model.

Container

An Active Directory *object* that holds other objects and containers. *Sites, domains,* and *organizational units (OUs)* are all containers.

Cost

In the context of Active Directory sites, *cost* is a measurement that the system administrator assigns to each *site link*. The cost value helps Active Directory determine which site link is a primary route (assigned a low cost, such as 1) and which is a secondary route (assigned a higher cost, such as 100) between *sites.*

Cross-link trust

A relationship that you establish to shorten the path between *domains* in the same *forest.* These relationships are *transitive trusts* that you manually create.

Datastore

A database file.

Data table

Stores all the specific data in Active Directory about users, groups, printers, and so on.

Defragmenting

The process by which the database file rearranges the pages of the file into a more compact format. This process is very similar to what you go through if you defragment the hard drive of your PC.

Digital certificate

An electronic ID card that verifies a user's credentials so that the user can communicate with network resources.

Directory-enabled network (DEN)

A network containing devices (routers and switches) that can take advantage of the Active Directory service. In a directory-enabled network, administrators can create policies that control configuration of network devices.

Distinguished name (DN)

An X.500-based naming convention that uses particular abbreviations to define the path leading to an Active Directory *object*. The path DC=com/DC=corp/CN=Users/CN=User1, for example, is a distinguished name.

Distributed application

Applications that run on computers spread throughout the network.

DNS table

A listing of *resource records* that match a host's *IP* address to its name. Together, these resource records make up the DNS table that the *Domain Name Service (DNS)* references.

Domain

Within Active Directory, a boundary encompassing Active Directory *objects* for security or administrative purposes.

Domain controller (DC)

A server that authenticates users seeking access to the *domain*.

Domain Name Service (DNS)

A network's name-resolution service. A network client uses DNS while searching for a host's *IP* address. DNS can determine the IP address from the host's name.

Dynamic DNS (DDNS)

Dynamic DNS enables hosts to update the *DNS table* with host names and addresses as they are added to the network.

Explicit trust

A one-way relationship, which means that Tree A can access the resources of Tree B, but Tree B can't access the resources of Tree A.

Extensible

You can add to or expand it. The Active Directory database, for example, is extensible because it can be expanded to include new network *objects*.

Extensible Storage Engine (ESE)

The Microsoft database engine on which Active Directory is based.

External trust

A relationship that the system administrator creates for *domain* users to access resources in a domain outside a *tree* or *forest*, between other Windows 2000 domain trees and forests, or between a Windows 2000 domain and a Windows NT domain. External trusts are always one-way, *nontransitive trusts*.

Fault tolerance

Redundant components that you configure to prevent lost data or services in the event of a system crash or network outage.

Flexible Single Master Operation (FSMO)

The master copy of data for service changes that can take place on only one *domain controller* at a time. The first domain controller on-line is the operations master, and the arrangement is known as the Flexible Single Master Operation (FSMO).

Forest

A grouping of domain *trees* that you join together by *transitive-trust* relationships. The domain trees are separate *namespaces* rather than a contiguous namespace. Corp.com and xyz.com, for example, are both separate namespaces, but you can join them by transitive trusts to form a forest.

Fragmentation

Just as disk drives become fragmented as you add and remove files, databases become fragmented as you move data in and out. If the database is fragmented, it takes up more disk space and isn't as efficient. The system administrator then uses a database utility to *defragment* the database.

Fully qualified domain name (FQDN)

The entire path leading to a network *object* is its fully qualified domain name. User1.namerica.corp.com, for example, is a FQDN.

Functional model

A method that you use for designing an Active Directory structure that you can adapt to a variety of organization charts. By using a functional model, you may group *domains* by department, division, or project.

Garbage collection

Active Directory's automated database cleanup that occurs, by default, every 12 hours and takes care of deleting old log files and *tombstones* and *defragmenting* the database file.

Geographic model

A popular method that you use for designing an Active Directory structure for an organization with specific geographic boundaries, such as a company with international divisions. Administrative functions within one location function separately from those in other locations.

Global catalog

A searchable index that enables users to search for network *objects* without knowing their *domain* locations. The global catalog is a partial replica of the Active Directory.

Group policy

User and computer settings that apply to a specific group of users within a *site,* a *domain,* or an *OU* on the network.

Group Policy Object (GPO)

A Group Policy Object is a set of user and computer configuration settings that you store as an *object* in the Active Directory. You apply the policy settings to computers within a *site,* a *domain,* or an *OU* to impose settings on the user or the computer.

Hierarchical

A logical, top-down structure.

Inheritance

In a *tree* hierarchy, *parent domains* and *OUs* pass along properties, such as *GPOs* and permissions, to their *child domains*. This process is known as inheritance.

Installation

In the context of Active Directory, loading Windows 2000 Server onto a partition that doesn't currently hold an operating system. Sometimes known as a fresh build.

Internet Engineering Task Force (IETF)

An Internet standards governing organization.

Internet Protocol (IP)

A protocol that you use to address and route packets to network destinations.

Intersite replication

Directory updates between *domain controllers* in different *sites*.

Intrasite replication

Directory updates between *domain controllers* in the same *site*.

Kerberos

The default security-authentication protocol in Windows 2000.

Key Distribution Center (KDC)

A *Kerberos* security service running on *domain controllers*. It gives out tickets and keys to control resource access on the network.

Leaf

An Active Directory *object* that, unlike a container object, can't contain other objects. Printers and users are examples of leaf objects.

Lightweight Directory Access Protocol (LDAP)

An Internet standard that enables Web browsers to find and access information in a directory service database. LDAP is based on the X.500 Directory Access Protocol (DAP) but is more efficient and more widely used.

Link table

Stores links between *objects* and *attributes* in the Active Directory.

Logical structure

The conceptual framework for Active Directory in which you match the Active Directory configuration to the business processes of a corporation or organization.

Mixed mode

A network operating with a mixture of Windows 2000 servers and NT 3.51 or 4.0 servers in the same *domain*.

Multiple-master domain model

One of the four methods in Windows NT that you use to group *domains* for administrative purposes. This model is very similar to the *single-master domain model*. The usual configuration consists of two *account domains* and multiple *resource domains*. The resource domains *trust* the account domains, and both account domains trust each other.

Namespace

A *logically structured* naming convention in which all *objects* are contiguous, or connected in an unbroken sequence. All the names within a *namespace* share the same *root domain*.

Native mode

A network in which all *domain* servers are running Windows 2000.

Nested containers

A *container* inside a container is a nested container.

Nontransitive trust

The type of *trust relationship* found between Windows NT *domains*. If Domain A trusts Domain B, and Domain B trusts Domain C, this relationship doesn't imply that Domain A also trusts Domain C. The trust between Domains A and B is *explicit* to those domains and Domain C doesn't inherit that trust just because B trusts C. In this scenario, the system administrator needs to provide Domain A with a specific trust relationship with Domain C for such a relationship to exist between these two domains.

Object

A user, group, printer, or any other Active Directory component with descriptive parameters or *attributes*.

Object class

A set of mandatory *attributes* and optional attributes that combine to define a particular class of Active Directory *objects*. A user is one object class and a printer is another. Object classes are sometimes known as *schema objects* or metadata.

Object identifiers

Dotted decimal numbers that the *American National Standards Institute (ANSI)* assigns to each *object class* and *attribute*. ANSI assigns a specific root identifier to a U.S. corporation, and the corporation then assigns variations of its root identifier to the *objects* and attributes that it creates.

Open Database Connectivity (ODBC)

A Microsoft interface for accessing data from relational and nonrelational database management systems.

Open-file backup

The process of backing up database information while the database remains online.

Organizational unit (OU)

A logical *container* within a *domain* that you use to organize *objects* for easier administration and access. A domain contains OUs. They can't span multiple domains nor can they contain objects from other domains.

Parent-child trust

A *transitive trust* relationship between a parent *container* and its child container.

Parent domain

A *domain* with subordinate domains. The *root* of the *tree* is a parent domain. See *root domain*.

Physical structure

A framework for Active Directory that encompasses the network configuration, network devices, and network *bandwidth*.

Propagating updates

The process of forcing *replication* — the exchange of database information between the *domain controllers* within a *domain* — to occur.

Relative distinguished name (RDN)

The portion of an *object*'s name that is distinct from the object's path. The RDN is an X.500-based convention that is a kind of subset to the *distinguished name (DN)* convention. A relative distinguished name is sometimes known simply as a relative name. User1.namerica.corp.com, for example, is a distinguished name. The relative distinguished name is simply user1.

Replication

The periodic exchange of database information between the *domain controllers* within a *domain,* which ensures that all domain controllers contain updated, consistent data.

Replication latency

The time frame between the beginning and end of *replication* to all *domain controllers,* which can result in the directory information between domain controllers being temporarily out of synch.

Resource domain

In a Windows NT *domain* model, you group resources together — computers, printers, servers, and so on — into resource domains that have *trust relationships* with account domains. You group user accounts into *account domains*.

Resource record

Resource records are individual *DNS* entries in the DNS database that clients use to access *domain* services. An Active Directory server, for example, has an SRV (service) record in its DNS entry. Clients use the SRV record to locate an Active Directory server.

Root domain

The first *domain* that you create in your Active Directory structure. The root domain is the topmost level of your domain.

Safe mode

A method of starting Windows 2000 Server without the networking components. The system loads only basic drivers. You use this mode for troubleshooting the computer.

Schema

Definitions of all *object classes* or *object* categories and their *attributes* that are stored in the Active Directory.

Schema cache

The copy of Active Directory that loads into memory each time a computer running Active Directory boots up. The schema cache serves as a performance enhancement by storing the information in RAM, which provides faster access than reading from disk.

Security Accounts Manager (SAM)

The Windows NT database that contains user accounts and related security information.

Security Identifier (SID)

A unique identification number for an *object* on the network. Users, groups, and resources all have a unique SID that distinguishes them from all other objects.

Sequential log

A log that records service transactions and events in the order in which they occur. Unlike a *circular log* file, the information in a sequential log file isn't overwritten when the log file reaches a certain size or age. If the sequential log file fills, it creates a new log file or the service halts, depending on how you configure the service.

Session ticket

Encrypted information that the server examines to validate the client as an authenticated *domain* member. If a domain client requests access to a server resource, the *Key Distribution Center* returns a session ticket to the client computer. The server then determines whether to validate the client for access to that resource.

Single domain model

One of the four methods in Windows NT that you use to group *domains* for administrative purposes. In the single domain model, all servers, users, and other resources reside within one domain. The domain contains a single primary domain controller (PDC) and one or more backup domain controllers (BDC), depending on the size of the domain and its geographic makeup.

Single-master domain model

One of the four methods in Windows NT that you use to group *domains* for administrative purposes. A single-master domain model groups user accounts and groups into one domain, usually known as the *account domain,* and groups printers and servers into *resource domains*. One-way *trust relationships* enable users to access resources in all the account domains (subject to access rights, of course). This model is suitable for all but the largest corporations.

Site

A grouping of *IP subnets* connected by high-speed or high-*bandwidth* links. Sites are part of your network's physical *topology*.

Site link

A connection between two *sites* over which *replication* occurs.

Site link bridge

A connector between two *site links*. A site link bridge essentially creates a *replication* path among available site links.

Subdomain

See *child domain*.

Subnet

A portion of a segmented network.

Synchronization

Adjusting disparate directory services so that they're in tune or their database information matches.

Ticket Granting Ticket (TGT)

A *Kerberos object* that contains authentication information and key information for accessing resources. Whenever a user authenticates, the *Key Distribution Center* sends a Ticket Granting Ticket (TGT) with authentication information. The client caches the TGT until it needs to access a *domain* resource and then presents the TGT and requests access to the resource.

Tombstone

An *object* that you mark for removal from the database. Suppose, for example, that you remove several computers from the *domain*. You tombstone each computer object to show that it's obsolete. Each tombstoned object remains in the database for 60 days from the time you mark it.

Topology

The physical shape or design of a network. Bus, ring, and star are all network topologies.

Transitive trust

Bidirectional trust relationship between two *domains* that extends to other trusted domains in the domain *tree*.

Tree

Hierarchical grouping of *domains* within a contiguous *namespace*.

Tree-root trust

The _transitive trust_ relationship between two _trees_ in a _forest_.

Trust relationship (or trust)

The method that Windows NT uses to join separate _domains_ into an administrative model. A Windows NT trust relationship enables users in one domain to access resources in another domain without merging administrative control of the two domains.

Windows NT trust relationships are one-way only, meaning that the trust works in only one direction. One domain, the trusted domain, holds the users who require access. The second, or trusting domain, holds resources that the users in the trusted domain want to access. For both domains to trust each other, you must create a second trust relationship.

NT administrators create trust relationships between specific domains — they don't exist by default if you create multiple domains. Active Directory, however, automatically creates _transitive trusts_ that are bidirectional rather than one way between domains, so the system administrator no longer has to create them.

Upgrade

In the context of Active Directory, loading Windows 2000 Server over an existing operating system, thus overwriting the previous operating system's system files.

User principal name (UPN)

The portion of an _object_'s name that's generally recognized as an e-mail address. The UPN consists of the user's logon name and the name of the _domain_ in which the user object resides.

Appendix E

About the CD

*O*n the CD-ROM:

- ✔ Visio Professional 5.0 Test Drive, 60-day evaluation version, a diagramming application that helps you create professional looking flowcharts, network diagrams, organization charts, and other business diagrams.

- ✔ Visio Enterprise 5.0 Test Drive, 60-day evaluation version. Visio Enterprise is based on Visio Professional but provides the AutoDiscovery feature to help you "discover" the devices on your network. Visio Enterprise includes 14,000 exact-replica network equipment shapes to help you accurately and professionally create network diagrams.

- ✔ The Visio drawings I created for this text. (My Visio drawings were the basis of the final line art you see in the book.)

- ✔ DirectMigrate 2000 from Entevo, demo version, a powerful migration tool for a painless enterprise class migration from Windows NT to Windows 2000.

- ✔ EtherPeek 4.0 and TokenPeek, trial versions, powerful network traffic and protocol analysis tools.

- ✔ EtherHelp and TokenHelp, trial versions, feature-rich remote packet capture utilities that interface with EtherPeek and TokenPeek to help you plan and design your network.

- ✔ NetSense for EtherPeek and TokenPeek, trial version, a tool that performs expert analysis of the traffic captured by EtherPeek and TokenPeek for statistical representation of your network traffic.

System Requirements

Make sure that your computer meets the minimum system requirements provided in the following list. If your computer doesn't match up to most of these requirements, you may have problems using the contents of the CD.

- ✔ A PC with a Pentium/166 processor or higher.
- ✔ Microsoft Windows 95, Windows 98, Windows NT 4.0 with Service Pack 3 or higher, or Windows 2000.
- ✔ At least 128MB of total RAM installed on your computer.
- ✔ At least 450MB of hard drive space available to install all the software from this CD. (You need less space if you don't install every program.)
- ✔ A CD-ROM drive — quad-speed (4x) or faster.
- ✔ A monitor capable of displaying at least 256 colors or grayscale.

If you need more information on the basics, check out *PCs For Dummies,* 6th Edition, by Dan Gooking, or *Windows 98 For Dummies* or *Windows 95 For Dummies,* 2nd Edition, by Andy Rathbone (all published by IDG Books Worldwide, Inc.).

Using the CD with Microsoft Windows

To install the items from the CD to your hard drive, follow these steps.

1. **Insert the CD into your computer's CD-ROM drive.**

   Give your computer a moment to take a look at the CD.

2. **When the light on your CD-ROM drive goes out, double-click the My Computer icon (it's probably in the top-left corner of your desktop).**

   This action opens the My Computer window, which shows you all the drives attached to your computer, the Control Panel, and a couple of other handy things.

3. **Double-click the icon for your CD-ROM drive.**

   Another window opens, showing you all the folders and files on the CD.

4. **Double-click the file called License.txt.**

   This file contains the end-user license that you agree to by using the CD. When you are done reading the license, close the program, most likely Notepad, that displayed the file.

5. **Double-click the file called Readme.txt.**

This file contains instructions about installing the software from this CD. It might be helpful to leave this text file open while you're using the CD.

6. **Double-click the folder for the software you are interested in.**

Be sure to read the descriptions of the programs in the next section of this appendix (much of this information also shows up in the Readme file). These descriptions will give you more precise information about the programs' folder names and about finding and running the installer program.

7. **To install programs to your computer, find the file called Setup.exe, Install.exe, or something similar, and double-click that file.**

The program's installer will walk you through the process of setting up your new software.

What You'll Find

Shareware programs are fully functional, free trial versions of copyrighted programs. If you prefer a particular program, register with that program's author, pay a nominal fee, and receive licenses, enhanced versions, and technical support for the program. **Freeware** programs are free, copyrighted games, applications, and utilities. You can copy freeware programs — for free — to as many PCs as you like, but be aware that freeware programs usually have no technical support. **GNU** software is governed by a General Public License (GPL), which is included inside the folder of the GNU software. The only restriction for using or distributing GNU software is a big one — you can't restrict anyone else's use of the GNU software. (See the GPL for more details.) Trials, demos, or evaluation versions are usually limited, either by time (30 days from installation, for example) or functionality (such as not being able to print or save your projects).

The following sections provide a summary of the software on this CD, arranged by category.

Diagramming Tools

Visio Test Drive, from Visio Corporation
For Windows 95, 98, and NT. 60-day evaluation version.

Note: The 60-day evaluation period begins at the time of installation. If installed after January 1, 2001, however, the software will no longer work.

Use Visio Professional to create network, software, and database diagrams. Save them in a variety of graphic formats, and then embed them in your Word or PowerPoint files.

Based on Visio Professional, Visio Enterprise adds 14,000 network equipment shapes and the AutoDiscovery feature to help you in diagramming conceptual, logical, and physical network models.

For additional information about Visio Enterprise, visit www.visio.com/.

Sample files from the book, by the author
They're far from perfect, but for your convenience I've included the Visio diagrams that I created for this book. Use them as a jumping-off point for starting your own Windows 2000 implementation.

Migration Tools

DirectMigrate2000, from Entevo Corporation
For NDS and Windows NT 4.0. Trial version.

DirectMigrate2000 handles a wide array of migration scenarios. The program is flexible enough to handle NT-to-Windows 2000 migrations from a variety of domain models. Using the DirectMap virtual directory, you can model your Active Directory structure before beginning to move users and resources. DirectMigrate 2000 accurately transfers NT group memberships, access rights, and permissions to Windows 2000.

For additional information on DirectMigrate2000, visit www.entevo.com/.

Network Tools

EtherPeek 4.0, from AG Group, Inc.
Windows 95, 98, and NT 4.0. Trial version.

A powerful network traffic and protocol analyzer for Ethernet networks.

Note: To obtain a serial number that enables you to use EtherPeek, go to www.aggroup.com and click Demos/Registration.

For additional information, visit the Web site at www.aggroup.com/.

TokenPeek, from AG Group, Inc.
Windows 95, 98, and NT 4.0. Trial version.

A powerful network traffic and protocol analyzer for Token Ring networks.

Note: To obtain a serial number that enables you to use TokenPeek, go to www.aggroup.com and click Demos/Registration.

For additional information, visit the Web site at www.aggroup.com/.

EtherHelp, from AG Group, Inc.
Windows 95, 98, and NT 4.0. Trial version.

Captures packets on remote network segments for analysis with EtherPeek.

For additional information, visit the Web site at www.aggroup.com/.

TokenHelp, from AG Group, Inc.
Windows 95, 98, and NT 4.0. Trial version.

Captures packets on remote network segments for analysis with TokenPeek.

For additional information, visit the Web site at `www.aggroup.com/`.

NetSense for EtherPeek and TokenPeek, from AG Group, Inc.
Windows 95, 98, and NT 4.0. Trial version.

Analyzes important information gathered from the EtherPeek and TokenPeek trace files. Provides a graphical representation of network traffic.

For additional information on these products by AG Group, Inc., visit `www.aggroup.com/`.

If You've Got Problems (Of the CD Kind)

I tried my best to compile programs that work on most computers with the minimum system requirements. Alas, your computer may differ, and some programs may not work properly for some reason.

The two most likely problems are that you don't have enough memory (RAM) for the programs you want to use, or that you have other programs running that are affecting the installation or running of a program. If you get error messages like `Not enough memory` or `Setup cannot continue`, try one or more of the following methods and then try using the software again:

✔ **Turn off any anti-virus software that you have on your computer.** Installers sometimes mimic virus activity and may make your computer incorrectly believe that it is being infected by a virus.

✔ **Close all running programs.** The more programs you're running, the less memory is available to other programs. Installers also typically update files and programs; if you keep other programs running, installation may not work properly.

✔ **In Windows, close the CD interface and run demos or installations directly from Windows Explorer.** The interface itself can tie up system memory, or even conflict with certain kinds of interactive demos. Use Windows Explorer to browse the files on the CD and launch installers or demos.

✔ **Have your local computer store add more RAM to your computer.** This is, admittedly, a drastic and somewhat expensive step. However, if you have a Windows 95 PC, adding more memory can really help the speed of your computer and enable more programs to run at the same time.

If you still have trouble installing the items from the CD, please call the IDG Books Worldwide Customer Service phone number at 800-762-2974 (outside the U.S.: 317-596-5430).

Index

• *J* •

• *K* •

• *R* •

Notes

IDG Books Worldwide, Inc., End-User License Agreement

READ THIS. You should carefully read these terms and conditions before opening the software packet(s) included with this book ("Book"). This is a license agreement ("Agreement") between you and IDG Books Worldwide, Inc. ("IDGB"). By opening the accompanying software packet(s), you acknowledge that you have read and accept the following terms and conditions. If you do not agree and do not want to be bound by such terms and conditions, promptly return the Book and the unopened software packet(s) to the place you obtained them for a full refund.

1. **License Grant.** IDGB grants to you (either an individual or entity) a nonexclusive license to use one copy of the enclosed software program(s) (collectively, the "Software") solely for your own personal or business purposes on a single computer (whether a standard computer or a workstation component of a multiuser network). The Software is in use on a computer when it is loaded into temporary memory (RAM) or installed into permanent memory (hard disk, CD-ROM, or other storage device). IDGB reserves all rights not expressly granted herein.

2. **Ownership .** IDGB is the owner of all right, title, and interest, including copyright, in and to the compilation of the Software recorded on the disk(s) or CD-ROM ("Software Media"). Copyright to the individual programs recorded on the Software Media is owned by the author or other authorized copyright owner of each program. Ownership of the Software and all proprietary rights relating thereto remain with IDGB and its licensers.

3. **Restrictions on Use and Transfer.**

   (a) You may only (i) make one copy of the Software for backup or archival purposes, or (ii) transfer the Software to a single hard disk, provided that you keep the original for backup or archival purposes. You may not (i) rent or lease the Software, (ii) copy or reproduce the Software through a LAN or other network system or through any computer subscriber system or bulletin-board system, or (iii) modify, adapt, or create derivative works based on the Software.

   (b) You may not reverse engineer, decompile, or disassemble the Software. You may transfer the Software and user documentation on a permanent basis, provided that the transferee agrees to accept the terms and conditions of this Agreement and you retain no copies. If the Software is an update or has been updated, any transfer must include the most recent update and all prior versions.

4. **Restrictions on Use of Individual Programs.** You must follow the individual requirements and restrictions detailed for each individual program in Appendix E of this Book. These limitations are also contained in the individual license agreements recorded on the Software Media. These limitations may include a requirement that after using the program for a specified period of time, the user must pay a registration fee or discontinue use. By opening the Software packet(s), you will be agreeing to abide by the licenses and restrictions for these individual programs that are detailed in Appendix E and on the Software Media. None of the material on this Software Media or listed in this Book may ever be redistributed, in original or modified form, for commercial purposes.

5. **Limited Warranty.**

   (a) IDGB warrants that the Software and Software Media are free from defects in materials and workmanship under normal use for a period of sixty (60) days from the date of purchase of this Book. If IDGB receives notification within the warranty period of defects in materials or workmanship, IDGB will replace the defective Software Media.

   (b) **IDGB AND THE AUTHOR OF THE BOOK DISCLAIM ALL OTHER WARRANTIES, EXPRESS OR IMPLIED, INCLUDING WITHOUT LIMITATION IMPLIED WARRANTIES OF MERCHANTABILITY AND FITNESS FOR A PARTICULAR PURPOSE, WITH RESPECT TO THE SOFTWARE, THE PROGRAMS, THE SOURCE CODE CONTAINED THEREIN, AND/OR THE TECHNIQUES DESCRIBED IN THIS BOOK. IDGB DOES NOT WARRANT THAT THE FUNCTIONS CONTAINED IN THE SOFTWARE WILL MEET YOUR REQUIRE-MENTS OR THAT THE OPERATION OF THE SOFTWARE WILL BE ERROR FREE.**

   (c) This limited warranty gives you specific legal rights, and you may have other rights that vary from jurisdiction to jurisdiction.

6. **Remedies.**

   (a) IDGB's entire liability and your exclusive remedy for defects in materials and workman-ship shall be limited to replacement of the Software Media, which may be returned to IDGB with a copy of your receipt at the following address: Software Media Fulfillment Department, Attn.: *Active Directory For Dummies*, IDG Books Worldwide, Inc., 7260 Shadeland Station, Ste. 100, Indianapolis, IN 46256, or call 800-762-2974. Please allow three to four weeks for delivery. This Limited Warranty is void if failure of the Software Media has resulted from accident, abuse, or misapplication. Any replacement Software Media will be warranted for the remainder of the original warranty period or thirty (30) days, whichever is longer.

   (b) In no event shall IDGB or the author be liable for any damages whatsoever (including without limitation damages for loss of business profits, business interruption, loss of business information, or any other pecuniary loss) arising from the use of or inability to use the Book or the Software, even if IDGB has been advised of the possibility of such damages.

   (c) Because some jurisdictions do not allow the exclusion or limitation of liability for conse-quential or incidental damages, the above limitation or exclusion may not apply to you.

7. **U.S. Government Restricted Rights.** Use, duplication, or disclosure of the Software by the U.S. Government is subject to restrictions stated in paragraph (c)(1)(ii) of the Rights in Technical Data and Computer Software clause of DFARS 252.227-7013, and in subparagraphs (a) through (d) of the Commercial Computer@ndRestricted Rights clause at FAR 52.227-19, and in similar clauses in the NASA FAR supplement, when applicable.

8. **General.** This Agreement constitutes the entire understanding of the parties and revokes and supersedes all prior agreements, oral or written, between them and may not be modified or amended except in a writing signed by both parties hereto that specifically refers to this Agreement. This Agreement shall take precedence over any other documents that may be in conflict herewith. If any one or more provisions contained in this Agreement are held by any court or tribunal to be invalid, illegal, or otherwise unenforceable, each and every other pro-vision shall remain in full force and effect.

Installation Instructions

The *Active Directory For Dummies* CD offers helpful programs and tools that you won't want to miss. To install the items from the CD to your hard drive, follow these steps.

1. **Insert the CD into your computer's CD-ROM drive.**

   Give your computer a moment to take a look at the CD.

2. **When the light on your CD-ROM drive goes out, double-click the My Computer icon (it's probably in the top-left corner of your desktop).**

   This action opens the My Computer window, which shows you all the drives attached to your computer, the Control Panel, and a couple of other handy things.

3. **Double-click the icon for your CD-ROM drive.**

   Another window opens, showing you all the folders and files on the CD.

4. **Double-click the file called License.txt.**

   This file contains the end-user license that you agree to by using the CD. When you are done reading the license, close the program, most likely Notepad, that displayed the file.

5. **Double-click the file called Readme.txt.**

   This file contains instructions about installing the software from this CD. It might be helpful to leave this text file open while you're using the CD.

6. **Double-click the folder for the software you are interested in.**

   Be sure to read the descriptions of the programs in the next section of this appendix (much of this information also shows up in the Readme file). These descriptions will give you more precise information about the programs' folder names and about finding and running the installer program.

7. **To install programs to your computer, find the file called Setup.exe, Install.exe, or something similar, and double-click that file.**

   The program's installer will walk you through the process of setting up your new software.

For more information, see Appendix E, "About the CD."

Discover Dummies Online!

The Dummies Web Site is your fun and friendly online resource for the latest information about ...*For Dummies*® books and your favorite topics. The Web site is the place to communicate with us, exchange ideas with other ...*For Dummies* readers, chat with authors, and have fun!

Ten Fun and Useful Things You Can Do at www.dummies.com

1. Win free ...*For Dummies* books and more!
2. Register your book and be entered in a prize drawing.
3. Meet your favorite authors through the IDG Books Author Chat Series.
4. Exchange helpful information with other ...*For Dummies* readers.
5. Discover other great ...*For Dummies* books you must have!
6. Purchase Dummieswear™ exclusively from our Web site.
7. Buy ...*For Dummies* books online.
8. Talk to us. Make comments, ask questions, get answers!
9. Download free software.
10. Find additional useful resources from authors.

Link directly to these ten fun and useful things at
http://www.dummies.com/10useful

For other technology titles from IDG Books Worldwide, go to
www.idgbooks.com

Not on the Web yet? It's easy to get started with *Dummies 101*®: *The Internet For Windows*® *98* or *The Internet For Dummies*®, 6th Edition, at local retailers everywhere.

Find other ...*For Dummies* books on these topics:
Business • Career • Databases • Food & Beverage • Games • Gardening • Graphics • Hardware
Health & Fitness • Internet and the World Wide Web • Networking • Office Suites
Operating Systems • Personal Finance • Pets • Programming • Recreation • Sports
Spreadsheets • Teacher Resources • Test Prep • Word Processing

IDG BOOKS WORLDWIDE
BOOK REGISTRATION

We want to hear from you!

Visit **http://my2cents.dummies.com** to register this book and tell us how you liked it!

- Get entered in our monthly prize giveaway.

- Give us feedback about this book — tell us what you like best, what you like least, or maybe what you'd like to ask the author and us to change!

- Let us know any other *...For Dummies*® topics that interest you.

Your feedback helps us determine what books to publish, tells us what coverage to add as we revise our books, and lets us know whether we're meeting your needs as a *...For Dummies* reader. You're our most valuable resource, and what you have to say is important to us!

Not on the Web yet? It's easy to get started with *Dummies 101*®: *The Internet For Windows*® *98* or *The Internet For Dummies*®, 6th Edition, at local retailers everywhere.

Or let us know what you think by sending us a letter at the following address:

...For Dummies Book Registration
Dummies Press
7260 Shadeland Station, Suite 100
Indianapolis, IN 46256-3917
Fax 317-596-5498

™

BESTSELLING
BOOK SERIES